AF600450

AWFUL PARENTHESIS

Suspension and the Sublime in Romantic and Victorian Poetry

ANNE C. McCARTHY

Awful Parenthesis

Suspension and the Sublime in Romantic and Victorian Poetry

UNIVERSITY OF TORONTO PRESS
Toronto Buffalo London

Toronto Buffalo London
utorontopress.com

ISBN 978-1-4875-0291-1

Library and Archives Canada Cataloguing in Publication

McCarthy, Anne C., author
Awful parenthesis : suspension and the sublime in romantic and Victorian poetry / Anne C. McCarthy.

Includes bibliographical references and index.
ISBN 978-1-4875-0291-1 (cloth)

1. English poetry – 19th century – History and criticism. 2. Sublime, The, in literature. I. Title.

PR595.S77M33 2018 821′.809 C2017-907454-7

This book has been published with the assistance of the College of Liberal Arts at Pennsylvania State University.

University of Toronto Press acknowledges the financial assistance to its publishing program of the Canada Council for the Arts and the Ontario Arts Council, an agency of the Government of Ontario.

Canada Council for the Arts Conseil des Arts du Canada

Funded by the Government of Canada | Financé par le gouvernement du Canada

Contents

Abbreviations

AR Samuel Taylor Coleridge, *Aids to Reflection*, ed. John Beer (Princeton: Princeton University Press, 1993)

BL Samuel Taylor Coleridge, *Biographia Literaria*, 2 vols., ed. James Engell and W. Jackson Bate (Princeton: Princeton University Press, 1983)

CCH *Coleridge: The Critical Heritage*, ed. J.R. de J. Jackson (New York: Barnes & Noble, 1970)

CL *Collected Letters of Samuel Taylor Coleridge*, 6 vols., ed. Earl Leslie Griggs (Oxford: Clarendon Press, 1956–71)

CN Samuel Taylor Coleridge, *Notebooks*, 5 vols., ed. Kathleen Coburn, Merton Christensen, and Anthony John Harding (Princeton: Princeton University Press, 1957–2002)

CPP *Coleridge's Poetry and Prose*, ed. Nicholas Halmi, Paul Magnuson, and Raimonda Modiano (New York: W.W. Norton, 2004)

CPW *Coleridge's Poetical Works*, 2 vols., ed. J.C.C. Mays (Princeton: Princeton University Press, 2001)

Friend Samuel Taylor Coleridge, *The Friend*, 2 vols., ed. Barbara E. Rooke (Princeton: Princeton University Press, 1967)

HSWT *History of a Six Weeks' Tour through a Part of France, Switzerland, Germany, and Holland* (London: T. Hookham, 1817)

SPP *Shelley's Poetry and Prose*, 2nd ed., ed. Donald H. Reiman and Neil Fraistat (New York: W.W. Norton, 2002)

SWF Samuel Taylor Coleridge, *Shorter Works and Fragments*, 2 vols., ed. H.J. Jackson and J.R. de J. Jackson (Princeton: Princeton University Press, 1995)

Acknowledgments

The lineaments of this project emerged nearly a decade ago while I was a student at the Graduate Center of the City University of New York. My first group of interlocutors – Anne Humphreys, Gerhard Joseph, Alan Vardy, and Nancy Yousef – encouraged my early explorations of suspension and the sublime, allowed me to cross Romantic and Victorian boundaries more or less at will, and believed in the project from its very beginning. New York remains, in many ways, my intellectual homeland, and they formed the centre of what was, for me, a truly transformative scholarly community that included the CUNY Victorian Seminar, the New York Romanticists Group, and, of course, the Long Nineteenth-Century Student Colloquium. My intellectual and social lives have been vastly improved by the friendship, support, conversation, and general wonderfulness of Emily Stanback, Leila Walker, Mia Chen, Sharmaine Browne, Rob Faunce, Jonathan Gray, Maggie Galvan, Kiran Mascarenhas, Adele Kudish, Caroline Conoly, Jason Schneiderman, and Jesse Schwartz, as well as Tanya Agathocleous, Richard Kaye, Talia Schaffer, Jonah Siegel, Rich McCoy, and Carrie Hintz.

At Penn State I've been fortunate to be surrounded by some of the best, most brilliant, and most supportive colleagues anyone could want. Robert Caserio, Chris Castiglia, Chris Reed, Janet Lyon, and Michael Bérubé have read much of this book at different stages and have provided thoughtful comments and tough love at key moments in the process. Susan Squier, Lisa Sternlieb, Daniel Purdy, Julia Kasdorf, Ben Schreier, Jonathan Eburne, Hester Blum, and Matt Tierney have been ongoing sources of encouragement and stimulating conversation. The friendship of Kate Anderson, Carrie Hritz, and Kate Baasch has seen me through good times and bad. Claire Colebrook has consistently gone above and beyond in her mentorship, advocacy, and friendship – and for this I am utterly grateful.

The ideas I develop in this book have been worked out over years of conference presentations, informal discussions, and country walks. Chip Tucker, David L. Clark, Jennifer Jones, and Caroline Levine were early supporters of my work and were instrumental in helping me bring my ideas to a wider scholarly audience. Tim Fulford provided timely advice on Coleridge. Dave Collings has long been a friend and an eminently generous reader. Kerri Andrews, Rachel Feder, Sebastian Lecourt, Daniel Robinson, and Chris Washington have never failed to improve my life and work. I've been especially lucky to work with some spectacular people at the Keats Letters Project: Ian Newman, Brian Rejack, Kate Singer, Emily Stanback, and Michael Theune.

Mark Thompson and the anonymous readers at the University of Toronto Press saw the potential in this book and helped me shape it into what it is; I am also grateful for the expert assistance of Barb Porter and my copy editor, Judy Williams. Lingering infelicities are, of course, my own.

At the Graduate Center, my work was supported financially by a Robert E. Gilleece Fellowship, a university Writing Fellowship, and the B. Altman Dissertation Year Fellowship. At Penn State, I have benefited from a junior faculty research leave in the College of Liberal Arts and a semester-long fellowship at the erstwhile Institute for the Arts and Humanities.

Earlier versions of chapters 3 and 4 were published in *Studies in Romanticism* and *Victorian Poetry*, respectively. I am grateful to the Trustees of Boston University and to the University of West Virginia Press for permission to use that material here.

Marilyn McCarthy provided significant help throughout all stages of this process, but particularly with the final proofreading and indexing. She and my father, Tom, have been consistently supportive over the years and are no doubt as happy to see this book come to fruition as I am.

Awful Parenthesis is dedicated to Fred Ulfers, whose friendship and joyful wisdom I have been lucky enough to share over the last twenty years. As one of the first professors I had as an NYU undergraduate, he was instrumental in helping me find the language I needed at the times that I needed it most. I hope this book does some justice to the many conversations we've had over coffee and pecan pie. May it be an invitation to many more.

AWFUL PARENTHESIS

Suspension and the Sublime in Romantic and Victorian Poetry

Approaching Suspension

The main title of this book – *Awful Parenthesis* – comes from Thomas De Quincey's "On the Knocking at the Gate in *Macbeth*" (1823). In this essay, De Quincey sets out to theorize a certain "perplexity" in his response to the murder of Duncan in Shakespeare's Scottish play. Representations of murder on the stage or in literature, he reasons, generally focus the audience's attention on the victim, emphasizing the "natural but ignoble instinct by which we cleave to life."[1] Duncan's murder in *Macbeth*, on the other hand, impresses De Quincey with "a peculiar awfulness and a depth of solemnity" (3.150) because it foregrounds the heightened mental and external conditions that make the murder possible. In other words, the structure of the play makes the act of murder available as an object of sublime contemplation. The knocking at the gate to which the essay's title refers is what effects this radical reorientation. It makes explicit the unusual atmosphere and state of mind that had allowed the murder to be carried out in the first place, even though the sound simultaneously initiates the cessation of those conditions and marks a return to "ordinary life." The knock distends temporality – in that it prompts reflection on what has just happened rather than on what is happening now – and its effects operate beneath, even against, the linguistic registers of the play-text. More than that, it evades the representational codes of reality itself, for once the audience becomes aware that such a pause has occurred, it is already over.

De Quincey claims that such scenes are not unknown in accounts of real-life crimes – he cites an anecdote about the Ratcliffe Highway murders in this regard – but it is clear that he is most interested in the phenomenon of the pause itself, rather than anything particular that occurs during the interval. He compares the affective jolt of the

Shakespearean knock to the moment a "wife, a daughter, or sister" recovers from a fainting fit and to an urban street just after the passage of a funeral cortège, when "the death-like stillness [is] broken up by the sound of wheels rattling away from the scene, and making known that the transitory vision was dissolved" (3.152). Even with these examples, however, the pause and its effects remain elusive. Returning to his description of the play, De Quincey once again meditates on the strangeness of this interval:

> [T]he world of ordinary life is suddenly arrested – laid asleep – tranced – racked into a dread armistice: time must be annihilated; relation to things without abolished; and all must pass self-withdrawn into a deep syncope and suspension of earthly passion. Hence it is that when the deed is done … the knocking at the gate is heard; and it makes known audibly that the reaction has commenced … the pulses of life are beginning to beat again: and the re-establishment of the goings-on of the world in which we live, first makes us profoundly sensible of the awful parenthesis that had suspended them. (3.153)

The very overdetermination of these images imbues suspension with a palpable intensity: it is not the absence of activity that one feels, but the overwhelming sense of interruption and possibility – a form of hovering, the alternation of resistance and yielding. The proliferation of terms – "arrested," "laid asleep," "tranced," "armistice," "syncope," and "suspension," among others – amplifies the essay's elliptical effects, producing what it describes. These terms accumulate at an experiential threshold, naming a condition of both knowing and not-knowing, and of not-knowing at the very moment in which knowledge becomes possible. Of course, "On the Knocking at the Gate" is not the only text in which De Quincey explores the possibilities and the terrors of suspension. The life of the opium eater is one that is lived largely through various modalities of trance, both deliberate and unexpected. These experiences in turn engender a heightened awareness of other forms of pause and paralysis that populate *Confessions of an English Opium-Eater* (1821) and *Susperia de Profundis* (1845): the dead body of his young sister on a summer's day, the art of Piranesi, the eerie calm of the submerged city of Savannah-La-Mar. "On the Knocking at the Gate" thus affirms, in a highly concentrated form, De Quincey's status as one of the most astute readers of suspension in nineteenth-century discourse. The essay provides an unusually sustained, deliberate meditation on the meaning of suspension as such in the early nineteenth century. And words such as "tranced," "syncope," and the "pulses of life" underline the irreducibly physical dimensions of suspension. It is an aesthetics that is always already felt, as William Wordsworth remarks in "Lines Written a Few Miles above Tintern Abbey" (1798), "in the blood, and felt along the heart" (29).[2]

"Tintern Abbey" is, in fact, a significant intertext for De Quincey's essay. The phrase "laid asleep" echoes Wordsworth's description of the "serene and blessed mood" in which "the motion of our human blood / Almost suspended, we are laid asleep / In body, and become a living soul" (42, 45–7). For Wordsworth, the suspension is a salutary one, the enabling condition of the visionary experience of the sublime. For De Quincey, as David Bromwich suggests, the meaning is more ambivalent: "the mood of Wordsworth's sublime moment ... evoked ... a sudden retreat from violence and terror."[3] Yet, the allusion to Wordsworth's poem – and I agree with Bromwich's view that this must be deliberate on De Quincey's part – does not seem to signal a "retreat" from the darker possibilities of this figure. It is the poem, rather than the essay, that seems to recoil from its own suspension, seeing in the visionary trance the possibility of a more permanent and deadly stasis. As Thomas Weiskel has argued, "The poem is always in danger of coming to a dangerous halt, and does so, four times. Each of the paragraphs begins anew, in reaction to a hidden sense of presence which cannot be signified but which is located in those mysterious breaks."[4] If anything, "On the Knocking at the Gate" signals De Quincey's desire to pause in this space of dangerous possibility – to pause, that is, in the "awful parenthesis" that succinctly links suspension and the sublime – and to explore what arises outside of the temporalities and signifying processes of so-called ordinary life. This is not merely, as Timothy Corrigan holds, an instance of "energetic redundancy ... where the accumulation of words is able to signify, only through their superfluity, what is beyond language."[5] Nor is this accretion explicable in exclusively psychoanalytic or cognitive terms, though these remain among the most important conceptual frameworks in De Quincey scholarship.[6] Rather, the essay attempts to account for suspension as such, understood as part of a constellation of meanings and images that that "gradually – if only through insistent repetition – take on increasingly general force"[7] in the Romantic and early Victorian eras.

"On the Knocking at the Gate," therefore, is concerned not merely with the suspension *of* some process or other object, nor is it exclusively focused on associations with paralysis and passivity. Suspension, as it is rendered in this essay, interrupts linear time, turning the spectator inward to reflect upon a situation that has just occurred. Taken as a whole, the essay represents something of an abstract for the concerns of this book, offering an unusually comprehensive catalogue of the modalities of suspension available to writers and readers in early nineteenth-century Britain.

Awful Parenthesis argues that suspension – this seemingly paradoxical concatenation of activity and passivity, of presence and absence – marks an aesthetic response to the ontological crisis of contingency and discontinuity as it was experienced in the literature of the nineteenth century. Drawing attention to the ways the world does not necessarily coincide with itself, suspension responds to radical contingency and to a sense of ever-expanding connection and estrangement. The poets in this study – Samuel Taylor Coleridge, Percy Bysshe Shelley, Alfred Tennyson, and Christina Rossetti – employ images, forms, and mental practices of suspension in order to function within a constitutively contingent world. At different times, this contingent reality may be reflected in the contradictory nature of the self, in the perilous ambiguity of a cataleptic body that may or may not be dead, or in a natural world whose laws are much less legible than they initially appear. Suspension rejects the impulse to cling to the known and the knowable, as well as the resigned ennui that would leave us, like Matthew Arnold in "Stanzas from the Grande Chartreuse" (1855), "Wandering between two worlds, one dead, / The other powerless to be born" (85–6).[8] As something other than a negative form of knowing, suspension resists the urge to conflate the unknown with the unimportant, to react with hostility to that which seems to threaten the claims of epistemology, or, for that matter, to fall into the paralysis of a recursive scepticism. Rather than assuming the existence of a stable external reality that may be represented or misrepresented depending on the skill of the observer, suspension responds to a world that is constituted by its own discontinuity and unreliability. Even the seemingly simple attempt to account for one's present circumstances – whether in the context of a sweeping nineteenth-century novel or a synchronic description of a particular historical moment – loses itself in a potentially infinite recursion of causes, contingencies, confrontations, and obscured connections.

De Quincey's essay theorizes suspension as one term among others. However, the word "suspension" offers a broader – and less overdetermined – array of meanings and connotations than many of these other terms. "Laid asleep," for instance, can be associated with both the visionary trance of Wordsworth and a popular discourse about death, but it does not capture the same resonances of ruptured time that are at work elsewhere in "Knocking." Suspension is also used in conjunction with its verb form, a juxtaposition that discloses some of its active potential. Ultimately, though, my decision to focus on suspension, rather than a term like "armistice" or even "trance," has to do with the presence of that word in some of the key formulations of nineteenth-century thought. I am thinking here of concepts like "suspended animation," the "willing suspension of disbelief" (a term that Coleridge introduces in the *Biographia Literaria*), and the "suspension of judgment" long associated with the Victorian frame of mind.[9] Granted, every decision of this kind ends up foreclosing certain avenues of inquiry as well, rendering them parallel rather than intersecting lines of thought. Readers may notice, for instance, that this study has surprisingly little to say about the concept of negative capability, first articulated by John Keats in a letter of 1817. At one level, the capacity for "being in uncertainties, Mysteries, doubts, without any irritable reaching after fact & reason" undoubtedly resonates with the forms of suspension that I discuss, though Keats himself cites Coleridge as an example of someone who lacks this aptitude.[10] Nevertheless, the reception of this concept in the later nineteenth century and beyond – a trajectory that has been studied in great detail by scholars such as Ou Li – means that "negative capability" occupies a place in literary and popular discourse both specific and diffuse. As a result, negative capability functions in ways that depart rather significantly from the forms of suspension that are at the centre of this study, even as they remain, in other ways, intimately entwined.[11]

Of the poets who make the most significant contributions to understanding suspension, Coleridge has perhaps the most complicated attitudes. Figures of suspension pervade his poetic, philosophical, and theological texts, structuring the relationship between his unsettled mind and frequently disordered body. Though suspicious of certain manifestations of paralysis, particularly those that afflict the powers of volition or motion, Coleridge understands suspension in a capacious sense, as both an epistemological and an existential condition. He is among the first Romantic-era authors explicitly to theorize the experience of the sublime as one where the human powers of comparison are suspended: a central, though often overlooked, intervention. The chapters on Shelley, Tennyson, and Rossetti each elaborate the connections between suspension and the sublime. For Shelley, forms of bodily and mental suspension provide the conditions of an ecstatic sublime able to respond to a contingent and sometimes inhuman universe. Yet, far from using suspension to evade the problems of the sensible world, the Shelleyan sublime, at least as far as it is articulated in "Mont Blanc," ultimately refuses to "rise above." Tennyson treats suspension largely as an epistemological problem symptomatic of an age in which the grounds of truth were increasingly elusive. At a time when real and reasonable doubts existed about the medical profession's ability to define clearly the signs of death, Tennyson uses tropes of live burial and suspended animation to explore his own fears of insignificance. Finally, Rossetti's poetry returns to the idea that suspension and its radical uncertainty are part of a broader existential condition – a condition that does not, however, provoke the same kinds of agonized responses that it did in the work of Coleridge and others. At once orthodox and idiosyncratic, Rossetti's religious faith responds to a world whose uncertainties are not the result of fallenness, but rather are its constitutive condition.

Defining Suspension

At the end of the 1860s, the essayist Henry Sidgwick claimed that he and his contemporaries shared a number of identifiable habits of mind: "We are growing more sceptical in the proper sense of the word: we suspend our judgment much more than our predecessors, and much more contentedly: we see that there are many sides to questions: the opinions that we do hold we hold if not more loosely, at least more at arm's length."[12] Sidgwick is not the only observer to have identified scepticism, manifested in the suspension of judgment, as a defining feature of the nineteenth century. Indeed, for many thinkers, suspension of judgment came to represent the best of the Victorian mind: the possibility of objective inquiry, and the sober weighing of the facts without regard to prejudices. As Caroline Levine argues, scepticism and suspended judgment were not limited to intellectual inquiry; the realist novel and detective story helped educate readers in these scientific casts of mind. Narrative suspense is a form that is perhaps uniquely important in the study of Victorian literature, structuring, as Levine argues, not only aesthetic creation but also productive mental activity more generally: "Nineteenth-century scientists and philosophers insisted that a doubtful pause was absolutely essential to the pursuit of knowledge … From this epistemological perspective, novelistic suspense performed a crucial cultural role: narrative enigmas and delays could help to foster habits of hesitation and uncertainty."[13] Narrative suspense, understood as a contingent feature of plot, encourages the reader to anticipate and imagine what comes next, promising either implicitly or explicitly that the mystery will be revealed in due time. In short, it creates an object of knowledge to be discovered through the application of appropriately careful and patient reading practices. Within the archetypal narrative of experimentation and discovery, suspense and the suspension of judgment are means to an end, moments of uncertainty that will realize the satisfactions of knowledge and mastery or, at the very least, yield the knowledge of what one does not know.

At first glance, Sidgwick's encomium to the suspension of judgment and the holding of opinions "at arm's length" appears to have little relationship to the affective intensities that characterize De Quincey's "awful parenthesis." There appears to be little room in De Quincey's theatrical scene for the kinds of measured investigation carried out in a scientific laboratory or even in a detective novel; it is difficult to see how deliberate "habits of hesitation" cultivated by narrative suspense could be similarly encouraged by the involuntary shocks and surprises of the syncope. Nevertheless, I argue that these conceptualizations are, essentially, part of the same constellation of meanings. When suspension – rather than one of its local articulations, be it suspended animation, narrative suspense, or the suspension of judgment – is rendered the overarching term, we can see those connections most clearly. In other words, the pedagogical or ethical claims that attach to a relatively circumscribed notion like suspended judgment depend upon a more capacious and uncertain understanding of suspension as it appears at different sites of intensity at certain crucial moments in the work of early nineteeth-century authors.

In its most general meaning, suspension denotes a temporary pause, hesitation, deferral, or delay. It refers to withdrawals and omissions, abbreviations, interruptions, and intervals. When used in a physical sense, suspension can refer both to the state of being hung up or hanging by a thread and, perhaps more strikingly, to the "action of holding up or state of being held up without attachment."[14] More than just a pause among other pauses, suspension pushes back against inertia and interrupts habitual modes of existence. As form and practice, mental and physical, temporal and spatial, suspension calls attention to what it places in abeyance: habits of scepticism or credulity, up to and including the "*lived belief* in the world's continued holding-together across its gaps."[15] Despite a colloquial affinity with terms such as paralysis, passivity, and deprivation, the act itself frequently requires an active application of energy. This conception of suspension's intensity affirms Stefanie Markovits's understanding of nineteenth-century "inaction" as "both frustrated external action and heightened internal action."[16] Indeed, many of the moments of suspension that this book will consider are also sites of what Elisha Cohn calls "a paradoxically static intensity – still life, vibrant in its absorptive movelessness."[17] Suspension is the exception to the rule, a gesture directed against the law. It is both a punishment (the temporary removal of a privilege) and the mitigation of punishment (a suspended sentence). The art historian Jonathan Crary describes suspension as "the state of being suspended, a looking or listening so rapt that it is an exemption from ordinary conditions, that it becomes a suspended temporality, a hovering out of time ... It implies the possibility of a fixation, of holding something in wonder or contemplation, in which the attentive subject is both immobile and ungrounded."[18] In the context of literature, suspension is a catalyst for defamiliarization, as theorized by Victor Shklovsky: "A work is created 'artistically' so that its perception is impeded and the greatest possible effort is produced through the slowness of the perception. As a result of this lingering, the object is perceived not in its extension in space, but, so to speak, in its continuity."[19] Ultimately, however, the logic of suspension emerges in response to that of the aporia; it is the means through which the impasse may be crossed without erasing or ignoring the genuine discontinuity that gave rise to it in the first place.

Awful Parenthesis joins a number of recent critical investigations into modalities of suspension in nineteenth-century literature and culture. Robert Mitchell's *Experimental Life*, for instance, traces the way that the science of suspended animation opened up new artistic possibilities for Romantic-era writers. Not only did the body in suspended animation figure the "dislocations between an individual lifespace and the temporalities of modern social change," it also provided a way of thinking about how to "alter the nature of lived time, enabling states that merged life and death, dreaming and waking, past and future."[20] Cultural critics such as Gavin Budge and Simone Natale, moreover, have recently explored the connections between suspension and the supernatural in Romantic and Victorian medicine and popular culture.[21] Most notably, perhaps, Cohn's *Still Life* examines "states of diminished consciousness [that] suspend the arduous framework of self-culture in Victorian narratives." Representations of trance, reverie, and dream in otherwise actively forward-moving texts offer, she argues, an opportunity for unconscious development, even as they threaten to undo the integrity of the conscious individual will. As the writers in the present study similarly discover, doing nothing often requires a surprising amount of intention, and early to mid-nineteenth-century readers needed little convincing that a body in a state of "death-like stillness" could house a living, terrified individual. However, for Cohn, as for Mitchell, suspension remains a relatively circumscribed moment within broader narratives of development: instances of suspension reframe "received categories of thinking, knowing, and doing," but do not alter a fundamental faith in the coherence of the world.[22]

The forms of suspension in which this book is most interested resist, rather than anticipate, the closure of experiment and narrative alike. As such, they are aligned with poetry rather than narrative. Here, I draw upon Jonathan Culler's well-known argument that "the lyric is characteristically the triumph of the apostrophic," a mode that "works against narrative and its accompaniments: sequentiality, causality, time, teleological meaning."[23] A number of comparative studies of nineteenth-century poetry and the novel have used this distinction as a starting point for developing increasingly nuanced understandings of realist fiction and of the relation between Romantic and Victorian literature. Monique R. Morgan, for instance, follows Culler's lead in characterizing lyric as the genre capable of instantiating "a timeless present, an infinitely suspended moment, which contrasts with narrative's past progression of events."[24] The structural features of poetry, such as line breaks, metre, and caesura, further enact what J. Hillis Miller has called the "linguistic moment": a "suspension of the forward-moving working of language toward the production of meaning, in a prolonged, hovering instant of self-reflection" in ways that tend not to appear as frequently in narrative forms.[25] While I do not engage directly with recent scholarly developments in the field of historical poetics, it is worth noting that suspension operates even within this discourse. For instance, Meredith Martin and Yisrael Levin have discovered fundamental, even constitutive disagreements in nineteenth-century prosody manuals. The discovery of these radical uncertainties, they write,

> allows a frightening, indeed, a destabilizing amount of freedom. What if, instead of a border, a boundary, a measure, delineation, a container, a shape, meter was more of a discursive in-between space? A no-man's land, a battlefield, a mediator between the writer and the reader – a mediator between the self and the world – but what about a mediator between the self and the self?[26]

The structure of this passage with its accumulation of similar, though not identical, terms is reminiscent of the style of De Quincey's essay. Particularly intriguing is the distinction that Martin and Levin make between, on the one hand, "a border, a boundary, a measure," and, on the other, "a discursive in-between space" or "no-man's land." The latter set of categories, to which prosody belongs, suggests an uncertainty of a different order from the former: a zone of possibilities and overlapping though mutually exclusive meanings, rather than a clear-cut distinction. Metre, that is, does not consistently offer enough information for definitive decisions about meaning. Rather, it opens a space in which the possibility of certainty is held in abeyance. Binary thinking and formal determination are perpetually suspended. The broader claims that Martin and Levin make for prosody, namely that it "can teach us as much about ambivalence and the desire for stability as it can about experiment and disruption,"[27] imply that in addition to naming a set of practices having to do with the formal dimensions of poetic discourse, prosody could also provide a conceptual category for thinking about forms of suspension that respond to constitutive, rather than contingent, gaps in knowledge. Perhaps most significantly, the "no-man's land" makes space for an understanding of suspension as a relation without relation. When the object of suspension is no longer subject to epistemological investigation – as it is in conventional narrative forms – it enables a different order of experience, one described by Anne-Lise François: "the suspension of relation between the two hands, which releases the gift of alms, however temporarily, from the circuit of exchange (anticipation and return, sacrifice and reward) in which charity is usually caught, might be taken as a figure for the numerous tropes of passive agency, singularity, and nonrelation informing postmodern ethical thought."[28] Suspension, that is, marks that which can never become reified into an object of knowledge. It remains, rather, something that can be "known" only in its passing away, only in its difference from the moment in which it becomes known.

Suspension and the Sublime

The associative link between suspension and the sublime – the conception, that is, of an *awful* parenthesis – is one of the central interventions of this study. The sublime has, at least since Immanuel Kant, been considered to offer a privileged insight into the status of the human being in the world, revealing "the subjective purposiveness of our mind, in the use of our imagination, for the mind's supersensible vocation."[29] The language of suspension has largely been taken for granted in discussions of the aesthetics of the sublime, treated as a way station on the journey to some other kind of experience.[30] In the *Critique of Judgment* (1790), Kant dictates that the sublime consists in "a momentary inhibition of the vital forces followed by an outpouring of them that is all the stronger."[31] He minimizes that "momentary inhibition" or suspension, preferring instead to dwell on the "outpouring" that comes after: the elevation, the transcendence, the recognition of the superior force of reason. To emphasize the connection between suspension and the sublime, however, pauses the upwardly focused drive towards transcendence and mental escape, dwelling instead with the inhibition itself, a violence that is able to "jolt us momentarily out of a perspective constructed by reason and language."[32] Thus, understanding suspension as the constitutive movement of the sublime discloses the essential discontinuity of the world – a discontinuity that cannot be fully recovered or resolved. From this perspective, the suspension of certainty is not a temporary pause, but becomes, rather, the paradigmatic posture for meeting a world of "constitutive discontinuity." This term appears in Jean-François Lyotard's *The Differend*, relating to the "abyss of Not-Being which opens between phrases" and the "constitutive discontinuity (or oblivion) of time."[33] The space of suspension opened by the aesthetic experience of the sublime is a space of radical possibility: anything could happen, or – as Lyotard claims elsewhere – nothing at all.[34] Thus too does Philippe Lacoue-Labarthe describe the feeling of "drawing a blank": "What is suspended, arrested, tipping suddenly into strangeness, is the presence of the present (the being-present of the present). And what then occurs without occurring (for it is by definition what cannot occur) is – without being – nothingness, the 'nothing of being.'"[35] Suspension, that is, hovers at the edges of the sublime and the unspeakable, part of a shared discourse that unites the aesthetics of Romanticism with those of deconstruction.

While a dominant discourse on the sublime emphasizes the transcendence of a discontinuous sensible world in favour of the mind's identification with supersensible reason, the sublime aesthetics of suspension presents an alternative trajectory that remains within the contradictions and impasses, dealing with the moment of crisis as it arises. Images of bodies in suspended animation, rapt in trance, or caught in the ellipsis of thwarted speech index an aesthetic response to the ontological conditions of contingency and discontinuity in the self as well as in the world. In short, suspension is the occasion of the sublime, and of a particular kind of sublime experience that shatters narrative consciousness and faith in what Percy Shelley will call, in "Mont Blanc," "the secret strength of things / Which governs thought" (139–40). Outside of determinate narrative structures, suspension operates in ways that are unpredictable and disruptive. As this book argues, even something as quintessentially "Victorian" as the suspension of judgment finds its condition of possibility in these earlier, often fraught, excursions into the suspension at the core of the sublime. The experiences that I privilege in this study are those that reveal this abyssal reality, this truth of disjunction, whether such disjunctions are to be ecstatically embraced (Shelley, Rossetti), feared (Tennyson), or ambivalently and agonistically registered (Coleridge).

By arguing that suspension mediates the experience of an inherently unstable reality, *Awful Parenthesis* attributes to its central figures a proto-deconstructive sense of a world constituted by its own discontinuity with itself. In doing so, I build upon a long tradition in Romantic studies that shows the extent to which the writers of the period avoided taking the world's coherence for granted. Angela Esterhammer reminds us that writers of the period anticipate poststructuralist insights about "the retroactive and self-referential structures, the vulnerability and the potential for failure" that attend performative speech but do not uniformly view such characteristics of language as shortcomings or crises. Romantic writers, she argues, "tend to describe the paradoxical temporality of declarative statements, not as a scandal, but as something like a miracle – a characteristic of human language that can be observed but not fully explained. Accordingly, Romantic theorists themselves are never too surprised when their attempts to analyze the operation of language run into ambiguities, gaps, or self-contradiction."[36] *Awful Parenthesis* comes to a different, though essentially complementary conclusion: that these contradictions and gaps are not – or not only – constitutive characteristics of human language but also reflect basic truths about reality itself. The more closely one observes the world, the less it holds together. This is, itself, a recognizably "Romantic" position. As Jerome Christensen argues, "Insofar as Romanticism holds together, then as now, it coalesces as a writing about how things or persons (or things *and* persons) hold together."[37] Both Anne Mellor's "romantic irony" and James Chandler's attention to anachronism (objects out of time) and anatopism (objects out of place) in Romantic writing reflect ways of responding to a world whose holding together cannot be guaranteed and to the potential for chaos and profound dislocation.[38]

As the nineteenth century progressed, the dominant discourse of the sublime became both muted and distant – an emotion to be experienced in the context of, say, a guided tour of Mont Blanc or in the contemplation of the faraway landscapes of empire.[39] Yet suspension – and its potential for sublimity – remains very much at home. Here, we may productively return to De Quincey. Among the examples he invokes to explain the affective phenomenon of the knocking at the gate is a domestic set piece: "If the reader has ever witnessed a wife, daughter, or sister, in a fainting fit, he may chance to have observed that the most affecting moment in such a spectacle, is *that* in which a sigh and a stirring announce the recommencement of suspended life" (3.152). The comparison is, at first glance, striking in its failure to correspond fully to the original object of inquiry. The suspended animation of a beloved female body – and the ending of that suspension in a return to life (here implicitly distinguished from the continuation of that suspension into death) – seems a purposefully inadequate analogue to the elaborately staged "retiring of the human heart" in *Macbeth* (3.153). What the image suggests, however, is the way in which suspension can make certain kinds of images newly available for theorization as versions of the sublime. In *Villette* (1853), for instance, Charlotte Brontë imagines Lucy Snowe's reawakening from a fainting fit in terms strikingly similar to De Quincey's: "The returning sense of sight came upon me, red, as if it swam in blood; suspended hearing rushed back loud, like thunder; consciousness revived in fear: I sat up appalled, wondering into what region, amongst what strange beings I was waking."[40] Just as Macbeth and the play's audience are startled into a resumption of activity that is also a kind of epistemological (and ontological) shock, Lucy's bodily suspension ends with dramatic violence – blood-red vision, thundering sounds, and an awareness of overwhelming fear. All of this mirrors her emotional derangement, yet it also in a certain sense anticipates and displaces it: that is, circumstances of her fainting fit are more slowly remembered. Delayed realization and seemingly deliberate misreading also characterize George Eliot's use of the fainting woman trope in *Scenes of Clerical Life* (1857). Describing the revival of Caterina after a long period of syncope, the narrator of "Mr. Gilfil's Love Story" remarks:

> It is a wonderful moment, the first time we stand by one who has fainted, and witness the fresh birth of consciousness spreading itself over the blank

> features, like the rising sunlight on the alpine summits that lay ghastly and dead under the leaden twilight. A slight shudder, and the frost-bound eyes recover their liquid light; for an instant they show the inward semi-consciousness of an infant's; then, with a little start, they open wider and begin to *look*; the present is visible, but only as a strange writing, and the interpreter Memory is not yet there.[41]

The rapturously contemplative description of Caterina's awakening appears at first to belong more to the ostensibly serene elevation of Romantic nature poetry ("rising sunlight on the alpine summits") than to the violent, gothically inflected awakening of *Villette*. Yet the references to the natural world elide the traumatic scene that had caused it in the first place. Caterina's fainting fit had been precipitated by her discovery of the dead body of Captain Wybrow, the man whom she loves and who had spurned her affections. When the "interpreter Memory" returns, it does so in a way that provokes a kind of deferred agony. First, Caterina questions what she has witnessed in terms that evoke a network of associations with bodies in suspended animation: "perhaps he was not really dead – only in a trance; people did fall into trances sometimes."[42] Moments later, she wonders whether she is responsible for having killed him, either by wishing him dead or through some unremembered violent action. What these two examples from later nineteenth-century literature share with the brief image in De Quincey's essay is not only the image of the fainting woman – and its sense of domestic spectacle – but also a dislocation so profound that definitive reading becomes impossible.

The catastrophes that came to overwhelm Victorian life, such as railway disasters, factory accidents, and wars of empire, did not so easily give rise to the contemplative and instructive transcendence associated with the Romantic nature sublime. As Jill Matus has argued, Victorian writers framed experiences of what would, in the twentieth century, come to be known as trauma in the conceptual language of suspension, although responses to overwhelming, catastrophic disruptions – both external and internal – became the object of medical, rather than philosophical or aesthetic, investigation. She frames her central questions in terms of suspension: "How did Victorians understand the effect on consciousness and memory of events and experiences that 'went beyond the range of the normal' – events so overwhelming and inassimilable that the ordinary processes of registration and representation were suspended or superseded? And what proposed architecture of mind would support a theory of ruptured or suspended registration?"[43] These are not exactly the same questions at work in the present study; nevertheless, they do parallel my sense that the field of nineteenth-century literary studies needs alternatives to the dialectic of inwardness and public responsibility that has long provided the dominant narrative of a "Victorian" sublime.[44] The structure of visionary suspension does not change, but such embodiments have a different resonance for Victorian poets.

Although this book is at one level organized along somewhat conventional temporal lines, so that Coleridge and Shelley appear before Tennyson and Rossetti, it is also an experiment in a discontinuous historicism that responds to the formal demands and opportunities of suspension. It proposes a version of the sublime that is capacious enough to function in readings of both Romantic and Victorian literature, without assimilating one into the other or reifying the still-dominant narrative that the later nineteenth century's "emphasis on morality (duty, propriety, work) as the restraint of emotional and bodily feeling functions in part as a direct reaction against the too-feeling Romantic body and morally transformable reader of sensibility."[45] Studies such as Morgan's demonstrate how a comparativist approach to genre can help creatively to bridge certain cultural and critical gaps between the Romantic and Victorian periods. In Morgan's case, this means using both Romantic and Victorian long poems as a way to think about "the confluence of two literary-historical trends: the increasing prestige of lyric poetry, and the increasing popularity of the novel."[46] Focusing on texts that are essentially hybrids of the two forms enables her to avoid repeating the standard narratives of Victorian reaction against Romanticism – an orientation that is also shared by Cohn, though her focus remains in the Victorian period. Similarly, Dino Franco Felluga makes a complementary cross-period argument about the way that "the rhetoric of pathology became increasingly disentangled from the novel and applied instead to poetry," examining as well how poets themselves became implicated in this transformation during the early nineteenth century.[47] The present study contributes to this work by holding space for the operations of contingency in ongoing discussions of periodization and, more broadly, for our ability to think "intersecting, overlapping, communicating and non-communicating sets of works, questions, genres, approaches, pedagogies"[48] in ways that take account of both proximity and discontinuity.

Method and Structure

The first half of this book examines Romantic articulations of suspension, particularly in relation to the sublime. Arguably no one explores the multiple, sometimes contradictory affordances of suspension better than Coleridge, the subject of this book's first two chapters. The first chapter offers a broad overview of Coleridge's uses of suspension, paying specific attention to his invocation of suspension to define the sublime (i.e., as the suspension of the comparing powers) as well as a broader context of encounter with a discontinuous world in texts that include the Scafell letter, "Frost at Midnight," and the *Biographia Literaria*. Chapter 2 turns this focus inward. "Christabel," whose heroine is frequently described as being unable to "tell," emblematizes Coleridge's fraught engagement with discontinuity of both the self and the world, raising problems that cannot be solved with the tools of narrative poetry. *Aids to Reflection*, Coleridge's commentary on the religious works of Robert Leighton, takes up the problems of a fragmented self and the gap between faith and knowledge that "Christabel" reveals; both texts, despite their differences, come to be concerned with a common set of questions. Yet, Coleridge remains profoundly ambivalent about suspension, largely because his apprehension of contingency is at odds with his intellectual and spiritual desire for unity. Chapter 3 elucidates a more affirmative sublime aesthetics of contingency in the poetry of Percy Bysshe Shelley. Reading "Mont Blanc: Lines Written in the Vale of Chamouni" in conversation with the *History of a Six Weeks' Tour* (the volume in which the poem was first published), *Frankenstein*, and "Mutability" ("We are as clouds"), I unfold the implications of his "trance sublime and strange" for a world that is constitutively contingent. Ultimately, I argue, the thrust of Shelley's poetry is not towards a triumphal transcendence, but towards a working-through of the intractable facts of catastrophe and loss.

The second half of the book turns to the Victorian era and finds that, within the seemingly secure narratives of closure and classification, suspended bodies index genuine perplexities about life, death, and the grounds of religious faith. The speaker of Tennyson's *Maud* (chapter 4), who believes that he has been buried alive, identifies himself with figures in both scientific and popular literature who suffer nightmarish fates because their bodies are at odds with the reading practices of those around them. While scientific treatises and narrative fiction sought more accurate methods of diagnosing death, Tennyson's poem suggests that the suspension of reference is a structural feature of signification – uncertainty remains even in the most careful readings. *Maud* thus directs readers' attention away from its plot in order to register a profound concern with bodies – and texts – that are held in suspension. Christina Rossetti is the subject of the fifth and final chapter. Her long narrative poem *The Prince's Progress* has often been dismissed as a creative failure because of the way it frustrates readers' generic, intertextual, and even metrical expectations. I reread the poem as one of Rossetti's most sustained poetic attempts to practise suspension in a world that often seems out of control. By refusing to resolve the inconsistencies of her own text, Rossetti reminds her readers of the dangers of both clinging to representations of truth and identifying too closely with the changing conditions of an imperfect world. In her devotional writings, she counsels her readers to "pray against roothold"; in *The Prince's Progress*, she suggests a parallel responsibility to read against roothold in order to avoid reducing the multiplicity of the world to a set of predetermined categories. Like Shelley in "Mont Blanc," she uses language to hold her readers in contemplative, suspended states that nonetheless require their critical participation.

Caroline Levine has recently demonstrated that individual forms "move across time and space," bringing with them "both the particular constraints and possibilities that different forms afford" – even though not every possibility or constraint will operate at every given moment.[49] The focus on the "affordances" of a form such as suspension enables my inquiry to move across the Romantic and Victorian periods without retelling familiar stories of anxiety, excess, or even the decline of the aesthetics of the sublime. At the same time, it also avoids combining these two periods into a "long" nineteenth century, remaining mindful that historical proximity, even adjacency, does not necessarily translate into continuity. The texts under discussion generate their own, often non-linear, temporalities as sites of composition, revision, publication, circulation, reading and rereading, collecting and recollecting. They indicate points of intensity in a longer history of suspension, and their significance unfolds in multiple directions in time and space. That said, this book engages a number of themes beyond those that I foreground in the title, particularly those of theology and embodiment, as well as – to a lesser extent – theories of the gothic and medical discourse. Many of these topics could, of course, be the subjects of their own monographs. Some of those studies have already been written, from Paul Youngquist's *Monstrosities* to Colin Jager's recent *Unquiet Things*.[50]

What has not previously been examined – and what this book begins to explore – is the formal structure of suspension that subtends a number of different methods of locating the unstable self in a contingent world. Far from being relegated to the margins of nineteenth-century discourse, suspension emerges at the centre of intellectual, creative, scientific, and religious thinking.

Chapter One

Coleridge, Suspension, and the Sublime

Among the most memorable incidents that Samuel Taylor Coleridge recounts in chapter 10 of the *Biographia Literaria* (1817) is a particular evening in Birmingham during his 1796 *Watchman* subscription tour when, against his initial objections, he agreed to smoke an after-dinner pipe with his host. Almost immediately, he was afflicted with "a giddiness and distressful feeling in my eyes," a description that plays ironically on his status as a self-proclaimed watchman. Upon arriving at his next engagement, Coleridge recalls that he "sunk back on the sofa in a sort of swoon rather than sleep," yet continued to interact with visitors. Only slowly did he return to a full command of his faculties:

> I at length awoke from insensibility, and looked round on the party, my eyes dazzled by the candles which had been lighted in the interim. By way of relieving my embarrassment one of the gentlemen began the conversation, with "*Have you seen a paper to day Mr. Coleridge*?" Sir! (I replied, rubbing my eyes) "I am far from convinced, that a christian is permitted to read either newspapers or any other works of merely political and temporary interest." This remark so ludicrously inapposite to, or rather, incongruous with, the purpose, for which I was known to have visited Birmingham, and to assist me in which they were all then met, produced an involuntary and general burst of laughter; and seldom indeed have I passed so many delightful hours, as I enjoyed in that room from the moment of that laugh to an early hour the next morning. (*BL* 1.183)

Coleridge emphasizes his own "insensibility," a tobacco-induced suspension of his motor skills, memory, and conscious presence, for comic effect. Not quite sleeping, but also not quite awake, he goes through the motions of interacting with others while also, in the retelling of this story, distancing himself from what he had been doing. Into the space created by the suspension of the conscious faculties that would otherwise be fully occupied with the political concerns of the moment, Coleridge's criticism of the periodical press arrives from some more authentic, enduring part of his identity not subject to the "temporary interest" of the subscription tour or the paralysing effects of accidental overindulgence. The "friends" in Birmingham who laugh – spontaneously – at Coleridge's confusion also have a more serious role to play. Having attempted to "dissuade" him from the *Watchman* scheme at the time, they are invoked in the pages of the *Biographia* to support the notion that Coleridge was never the radical he had then appeared to be. "They will bear witness for me," he declares, "how opposite even then my principles were to those of jacobinism or even of democracy" (*BL* 1.184). Although Coleridge cannot deny having participated in activities associated with radical politics since his body, at least, was going through the motions of the subscription tour in Birmingham, the story of his own suspension (and, crucially, of a truth spoken from a place beyond conscious volition) renders the question of his "presence" indeterminate. He was both there and not there.

The year before the *Biographia* was published, William Hazlitt described Coleridge as "a man of that universality of genius, that his mind hangs suspended between poetry and prose, truth and falsehood, and an infinity of other things, and from an excess of capacity, he does little or nothing."[1] Yet even Hazlitt, with his own prodigious essayistic powers, could not, in this case, say something about Coleridge that Coleridge had not already said about himself. Indeed, one of the secrets of Coleridge's self-presentation, in the *Biographia* and elsewhere, was his strategic use of suspension – including rendering his own body in a state of suspended animation. His suspensions are both salutary and dangerous, productive and paralysing. Though they may, as Hazlitt implies, be self-serving and evasive, they are just as likely to mark moments of radical vulnerability and risk. The elaborately constructed Birmingham episode, for instance, foregrounds, rather than effaces, the disjunction between a past and present Coleridge.

Coleridge's self-generated tropes of inactivity are legion: the writing promised but never produced; the frequent, sometimes rueful, references to William Wordsworth's superior productivity; and, of course, the figure of the poet entranced, held in thrall by the intoxicating effects of inspiration and other drugs. Within this complex of revisions and explanations, the *Watchman* tour anecdote appears as a canny rewriting of personal history at a crucial moment in Coleridge's later career. The story employs a set of strategic suspensions that affirm the image of Coleridge as a radically susceptible poet only partially responsible for the content of his inspirations. As Kenneth Johnston points out, this representation was part of a broader effort to distance himself from the 1790s and "to show securely that he was not involved in politics – not any more, anyway. And it worked very well, on that one point at least: the image of a dreamy Coleridge, lost in his clouds of opium and poetry, is a standard cultural reference point, however cliché."[2] Portraying himself as the object of a ludicrous physical suspension enables Coleridge to have the situation both ways. If he is guilty of anything in this episode, it is a too-great susceptibility to peer pressure: "the lamentable difficulty, I have always experienced, in saying, No! and in abstaining from what the people about me were doing" (*BL* 1.183). Nor is this the first time that Coleridge characterizes his youthful political adventures as the result of heightened susceptibility to external influences. Reflecting on his political activities in the early 1790s from the vantage point of the 26 October 1809 number of *The Friend*, Coleridge allows that his "feelings … and imagination did not remain unkindled in this general conflagration; and I confess I should be more inclined to be ashamed than proud of myself, if they had! I was a sharer in the general vortex, though my own little World described the path of its Revolution in an orbit of its own" (*Friend* 2.146). Even here, Coleridge maintains his separation in a way that strategically brackets certain of his faculties. He was pulled in to the "general vortex," yet only for the limited time when it crossed his own ultimately independent "orbit." Coleridge goes on to describe the Pantisocracy scheme as "the gradually exhausted Balloon of youthful Enthusiasm" (2.147) by whose means he was able to remain suspended above the excesses of Jacobinism (he is once again in but not of the political vortex), much as the effects of the tobacco in Birmingham prevent him from sinking into a belief in democracy.

By dramatizing his own suspended, ambivalently signifying body and his "incongruous" speech, Coleridge explores how it may be possible to occupy multiple subject positions at once and to speak, as it were, from within a contradiction that can neither be resolved nor denied. By failing to resolve the question of Coleridge's authentic political commitments, the passage remains true to an experience of constitutive discontinuity and an awareness of potentialities left untested – something very much like Hazlitt's "infinity of other things." Speaking from the borderlands of an altered state, Coleridge embodies an "authentic" identity that is distinguished by its apparent (and actual) discontinuity with observable reality. In other words, by leaving them both in suspension, the *Biographia* anecdote pointedly fails – or, perhaps, refuses – to reconcile the Coleridge of 1796 and the Coleridge of 1817. The effect of this layering of self and self parallels Coleridge's use of simile, a rhetorical figure that both compares and draws attention to dissimilarity and distance, in many of his poems. As Susan Wolfson argues, while Coleridge seeks "the more organic and consubstantial principles of unity" against a "merely 'formal' species of relation" in simile, he nonetheless avails himself of simile at certain moments because the figure "dramatizes the effort to find a language adequate to represent what is felt to escape representation."[3] If, however, Coleridgean simile lends itself to this straightforwardly deconstructive reading, the simile understood as one practice of suspension among others becomes an effort to register discontinuities and contingency within the world itself, and not simply within existing linguistic technologies of representation. From this perspective, Coleridgean suspension acknowledges, however reluctantly, the possibility that organic unity – let alone a notion of an integrated, deliberately willing self – is at least partially a fiction.

No one among the writers of the nineteenth century explored suspension more deeply or more variously than Coleridge. This chapter presents a "general history" of suspension in Coleridge's writings, tracing several threads of his thinking on the subject, from the poignant pauses of "Frost at Midnight" and "The Nightingale" to the strangely sublime "palsy" that strikes him on his descent from Scafell mountain in the summer of 1802, and concluding with a reconsideration of what the *Biographia* names "that willing suspension of disbelief for the moment, which constitutes poetic faith" (2.6). As the anecdotes in the *Biographia* and *The Friend* demonstrate, Coleridge understood suspension in bodily as well as intellectual, political, and spiritual terms. His approach to the concept was undoubtedly indebted to scientific investigations in the 1790s and beyond that dealt with topics such as physical paralysis, the status of the body and mind in dreams, and the possibilities of mesmeric influence.[4] Neither wholly paralytic nor merely evasive, his experiments in suspension attempt to come to terms with discontinuities and contingencies that refuse to be explained away. He returns to this form at times of crisis and ambiguity and also in moments of ecstasy and possibility. Never a singular concept, suspension enables Coleridge to move among various levels of intellectual and visionary experience, dilating and stretching time in order to bear witness to the discontinuities within the world and within himself. Broadly, then, this chapter argues that an emphasis on volition and the too-narrow focus on the suspension of bodily animation occlude much of what is interesting about suspension in Coleridge's discourse, particularly its centrality to his conception of the sublime. Coleridge's definition of the sublime as the suspension of the comparing powers offers a profound revision of more traditional versions of the aesthetic. Although Coleridge has been characterized by one scholar as "the foremost British advocate of the aesthetic of transcendence with which Romanticism is so often associated,"[5] this chapter reveals that what lies beneath this particular aesthetic is, more often than not, a marked ambivalence about transcendence – one that leads him to remain *within* the experience of suspension and discontinuity. In his hands, the moment of sublime ecstasy becomes dilated, suspended, and uniquely attuned to the workings of contingency. Suspension operates at the very centre of Coleridgean sublimity in a way that intensifies rather than transcends experience, and it operates most forcefully when Coleridge encounters a disjunction between the world as it is and the world as he either expected or wished it to be.

Suspended Poetics: "Frost at Midnight" and "The Nightingale"

By calling attention to what they place in abeyance, phrases such as the "willing suspension of disbelief" have a tendency to take suspension itself for granted, eliding a number of potential operations under that single word. Brief close readings of two of Coleridge's conversation poems – "Frost at Midnight" and "The Nightingale" – will help clarify the multiple operations of suspension, even within a relatively circumscribed context. Both of these well-known poems associate states of suspension with Coleridge's infant son Hartley. In "Frost at Midnight," for instance, the figure of the sleeping child amplifies the "mystery of life's continuance in the night's stillness," by embodying a "doubly inaccessible" (because preverbal) consciousness, as John Beer argues.[6] The original ending of "Frost at Midnight," however, shows how suspension is also a waking state, imagining that the sight of melting icicles will "suspend" Hartley's "little soul." The "father's tale" in "The Nightingale" reinforces the connection between suspension and awakening: Coleridge recounts how the sight of the moon prompted the infant to "suspend" his cries.

Taken together, these poems adumbrate a complex understanding of suspension as both paralysing and enabling, absorbing and jarring, as it structures both the poet's and the child's relations to the external world.

"Frost at Midnight" is a poem that both thematizes and enacts suspension. Critical discourse on the poem also draws upon the language of suspension to perform key conceptual work even when suspension itself is not the object of analysis. For Christopher Stokes, the excessive silence of midnight renders the poet "suspended in this most intimate and yet lonely of times, between one day and another";[7] Felicity James, meanwhile, observes that "the poem holds in delicate suspension the particular and the ideal."[8] The silent musings of the poet are nonetheless in some sense "overhead" by the reader, reproducing, as Tim Fulford has argued, "the suspension of the ordinary logic of communication which is its subject, replacing both by a discourse in which writing overcomes its remoteness from an audience by portraying its necessary silence as a speech beyond speech."[9] We might conclude from all of this that suspension is essentially a thematic and structural given in "Frost at Midnight": a way of drawing attention to the thoughts, activities, and decisions that are suspended, while the disruptive force of suspension itself becomes somewhat dissipated. Yet the apparent givenness of suspension in the poem is all the more reason to reexamine its force and complexity. Composed in February 1798 and published in the *Fears in Solitude* volume later that year, the reverie opens with a description of the frost's "secret ministry" unfolding in "that solitude, which suits / Abstruser musings" (1, 5–6).[10] Coleridge frames this interval when "the numberless goings on of life" (12) in Nether Stowey lie in abeyance as a productive emptiness, whose silence is broken only by the regular breathing of the sleeping child. Memories of childhood disappointment flutter at the fireplace grate, while icicles hang from the eaves of the house. The poem's first lines foreground what Judith Thompson characterizes as the "uneasiness, a creepy, creeping stagnancy"[11] of a domestic space constitutively disrupted by the political that thereby fails to coincide entirely with itself:

> 'Tis calm indeed! so calm, that it disturbs
> And vexes meditation with its strange
> And extreme silentness. (8–10)

Certain binary oppositions – past and present, sensation and imagination, sleep and dreams, sentience and non-sentience – dissolve into each other. The disturbing calm of the middle of the night, with its "extreme silentness," approaches something like the pure suspension that De Quincey sought in the *Macbeth* essay discussed in the Introduction. The sound of Hartley's breath marks the "interspersed vacancies / And momentary pauses of the thought" (46–7), while the father's musing comes to occupy the blankness left by the temporary cessation of the day's activities. The sleeping infant's "gentle breathings" emerge from a "deep calm" (45), but this is a relatively late correction. Earlier versions of the poem render the phrase as "dead calm," a poignant reminder of the close association of sleep and death as well as the vulnerability of young children in particular.[12]

Imagining the future life of the son who sleeps beside him, the father explicitly does not wish to transmit the after-effects of his own solitary childhood spent in the tortured anticipation of pleasures that never arrived, with a heart that "leaped up" each time "the door half opened" in the schoolroom (40, 39). If his son's heart leaps, Coleridge implies, it will be for reasons more typically associated with Wordsworthian joy – a version of the "other lore" (50) that Hartley will learn in nature, when his gentle breathing gives way to "that eternal language, which thy God / Utters" (60–1). However, despite Coleridge's attempts to plot an alternative life story for his son, the child figures a persistently illegible futurity that remains thinkable only as a modality of suspension. "Frost at Midnight," even as it tracks the poet's desire for connection and unbroken transmission, is very much a poem about discontinuity. The future in which "all seasons shall be sweet" (65) at first appears to designate a continuous, predictable cycle. Upon closer examination, however, it becomes radically unpredictable. At once binding and radically contingent, this discontinuous transmission includes the sound of "the eve-drops fall / Heard only in the trances of the blast" (70–1).[13] Within the suspended stillness of the poem's broader frame, these trances mirror the "interspersed vacancies" inside the cottage. Indeed, in its final lines, the father's hopes for his son are themselves left hanging, emblematized by the "silent icicles / Quietly shining to the quiet Moon" (73–4).

These pendulous hopes mark the ending of the poem in all versions published after 1798. This standard version is, as Thompson writes, "aesthetically and imaginatively satisfying in its organic unity, its circularity of theme and symbol," even though it "affirms the self-enclosure of the poetic imagination independent of others and of history."[14] The sense of poetic self-enclosure that leads Thompson to prefer the original version is further amplified by Coleridge's classification of "Frost at Midnight" among his "Meditative Poems in Blank Verse" in *Sibylline Leaves* (1817).[15] Yet, suspension as such disrupts even the enforced calm of the post-1798 poem. Its effects are similar to those that David Simpson, drawing upon the political events of the late 1790s, registers as portentous possibility:

> Uncertainty about what one is to others, about whether there are any friends to be expected, about the predictability of time passing from one moment to another ... is consonant with the odd, concluding imagery – in a poem Coleridge insisted (in 1817) was not political – a "secret ministry" changes the state of water drops and "hangs them up in silent icicles," a not-so-comforting sign of what can happen if one leaves the house for a public space where, in the mid-1790s, government ministries encouraged the stringing up of those deemed threatening to the national interest.[16]

For Simpson, the near-paralysis of the cold midnight scene initiates a trance that throws even the most basic assumptions about temporality into question, turning the poet towards an uncertain future. By connecting Coleridge's language to the discourse of political repression in the 1790s, Simpson recovers a very concrete figure of suspension – hanging – that haunted much early Romantic writing. Here, indeed, we may be reminded of Paul de Man's remark that "A full-fledged theory of metaphor as suspended meaning, as loss and restoration of the principle of analogy beyond sensory experience, can be elaborated on the basis of Wordsworth's use of 'hangs.'"[17] Yet, it is possible to read Coleridge's later disavowals and repositionings as versions of the *Biographia*'s description of him as an insensible watchman in Birmingham. Here again, Coleridge draws on the conceptual resources of suspension to position himself in relation to a previous, half-recognized self; as in the *Biographia*, this positioning is structured according to the protocols of suspension and constitutive discontinuity. The end result is not erasure, but something more like an overlay or suturing: a refusal entirely to close the gap between past and present selves, past and present intentions. If anything, the revision of the poem makes this discontinuity even more clear.

The version of the poem published in 1798 compares the "silent icicles" to

> those, my babe! which, ere to-morrow's warmth
> Have capp'd their sharp keen points with pendulous drops,

Will catch thine eye, and with their novelty
Suspend thy little soul; then make thee shout,
And stretch and flutter from thy mother's arms
As thou would'st fly for very eagerness. (*CPW* 1.1.456n74)

These final lines explicitly transform the icicles of the distant future into the substance of a more immediate – and far less quiet – tomorrow. Unlike the rest of the poem, which contemplates past and future in a more or less conventional lyric suspension, this passage creates what Heather Dubrow terms an "anticipatory amalgam": it "combine[s] qualities of narrative and lyric by referring to events that generally are explicitly or implicitly flagged as not having occurred in what is diegetically identified as a 'real' world – and that ... may or may not do so at some point."[18] In other words, Coleridge turns from describing what is actually happening – the quiet night, the sleeping child – to a future just beyond the poem's frame that may or may not take place. Unlike his earlier musings about his son's future, these lines have a concreteness and immediacy that propels the poem out of lyric contemplation. Fittingly, the trancelike suspension of the frost similarly gives way before the glittering warmth of an anticipated sun. The melting of the icicles is imagined in slow, dilated time that prolongs the moment before the "pendulous drops" of water fall to the ground. In fact, this anticipated moment is doubly suspended, for the child's perception belongs to the moment before – "ere" – the melting begins. At the almost imperceptible point where the icicles are illuminated by the sun but are not yet materially altered by it, Coleridge imagines that their "sharp keen points" will "suspend" the child's "little soul." The word here suggests the arousal of attention and focus, a kind of spiritual awakening, and even ecstasy.[19] Attempting to "fly" from his mother's arms, the child responds to this newly experienced attraction by beginning to move out of himself. His "shout" and physical restlessness (activities that belong to daylight) belie the midnight calm; attempting to escape his parent's grasp, Hartley also fractures whatever remains of the imagined continuity of the poem. This first glimmer of self, of a soul capable of rapture in the face of novelty, ruptures domestic space and pulls the poem out of its midnight idyll. This passage marks, moreover, an early articulation of the connection between suspension and the sublime. In his *Philosophical Enquiry into our Ideas of the Sublime and the Beautiful*, Edmund Burke declares curiosity – "whatever desire we have for, or whatever pleasure we take in novelty" – to be the "first and simplest emotion" of the human mind.[20] If novelty on its own is not fully capable of producing the series of mental events that amounts to the sublime proper, Coleridge nonetheless imagines his child's response to the melting icicles in a way that lays the groundwork for further aesthetic development. Where the sight of the sleeping child had previously reinforced the suspension of Coleridge's own conflicting thoughts and powers, securing a scene appropriate for "Abstruser musings," the sudden, sharp focus of this infant soul anticipates a different mode of attention that is no longer fully under his or his father's control. The final lines of the 1798 poem express a hope for the future symbolized by Hartley, but also underscore the contingency of that future.

In contrast to "Frost at Midnight," "The Nightingale," subtitled a "conversation poem" by Coleridge and printed in *Lyrical Ballads*, is a poem in motion that recalls a walk taken with William and Dorothy Wordsworth in Somerset. Coleridge is out of doors, while his child remains – as far as readers know – at home. Coleridge brings his son into the poetic space by telling a "father's tale" (106):

> once when he awoke
> In most distressful mood (some inward pain
> Had made up that strange thing, an infant's dream)
> I hurried with him to our orchard-plot,
> And he beheld the Moon, and, hush'd at once,
> Suspends his sobs, and laughs most silently,
> While his fair eyes, that swam with undropt tears
> Did glitter in the yellow moon-beam! (98–105)

The story draws upon many of the same images as "Frost at Midnight": a calm night, the sleeping child, the potential influence of the moon, and "undropt tears" that recall the "pendulous drops" of the icicles. Here again, Coleridge avails himself of the lexicon of suspension to describe the change from restlessness to calm and the silent joy that comes over his son at the sight of the moon. In both poems, "suspend(s)" indicates a moment of outward projection, where the child's mind – however unformed and inarticulate it may otherwise be – abruptly and permanently shifts its attention. Much in the same way that, earlier in the poem, Coleridge interrupts and alters a literary tradition that associates the song of the nightingale with the feeling of melancholy, Hartley's vision of the moon pauses his distress long enough for him to redirect his emotions even before he knows that he is having them. A version of this anecdote appears in a roughly contemporaneous entry in the *Notebooks*:

> – Hartley fell down & hurt himself – I caught him up crying & screaming – & ran out of doors with him. – The Moon caught his eye – he ceased crying immediately – & his eyes & the tears in them, how they glittered in the Moonlight! (*CN* 1.219)

The details are all the same, save for Coleridge's description of the incident that provokes Hartley's cries in the first place. The straightforward account of physical pain becomes more impenetrable when Coleridge attributes his son's cries to "some inward pain" resulting from "that strange thing, an infant's dream."[21] Though presented almost as an aside, this comment, like the multiplied suspensions in "Frost at Midnight," creates an indeterminate, uncrossable space between Hartley's distress and its alleviation. The parenthetical insertion into the poem visually and grammatically suspends the statement, marking it out as heterogeneous matter in an otherwise anodyne story of associationist child rearing. At this key moment, Coleridge reminds his readers that a sleeping infant is subject to multiple forms of suspension and illegibility. The radically individual and unrecoverable experience of the dream is further suspended in a pre-verbal or non-verbal mind. Like the "undropt tears" in his son's eyes – an image that reappears in the conclusion to part 1 of "Christabel" – the perpetual suspension indicated by the parenthetical introduction of the infant's dream trembles without dissipating the unease that subtends this scene, despite Coleridge's paternal confidence that "with the night / He may associate joy!" (108–9). One chain of associations – those that render the nightingale a "melancholy Bird" (14) and the dark night menacing – must be suspended so that another set of links may be forged.

"The Nightingale," for all its celebration of the potential pleasures afforded by the moonlit woods, expresses a fear of other forms of darkness and (self-)enclosure. It is a poem that wants to stay out as long as possible, to stay awake, to avoid going home. The father's tale is a delaying tactic, initiated by Coleridge at what was supposed to be a moment of parting; he has already promised "a short farewell!" (88). Lingering in the Somerset woodlands with William and Dorothy Wordsworth, Coleridge dilates upon the story of his son to put off his return to the cottage at Nether Stowey where, presumably, he will find Hartley himself, though perhaps, even at this early point, a recognizably different

Hartley from the infant in the poem. Whether his friends were equally reluctant to part remains an open question. For the "glitter" of the tears that Coleridge describes in his son's eyes cannot help but evoke the "glittering eye" (3) of the Ancient Mariner, who similarly holds his listener in thrall. At the same time, the image of the absently present infant anticipates Coleridge's self-presentation in "To William Wordsworth" (1807), where the reading of a draft of the *Prelude* finds him "In silence listening, like a devout child, / My soul lay passive" (95–6). Suspending the progress of an evening as it approaches the time of parting, he dwells for just one minute longer in the possibility of being both father and poet, while not having to choose between the two.

The Sublime as the Suspension of the Comparing Powers

"Frost at Midnight" and "The Nightingale" represent two relatively early poetic articulations of Coleridgean suspension. In both poems, Coleridge uses suspension to occupy multiple subject positions at once, bearing witness to fracturings and discontinuities in his own history and in the world more generally. There are hints of transcendence in the outward-reaching arms in "Frost at Midnight" and the overcoming of pain in "The Nightingale," but these scenes destabilize the poems they conclude – the former by breaking the "rondo" restored after 1798 and the latter by extending the conversation with the Wordsworths after the farewells have already begun. In this way, the endings of both poems also tell uniquely Coleridgean stories about the sublime: stories where the journey towards transcendence remains in a perpetual suspension. In "Frost at Midnight," the child's attention is abruptly caught by the light catching the melting icicles, while in "The Nightingale" the sight of the moon disrupts the sobs that are his habitual reaction to pain and fear. These events parallel the first two steps of the three-step experience of the Romantic sublime, as laid out by Thomas Weiskel: a more or less harmonious or habitual relationship to the object world gives way to a sudden and "immediate intuition of a disconcerting disproportion between inner and outer." It is more difficult to extend these structural resonances to the third movement in Weiskel's structure: the "reactive" phase, where "the mind recovers the balance of outer and inner by constituting a fresh relation between itself and the object such that the very indeterminacy which erupted in phase two is taken as symbolizing the mind's relation to a transcendent order."[22] Granted, Weiskel's version of the Romantic sublime is a fundamentally psychological and linguistic phenomenon that emerges from his reading of Immanuel Kant; all of this is unavailable to Hartley Coleridge, whose self-consciousness remains opaque to both the father-poet and the reader. For Weiskel, as for Kant before him, the uncertain rupture of suspension is a moment of passage within a broader narrative of sublime transcendence. But even though he stays within the broad outline of this narrative, Coleridge's sublime manifests a marked resistance to the "reactive" phase which, again following Kant, also represents the mind's turning away from the world and back to itself.

Such moments where transcendence is held in abeyance are characteristic of what Christopher Stokes describes as Coleridge's important but often overlooked sense of a "fragile sublimity, a sublimity that arises in the space where desire for transcendence is revised or relinquished."[23] Rather than seeing these instances of hesitation before transcendence as examples of failure or desublimation, Stokes argues that they should be understood as comprising a category of sublime experience. Stokes further observes that Coleridge defines the sublime in terms of suspension in a number of fragmentary comments, especially his notes on aesthetics in the mid-1810s. Though Coleridge never fully formalizes this dimension of his aesthetic theory, the frequency of the pairing suggests its significance. For instance, a series of notes on aesthetics dictated to John Kenyon posits: "Let there be (i.e. ~~in our~~ as Objects of our Conscious [? ~~At~~] Attention) neither Whole, or Parts, but in *All* suspending the Comparative Power, and there results the SUBLIME" (*SWF* 1.351). An approximately contemporary fragment echoes this understanding: "Where neither Whole nor Parts – but Unity as boundless or endless *Allness – Sublime*" (*SWF* 1.353). Coleridge's annotations to K.W.F. Solger's *Erwin* (which he read circa 1817) come to a similar conclusion: "No object of Sense is sublime in itself; but only as far as I make it a symbol of some Idea. The Circle is a beautiful figure in itself; it becomes sublime, when I contemplate eternity under that figure. – The Beautiful is the perfection, ~~of~~ the Sublime the suspension, of the Comparing Power" (*SWF* 1.596–7). Although at least one critic glosses this last musing as being "straight out of Kant,"[24] the centrality of suspension makes it emphatically Coleridgean. Stokes, too, identifies suspension as something that separates Coleridge's fragmentary attempts to define the sublime from that of Kant – he calls it the "key trope in all Coleridge's discussions of form."[25]

It is worth noting that Coleridge had associated visionary states with suspension long before his studies in critical philosophy. The sonnet

"As late I journey'd o'er th' extensive plain," which may have been written as early as September 1789,[26] provides an early example of suspension as the apotheosis of sublime ecstasy:

> New Scenes of Wisdom may each step display,
> And Knowledge open, as my days advance!
> Till what time Death shall pour th' undarken'd ray
> My eye shall dart thro' infinite expanse,
> While Thought suspended lies in Rapture's blissful Trance! (10–14)

At one level, Coleridge's youthful language anticipates the terms in which Kant will describe the sublime in the *Critique of Judgment*. The experience of what Kant calls the "mathematically sublime" consists in the encounter with absolute magnitude: that which, by definition, brooks no comparison to anything else, such as the "infinite expanse" in Coleridge's sonnet. Kant writes that "we do not permit a standard adequate to it to be sought outside it, but only within it. It is a magnitude that is equal only to itself." A few sentences later, he concludes: "*That is sublime in comparison with which everything else is small.*"[27] In keeping with Kant's insistence that the sublime properly names only an experience in the mind and not any specific object in the world, the sublime ruptures (often traumatically) the subject's relation with the external world and throws him back into the realm of absolute ideas that lie beyond sensory perception – something, perhaps, like "Rapture's blissful Trance" as understood by the young Coleridge.[28] However, where the role of suspension remains implicit in Kant's description of absolute magnitude, Coleridge's sonnet makes this action explicit.

In the *Biographia*, Coleridge recalls that Kant's works "took possession of me as with a giant's hand" (*BL* 1.153). However, as Monika Class has demonstrated in her revisionary account of the reception of Kant's work in Romantic-era Britain, this story of having been almost passively taken up by Kant's philosophy is itself part of the project of self-mythologizing that also produced the more ambiguous suspensions surrounding Coleridge's political activities. Class glosses the figure of the "giant's hand" as "conceptually indispensable for Coleridge's construction as a genius because it demonstrates that the act is not calculable, but unaware."[29] In other words, the "giant's hand" belongs to the same category of suspension that we have already seen at work, particularly in the *Biographia*; it provides an image of suspended passivity that both does and does not reveal the complexity of the situation. The conflation of the Kantian and Coleridgean sublimes also minimizes the degree to which Coleridge, as Alexander Schlutz has argued, was "troubled by the violent form this revelation [of the noumenal realm] took in the Kantian account of the sublime experience. The idea that the law of reason should only manifest itself in a violent power struggle with the phenomenal world of the senses and imagination, in which the mind demonstrated to itself its own superiority at the expense of nature, did not appeal to Coleridge's philosophical and religious sensibility."[30] In his description of the dynamical sublime – an encounter with natural force, rather than absolute magnitude – Kant claims that,

> though the irresistibility of nature's might makes us, considered as natural beings, recognize our physical impotence, it reveals in us at the same time an ability to judge ourselves independent of nature, and reveals in us a superiority over nature that is the basis of a self-preservation quite different in kind from the one that can be assailed and endangered by nature outside us. This keeps the humanity in our person from being degraded, even though a human being would have to succumb to that dominance [of nature].[31]

Taken by itself, this particular version of the sublime does not immediately seem like the relatively straightforward suspension of the comparing powers that takes place in the mathematical sublime. If anything, comparison appears to be even more entrenched in what is presented here as, essentially, a fight for true "superiority" that rigorously discriminates between "us" and the "nature outside us." Kant will go on, in fact, to claim further superiority over "nature within us."

Coleridge discovers an often-neglected space of suspension in Kant's dynamical sublime: the ability to consider nature as "a might that has no dominance over us."[32] Although this formula is usually read as another indication of the reversal of values that frees itself from dominance by engaging in domination, Coleridge implies that there might be an alternative reading, namely, that this ability consists in the suspension of the very distinction between the dominant and the dominated. The language of suspension enables Coleridge to remain within the general bounds of Kantian philosophical discourse without wholly endorsing the violence of sublime realization. Still, Coleridge's emphasis on the centrality of Kant's thought in his own early intellectual formation obscures the very real differences between them. And these differences are especially relevant, as I have been suggesting, when it comes to the linguistic and formal framing of the sublime. For what looks like "superiority" is, more often than not, an illusion of dominance. Such suspensions, as Coleridge knows, are most likely to happen in times of sudden crisis and unexpected contingencies, when everyday processes of perception, binary language, and the reliance on "solid ground" (physically and intellectually) have become ineffective if not outright dangerous.

As we have already seen, Kant's Analytic of the Sublime insists that suspension is a "momentary" feeling that lasts barely long enough to be registered as such. Coleridge, however, conceptualizes the sublime as an experience of suspension, or successive forms thereof. "Christmas out of Doors," a sketch first published in issue 19 of *The Friend* (28 December 1809) but that recalls his sojourn in Germany a decade earlier, shows how Coleridge reveals suspension to be central to the experience of the sublime and, in so doing, discloses a resistance to a more violent transcendence that would assert superiority over a contingent world:

> before the Thaw came on, there was a storm of wind; during the whole night, such were the thunders and howlings of the breaking ice, that they have left a conviction on my mind, that there are Sounds more sublime than any Sight *can* be, more absolutely suspending the power of comparison, and more utterly absorbing the mind's self-consciousness in it's total attention to the object working upon it. (*Friend* 2.257)

Seamus Perry cites this passage as an example of a lingering Burkean influence in Coleridge's sublime and observes that, "For Kantian interpreters of Coleridge, this kind of language is very difficult to explain: it is firmly counter-idealist."[33] The language of suspension amplifies many of the "counter-idealist" overtones in the passage by privileging absorption over elevation and dwelling in the moment of chaos rather than moving towards Weiskel's "reactive" or transcendent phase. Heard but not seen, the "thunders and howlings of the breaking ice" on Lake Ratzenberg evoke the threatening polar landscapes of the *Rime of the Ancient Mariner* rather than the safe places of Kantian reason. The suspension of the comparing powers operates with centripetal force: though Coleridge is not "out of doors" during the storm itself, his mind moves beyond the confines of his lodgings, exposing itself to the bitter cold and ice-breaking winds; whatever sense of elevation or superiority results is left unremarked. Rather, when the storm ceases on the following day, he recalls, "Part of the ice which the vehemence of the wind had shattered, was driven shore-ward and froze anew." At sunset, he continues to dwell on the natural scene – a version, perhaps, of Kubla Khan's "sunny pleasure-dome with caves of ice" (36) raised by something other than royal decree. He contrasts the "deep blue" of the frozen lake with "scattered Ice-islands ... of an intensely bright blood colour – they seemed blood and light in union!" Blood and light are not an obvious pair; their concatenation seems to emerge from gothic literature rather than natural philosophy. Thus the terms of this putative "union" remain equivocal – suspended – while the passage itself moves on to ice-fishermen and skaters.

Coleridge's Cliffhanger: Suspension on Scafell and Beyond

This suspended sublime – a sublime, that is, where the emphasis is on suspension rather than mastery – operates in exemplary fashion in Coleridge's epistolary account of a near-disaster on Scafell mountain in the late summer of 1802. Like many recreational mountain climbers, Coleridge had expended nearly all of his energy on reaching the summit of Scafell and was rewarded with "a chemical cocktail of endorphins, adrenaline, and dopamine" – the physical and mental sensations associated with a paradigmatically sublime experience.[34] The descent promised to be a "come-down" in more ways than one. In a letter addressed to Sara Hutchinson the next day, Coleridge confesses to having been "too indolent" (*CL* 2.841) on his return to pay much attention to his route, until he found himself stranded:

> every Drop increased the Palsy of my Limbs – I shook all over, Heaven knows without the least influence of Fear / and now I had only two more to drop down / to return was impossible – but of these two the first was tremendous / it was twice my own height, & the Ledge at the bottom was [so] exceedingly narrow, that if I dropt down upon it I must of necessity have fallen backwards & of course killed myself. My Limbs were all in a tremble – I lay upon my Back to rest myself, & was beginning according to my Custom to laugh at myself for a Madman, when the sight of the Crags above me on each side, & the impetuous Clouds just over them, posting so luridly & so rapidly northward, overawed me / I lay in a state of almost prophetic Trance & Delight – & blessed God aloud, for the powers of Reason & the Will, which remaining no Danger can overpower us! O God, I exclaimed aloud – how calm, how blessed am I now / I know not

> how to proceed, how to return / but I am calm & fearless & confident / if this Reality were a Dream, if I were asleep, what agonies had I suffered! what screams! – When the Reason & the Will are away, what remain to us but Darkness & Dimness & a bewildering Shame, and Pain that is utterly Lord over us, or fantastic Pleasure, that draws the Soul along swimming through the air in many shapes, even as a Flight of Starlings in a Wind. (*CL* 2.842)

Whatever panic Coleridge may have felt upon comprehending his predicament is, at least as far as his letter to Sara Hutchinson is concerned, displaced into an involuntary bodily affect. In other words, his body registers its perilous position before it becomes clear to Coleridge's conscious mind. Physical "palsy" – a trembling paralysis or suspension of the willed motion of the limbs – both anticipates the conscious acknowledgment of his predicament and intensifies when that acknowledgment takes place. Rather than being unambiguous signifiers of fear, paralysis and trembling become for Coleridge a way of registering his presence in a terrifying situation in a way that remains emotionally neutral. "Palsy," however, can refer, figuratively, to the suspension of sensibility in response to terror in addition to other physical symptoms.[35] Thus, "palsy" (i.e., the sensation of suspension and the suspension of sensation) is one of the terms that marks this passage as a description of the sublime. It is not the elevating, masterful sublime associated with the mountaintop, but the awakening of Coleridge's mind to his radical vulnerability and mortality. For much of this episode, Coleridge describes himself as having been flat on his back, a posture usually associated with sleep or a drug-induced "swoon." This proves to be the position best suited for redirecting his gaze from the vertiginous drop below to "the Crags above me on each side, & the impetuous Clouds just over them." Trembling on this narrow ledge, Coleridge comes to occupy, at least for a moment, an elusive zone of experience that allows him both to acknowledge the danger of his situation and his physical helplessness before the forces of nature and to respond without the fear which otherwise would constitute a mental flight from the very fact of his predicament.

In describing his physical and mental passage from terrified paralysis to overwhelming gratitude and freedom, Coleridge's sublime conforms to the general Kantian model of inhibition and release of the "vital forces." Terror and nervous laughter give way to "a state of almost prophetic Trance & Delight." The visionary trance reawakens his powers of reason and sense of humanity that, in spite of the continuing precariousness of his situation, allow him to focus instead on "higher" notions of independence and will that inhabit a space beyond sensation and calculation. From his physically prone position, he can recall feeling "calm" and "blessed," "calm & fearless & confident," even though he is no closer to finding a safe escape route. Nevertheless, he insists that this moment of apparent transcendence remains rooted in reality. Coleridge discovers something like a superiority to both external and internal nature, but his physical survival depends upon understanding his limitations. Moreover, despite the peril of his position on Scafell, Coleridge claims to have taken the greatest comfort from the awareness that what he is experiencing is all very real. Dreams, he reflects, call forth "agonies," "Darkness & Dimness & a bewildering Shame, and Pain that is utterly Lord over us." Even their pleasures are those of an absolute (and thus suspicious) passivity, a too-complete banishment of "Reason & Will." The open-ended, involuntary suspensions that affect the helpless dreamer are marked by an absence of will, by the sudden and abrupt paralysis of sleep, and by the subject's inability to do anything but be carried along, like "a Flight of Starlings in a Wind." Whatever the condition of his body and mind at that moment, he was not experiencing that "narcosis of the will"[36] he associates with unwilling suspensions of mind and body. But the afternoon on Scafell collapses these distinctions upon which Coleridge depends. The threat of a dreamer's suspended animation takes the manifestly active shape of a flock of birds. The "Flight of Starlings" suggests a kind of fragmentation – not simply a split between mind and body, but a more complete (and more perilous) fracturing and dissipation. By insisting that he was *not* dreaming, Coleridge asserts both the "unity of the self" and the "primacy of reason" – principles that were continually challenged by the kinds of dreams he experienced throughout his life.[37] Yet, it was an involuntary physical suspension that kept him from plunging headlong over the ledge in the first place – the palsy pulled him back. Coleridge's relief at finding himself to be awake and thus in the company of "Reason & Will" – a relief, of course, that is reported after a safe descent – emerges from the series of other involuntary suspensions that include both bodily palsy and the aesthetic trance triggered by the contemplation of the mountain and sky. Much in the way that the Ancient Mariner's transformation was effected by forces outside of himself, the truly transformative moment of Coleridge's situation – the encounter with a contingent reality – happens before he is fully conscious that such a moment is taking place.

A few weeks after he communicated the story in epistolary form to Sara Hutchinson, Coleridge published "Hymn before Sun-rise in the Vale of Chamouny" in the *Morning Post*, re-imagining his adventures on Scafell as a transcendent religious experience at the foot of Mont Blanc, a place he would never visit in person. In a well-known missive to William Sotheby, Coleridge recounts his compositional process: "accidentally lighting on a short Note in some swiss Poems, concerning the Vale of Chamouny, & it's Mountain, I transferred myself thither, in the Spirit, & adapted my former feelings to these grander external objects" (*CL* 2.865). The "swiss Poems" to which Coleridge alludes have long been identified as those of Friederike Brun, particularly "Chamounix beym Sonnenaufgange" (*CPW* 1.2.717–19).[38] To some extent, Brun's poem seems to have offered Coleridge a way out of the impasse of Scafell. The account of his desultory apprehension of the poem bears a striking resemblance to the Scafell letter's description of how he eventually found his way off the ledge: "I glanced my eye to my left, & observed that the Rock was rent from top to bottom – I measured the breadth of the Rent, and found that there was no danger of my being *wedged* in / so I put my Knap-sack round to my side, & slipped down as between two walls, without any danger or difficulty – " (*CL* 2.842). The offhanded report of the end of the crisis does not, in retrospect, dissipate the terror that he has just experienced; the effect is parallel to the unsettled endings of the 1798 "Frost at Midnight" and "The Nightingale." Even though the safe passage had existed all along, Coleridge still risked his life as he dropped from ledge to ledge. There is, though, a certain arbitrariness in the way he stages his escape, shrugging off the emotions of the moment before now that his reason has reasserted its control over the situation. This tone is echoed in his description of having "accidentally lighted" on a poem that was, in fact, much more crucial to the "Hymn" than he lets on. Both of these accounts instrumentalize suspension as a way of registering these enabling discontinuities – and, in a sense, preserving them – within the realization of a broadly unifying (if also inherently unstable) sublime discourse.

The Scafell letter tells a story of a dangerously interrupted descent and of a mind that trembles as palpably as the body. The "Hymn," by contrast, remains essentially stationary. This newly demarcated poetic space excludes many of the forms of suspension that had characterized the experience on Scafell. The poet's eye, when it is not turned inward in a posture of reverence, remains fixed on the "dread and silent Mount" (13), now viewed from a distance. His human body and the palsy of his limbs that had been so keenly felt on Scafell are nowhere to be found in this imagined Alpine scene. Most strikingly, the poem replaces the letter's ambiguous marking of discontinuity with an insistence on the unity imposed by the godhead and represented by the image of the inaccessible mountain. There is little room for anything else – not even a ledge on which to pause and consider one's next move. Thus, where the Scafell letter had registered the confrontation with contingency and vulnerability, the "Hymn" at least appears to do the opposite, insisting on a powerfully unifying divine force that brooks little dissent:

> Who made you glorious as the Gates of Heaven
> Beneath the keen full Moon? Who bade the Sun
> Cloath you with Rainbows? Who, with living flowers
> Of loveliest blue, spread garlands at your feet? –
> GOD! let the Torrents, like a Shout of Nations
> Answer! and let the Ice-plains echo, GOD!
> GOD! sing ye meadow-streams with gladsome voice!
> Ye Pine-groves, with your soft and soul-like sounds!
> And they too have a voice, yon piles of Snow,
> And in their perilous fall shall thunder, GOD! (54–63)

Addressed to the mountain itself, the climactic moment of the "Hymn" imagines nothing short of an apocalyptic unity. The vision of the natural world that cries out the name of its creator recalls Christ's entry into Jerusalem when, in response to the Pharisees' complaints about the noise of the multitude, he responds, "if these should hold their peace, the stones would immediately cry out."[39] The answers to the questions are known in advance. Stuart Curran describes "Hymn before Sunrise" as "the best of the hymns written from an orthodox perspective," though he finds it to be less "straightforward" and more doubtful than it first appears.[40] And, indeed, the natural-theological sublime of the "Hymn" stops short of presenting a fully totalizing vision. The poet praises God, but he does so indirectly, using the mountain as both a conduit and a detour. As Stokes remarks, "the expected address *to* God is continually deferred: the natural elements to which the speaker turns are, in a sense, turns away from the primary addressee; or at least a series of folds in this work of address." Stokes reads this deferral as evidence of Coleridge's anxiety about reverting to pantheism and the drive to place God just beyond the horizon of "a sensible, visible order."[41] Equally, that deferral instantiates an aporetic interval between question and answer. It may well be possible to respond, like the natural formations of Mont Blanc, with the affirmation of "GOD!" as the origin and ultimate meaning of existence, but, somehow, that affirmation stops short of knowledge. From this perspective, then, nothing is known in advance. This sublime epiphany must continually be renegotiated and reactivated around the site of suspension. Fittingly, then, in the poem's final lines, the mountain all but vanishes into thin air, its massive presence metaphorically sublimated into "a vapoury cloud" that "Rise[s] like a cloud of Incense, from the Earth!" (78, 80). If the natural formations of the "Hymn" are designed to make the presence of God more palpable, the poem ends with the implication that, in the presence of the extrasensory infinite, the finite itself de-materializes.

When he was not climbing fells in the Lake District or mentally projecting himself to more impressive Alpine landscapes, the Coleridge of 1802 was also working through recurrent intellectual and personal crises triggered by his love for Hutchinson – a personal impasse that did not admit of a tolerable compromise. "Dejection: An Ode," published in the *Morning Post* on 4 October 1802, marks his public articulation of these struggles, though, like "Hymn before Sun-rise," the published "Ode" had a more private beginning several months earlier in the epistolary "A Letter To – " (*CPW* 1.2.677–9). Contrasting his youthful happiness with his present depression, "Dejection" mourns the withdrawal of what Coleridge had considered to be his greatest poetic and intellectual gift:

> now afflictions bow me down to earth:
> Nor care I that they rob me of my mirth,
> But oh! each visitation
> Suspends what nature gave me at my birth,
> My shaping spirit of Imagination. (82–6)

The "visitation" of torpor seems to pull the imaginative spirit upwards and away from the poet bowed down by his "afflictions." In this context, suspension marks a reversion to a disappointing paralysis: the erstwhile genius turned to stone by the sheer horror of his own incapacities. However, as many of Coleridge's readers have recognized, there is a clear irony in writing an ode on the topic of one's inability to write. The suspension of the "shaping spirit" did not, it seems, prevent Coleridge from exercising some measure of his poetic powers. This is also, interestingly enough, true of the earlier and much longer version of the poem, where this passage appears more or less verbatim (save for the exchange of "Ill Tidings" for "afflictions" [238]). Though Coleridge claims not to be able to access his own powers of imagination, the "Ode" nonetheless offers alternative models of perception and creation that are themselves practices of suspension. To remain "still and patient" (88) in indeterminate space is not, perhaps, the preferred mode of interacting with the world for the poet elsewhere engaged in the pursuit of intellectual and physical transcendence and, indeed, in the shaping of his own reality. Still, the very form of the ode provides a way to resist the impulse to turn away and look upwards or imaginatively to reshape the experience at hand. An ode, that is, provides a structure for contemplation. Though experienced as inhibiting, the suspension of Coleridge's imaginative powers also, in this way, reveals itself to be enabling. More than that, the repeated invocations of his suspended "shaping spirit" create a space – a mental version of the mountain ledge – from which the poet may contemplate his younger days when "This joy within me dallied with distress, / And all misfortunes were but as the stuff / Whence Fancy made me dreams of happiness" (77–9). But the language belies a darker actuality: this is a time that will never return. So, too, does his comment that "hope grew round me, like the twining vine" (80) lend itself to an ambiguous reading, one that suggests dependence and parasitism as much as, if not more than, a productive interrelation.

What, then, remains when Coleridge contemplates the seemingly empty space where imagination used to be? He had welcomed the occasion for "abstruser musings" in the opening lines of "Frost at Midnight." In "Dejection," as Noel Jackson argues, "the poet makes moods of mental vacancy, the suspension of the shaping spirit of Imagination, the catalyst to a new kind of thinking."[42] Drawing upon Coleridge's later "Essays on the Principles of Genial Criticism" (1814) – a connection suggested by the poet's complaint that his "genial spirits fail" (39) – Jackson argues for the "productive disposition" of this state of "blank attachment" as rendered in "Dejection": a Kantian-inflected disinterestedness that remains attached to the aesthetic object even when it does not immediately produce pleasure or joy.[43] In the "Essay," Coleridge remarks, "We have sufficiently distinguished the beautiful from the agreeable by the sure criterion, that when we find an object agreeable, the *sensation* of pleasure always precedes the judgement, and is its determining cause. We *find* it agreeable. But when we declare an object beautiful, the contemplation or intuition of its beauty precedes the *feeling* of complacency, in order of nature at least: nay, in great depression of spirits may even exist without sensibly producing it" (*SWF* 1.380). Jackson's account of Coleridge's "blank attachment" accordingly places more emphasis on the perception of the beautiful than it does the sublime. Following a line of thought laid out by Anne-Lise François, Jackson draws attention to the "non-coercive command of the beautiful object."[44] Coleridge's "Dejection," that is, may be read as the dramatization of withdrawal symptoms, the consequence of feeling himself to be cut off from the grander emotions (and their attendant physical sensations) that had characterized the Scafell excursion. I argue, however, that rather than turning away from the sublime and towards the beautiful, the poem's thematization of suspension marks the vanishing point at which the sublime and beautiful are no longer fully distinguishable from one another. What remains is the suspension itself, the abrupt encounter with unexpected discontinuity – the precipitous edge, the failure of hopes and expectations – that, paradoxically, opens a kind of aesthetic breathing space in which the subject is able to reorient his relationship to a contingent reality. Interruption leads to insight, and transcendence remains perpetually deferred.

Willing and Unwilling Suspension in the *Biographia Literaria*

Particularly after the cathecting experiences of 1802, suspension offers to Coleridge a set of aesthetic practices that enable him to hold himself together while opening to the unknown and contingent. In the broadest sense – and in a way that looks back to the physical movements of the Scafell letter – suspension refers to double gesture of holding back and yielding as a prelude to the exercise of imagination, itself simultaneously active and passive. Suspension enables and deconstructs the movement of the will. It is from within this broader constellation of suspension and its related meanings that this chapter's final section will reconsider what is arguably Coleridge's most famous contribution to the discourse of aesthetic reception: the concept of the "willing suspension of disbelief."

In chapter 7 of the *Biographia*, Coleridge describes the process of leaping as a complex interplay of the will and its suspension. "We first resist the gravitating power by an act purely voluntary," he writes, "and then by another act, voluntary in part, we yield to it in order to light on the spot, which we had previously proposed to ourselves" (*BL* 1.124). The image is part of the passage that features his famous "water-bug" analogy for the conscious and unconscious workings of the mind, but where the insect is able to skim the top of the water by "alternate pulses of active and passive motion," the image of the leap suggests a different form of suspension. Here, a human body moves through the air, temporarily abrogating the laws of gravity, and – even if for an almost imperceptible moment – experiences the possibility of flight. Without ever fully escaping the determinism of physical laws, the leaper can nonetheless imagine what it might be like not to be bound by those laws. Such a sensation, however, comes at the price of vulnerability, the act of "yielding" to the same forces one is trying to escape.[45] Although the jumper in this passage alights in a "previously proposed" location, Coleridge knows from his mountaineering experiences that the relationship between intention and result may not always be as close as one would like. Indeed, when he again invokes the metaphor of leaping several chapters later, he does so in a way that emphasizes unpleasant surprises. In the latter passage, leaping becomes part of a point about the "aggregate influence" of poetic metre, even when its effects are not directly perceived. Coleridge describes metre as:

> a medicated atmosphere, or as wine during animated conversation; they act powerfully, though themselves unnoticed. Where, therefore, correspondent food and appropriate matter are not provided for attention and feelings thus roused, there must needs be a disappointment felt; like that of leaping in the dark from the last step of a stair-case, when we had prepared our muscles for a leap of three or four. (*BL* 2.66)

On the one hand, metre gives rise to a kind of hyper-consciousness and heightened attention that takes nothing for granted, the mental equivalent of walking carefully down a gloomy staircase, making sure to feel out each successive step in advance. At the same time, Coleridge likens metre to "a medicated atmosphere," such as might be created with nitrous oxide or, as we have seen previously, with tobacco, and "wine during animated conversation" – that is, to substances that have the ultimate effect of dulling sensation and which solicit the relinquishment of attention to details such as the passage of time or the quantity of substances consumed. In other words, when metre works appropriately, according to the expectations to which it gives rise, it has the ability to fade into the background and exercise its powers unobserved. Where the image of the water-bug described a more or less controlled process of suspension that enabled a continuous responsiveness to the changing conditions of a contingent world, the discussion of poetic metre draws attention to the ways that inner feelings and external conditions may fail to coincide. The result is an abrupt, presumably painful, landing.

These images of leaping, an action that requires both resistance and acquiescence in order to move across an uncertain surface or to hang in the air long enough to direct one's body to a place of safety, offer an important counterpoint to Coleridge's famous discussion of the "willing suspension of disbelief" in chapter 14:

> it was agreed, that my endeavours should be directed to persons and characters supernatural, or at least romantic; yet so as to transfer from our inward nature a human interest and a semblance of truth sufficient to procure for these shadows of imagination that willing suspension of disbelief for the moment, which constitutes poetic faith. (*BL* 2.6)

Coleridge's recollection of having staked his poetic claim to the supernatural in the early stages of planning the *Lyrical Ballads* is usually understood to be a retrospective commentary perhaps inspired by the reception of "Christabel" the year before. If the Scafell letter mobilized the language of trance to give way to the relieving knowledge that it was not a dream, the suspension of disbelief – as a "willing" suspension – provides the opposite consolation: the ability to wake up and say, "it was only a dream" (or an illusion, or a play). This willing suspension has been glossed as the "happy relinquishment of the reality principle"[46] but also as "the contumacious nod of temporary imaginative tolerance to an unenlightened or naïve poet" – or, for that matter, to a poor or disingenuous one.[47] Originally allied to the experience of reading a poem or being in the audience of a play, the term is now invoked in discussions of film theory to describe an experience of absorption.[48] Many discussions of the suspension of disbelief, however, put a great deal of emphasis on the idea of a "willing" suspension that keeps its voluntary power close at hand. This "willing suspension" is inherently partial, power "suspended, but not relinquished."[49] Michael Tomko, for instance, describes the suspension of disbelief as a "combination of active engagement and vulnerable receptivity [that] promises to provide not only a new perspective that comes from the other but also an experience otherwise unavailable."[50] It interrupts the rush to judgment and allows us to learn from others whose experience would otherwise be inaccessible to us. Tomko does not deny the potential pitfalls of suspended disbelief, yet he also establishes an active critical mind as a safeguard against epistemological embarrassment. Indeed, it can be difficult to escape the implication that the willing suspension of disbelief encourages a foolhardy holding back of one's judgment at the moment when that judgment is most necessary.

The danger is barely concealed in this passage, as the "shadows of imagination" for which Coleridge wishes to procure that "willing suspension" are the *Rime of the Ancient Mariner* and "Christabel" – two poems which place the very concept and possibility of agency in doubt. Readers may find themselves, like the wedding guest, held in thrall by the Ancient Mariner's "glittering eye," unable to do more than "liste[n] like a three year's child" (13, 15). As the following chapter will suggest, the suspension of disbelief may also manifest itself as something like the "forc'd unconscious Sympathy" (609) that robs Christabel of her autonomy and renders her little more than a puppet controlled by Geraldine. The emphasis on volition is intended, at least partially, as a way to distinguish between the productive and pleasurable suspensions that attend the reading of Coleridge's supernatural poetry – poems that dramatize the experience of a person who "has at any time believed himself to be under supernatural agency" (*BL* 2.6) – and the more dangerous aesthetically triggered suspension that becomes indistinguishable from outright delusion. This latter type of thoughtless consumption is illustrated in a footnote to chapter 3, where Coleridge invokes the figure of the "reading public." "For as to the devotees of the circulating libraries," he begins,

> I dare not compliment their *pass-time*, or rather *kill-time*, with the name of *reading*. Call it rather a sort of beggarly daydreaming, during which the mind of the dreamer furnishes for itself nothing but laziness and a little mawkish sensibility; while the whole *materiel* and imagery of the doze is supplied *ab extra* by a sort of mental *camera obscura* manufactured at the printing office, which *pro tempore* fixes, reflects and transmits the moving phantasms of one man's delirium, so as to people the barrenness of an hundred other brains afflicted with the same trance or suspension of all common sense and all definite purpose. (*BL* 1.48n)

In addition to being an uncanny anticipation of a twentieth-century movie theatre, this note attempts to establish a border between good and bad suspensions. In the degraded Platonic cave of "beggarly daydreaming," no semblances of truth or hints of human interest are to be had; it is pure absorption that erases individual distinctiveness of thought without supplying any concomitant feeling of shared purpose or endeavour in its stead.[51]

The coherence produced by acts of suspension is intrinsically unstable, and all the more so to the extent that suspension discloses a "semblance of truth." As we have seen, this is one of Coleridge's longstanding preoccupations. The attention that he gives to exploring different forms of suspension indicates the impossibility of maintaining the boundaries that he erects. The assent to the illusions of supernatural poetry is a necessary first step in the practices of Coleridgean suspension. The "willing suspension of disbelief" is as much – if not more – about the letting go of delusion, specifically those delusions that take the form of conditioned language and thought. Suspension – regardless of what other work it is performing – nearly always produces some sort of mental or physical vulnerability as its condition of possibility. One does not need to take a cynical view of Coleridge's motives for recommending the willing suspension of disbelief for his own supernatural tales in order to perceive the ease with which the assent to illusion may become a form of delusion. What distinguishes Coleridge's experiments in suspense from the more familiar practices of scientific experimentation and realist fiction is the fact that suspension for Coleridge is not an exclusively epistemological process: it may yield information and insight, but it is also something of an end in itself, a practice in which one engages for its own sake. Every leap is, to some extent, a leap of faith that requires both resistance and acquiescence to move across an uncertain surface – to hang in the air long enough to direct one's landing to a place of safety. Even the water insect is liable to sink if these alternations are not actively preserved. Suspension thus operates on both sides of the binary that opposes volition and passivity. It unifies but also separates. In so doing it leaves behind the intuition of constitutive discontinuity: the idea that reality itself requires a willingness to leap and, perhaps more importantly, to accept the possibility (and the actuality) of failure.

Coleridge centres suspension in his account of the sublime – an experience that is to some extent defined by its physical and epistemological danger. Suspension, as we have seen, is a highly mobile form in Coleridge's thought, one that offers a variety of possibilities at any given time. It is the posture that enables Coleridge's explorations of the frontier between dreaming and waking to intersect with his meditations on the sublime. The Scafell letter rigorously excludes the possibility of dreaming from the "trance" on the mountain, a distinction that is even more important to specify, since Coleridge's posture is, at that moment, that of a sleeper. The complete suspension of the powers of body and mind render the dreamer helpless before untrustworthy, illegible forces; the figure of "Night-Mair" haunts nearly every scene of "willing suspension," even if its presence is not made explicit. To the extent that Coleridge is able to produce or experience sensations of unity and wholeness, those sensations are themselves constituted by the presence of discontinuity – and the "susceptibility" of the suspended (or partially suspended) mind to surprise. Within the *Biographia* and elsewhere, Coleridge blurs the distinctions between willing and unwilling suspensions, sometimes – as we have seen in the Birmingham anecdote – in order to create a kind of ersatz unity of past and present selves that could not exist in a more determined context. More often than not, he presents suspension as *both* voluntary and involuntary. Coleridge agrees broadly with the Wordsworthian notion, from "Lines Written a Few Miles above Tintern Abbey," that the suspension of habitual processes of perception and even bodily positioning enables greater insight; in such moments, "We see into the life of things" (50).[52] It is an opening of the mind to externally produced images that affect the feelings through their own power, which is stronger for not having to contend with the judgment. The suspension of disbelief that Coleridge describes as the purpose of his supernatural poetry discloses, he argues, "human interest and a semblance of truth" – a truth that comes from "inward nature." Bridging the evident discontinuity between "reality" and a tale of the supernatural through an act of voluntary suspension results, Coleridge argues, in something more than the free play of images and thoughts. It tells us something about the discontinuous, sometimes unbelievable, form of reality itself.

Chapter Two

Semblances of Truth in "Christabel" and *Aids to Reflection*

One of the most notorious examples of suspension in the *Biographia Literaria* is a formal one: what Paul Hamilton calls the "disabling gap" in Coleridge's transcendental deduction of the imagination.[1] Located in the final chapter of the first volume, this hiatus marks the place where Coleridge abandons his efforts to complete that philosophical task. He inserts a letter from a friend as an explanation for this decision. Coleridge's correspondent describes the experience of reading the *Biographia*'s philosophical sections as something of a a violent displacement:

> *The effect on my* feelings ... *I cannot better represent, than by supposing myself to have known only our light airy modern chapels of ease, and then for the first time to have been placed, and left alone, in one of our largest Gothic cathedrals in a gusty moonlight night of autumn. "Now in glimmer, and now in gloom"; often in palpable darkness not without a chilly sensation of terror ...* (*BL* 1.301; italics in original)

In chapter 1, we saw how Coleridge was able to instrumentalize disruptions of mind and body to reframe the history of his political opinions in the *Biographia Literaria*. At the same time, the story fails convincingly to dissipate the discontinuity in his political beliefs, substituting a juxtaposition of competing views for a genuine resolution or a restoration of ideal wholeness. Along those same lines, chapter 13 of the *Biographia* offers an example of deliberate self-division: the "friend, whose practical judgement I have had ample reason to estimate and revere" and whose letter interrupts the longer deduction of the imagination, is none other than Coleridge himself (*BL* 1.300; 1.300n3). The sublime-like experience provoked by a reading of philosophy speaks less to elevation and insight than it does to an uncanny ontological disruption felt in mind and body. The heartbeat quickens, the sense of dread arises as though one is moving through a dark cathedral while the wind howls outside – a setting more appropriate to gothic fiction than critical theory. The letter formalizes a suspension that both separates and joins the *Biographia*'s two volumes. Coleridge closes this chapter by directing readers to a non-existent essay "on the uses of the Supernatural in poetry and the principles that regulate its introduction: which the reader will find prefixed to the poem of The Ancient Mariner" (*BL* 1.306). Yet it is "Christabel," the long-delayed sister-poem to the "Rime," that here reflects, with startling intimacy, this aporia in Coleridgean thought and that comes to represent a paradigmatic version of the paralysing encounter with discontinuity and its spiritual consequences. Although the poem is not named in the chapter, "Now in glimmer, and now in gloom" quotes part of the description of Christabel and Geraldine's surreptitious entry into the sleeping Sir Leoline's castle. "Christabel" is brought into an uneasy proximity with the *Biographia*'s philosophical sections that intensifies the strange suspension of authorial voice and rhetorical genre enacted by the letter.

"Christabel" is a text profoundly crossed by contingency: the ebbing and flowing of Coleridge's poetic powers; the capriciousness of William Wordsworth in his arrangement of *Lyrical Ballads;* the vagaries of more than a decade of recitation and manuscript circulation; and Coleridge's ongoing crises of opium addiction; not to mention the fluctuations in his emotional and spiritual life during the years that elapsed between the poem's composition in the late 1790s and its publication in 1816. *Christabel: Kubla Khan, a Vision; The Pains of Sleep* was Coleridge's first poetic collection in more than fifteen years. It featured only the three poems named in the title, along with prefaces that accounted (however unsatisfactorily) for their fragmentary and unfinished states. Yet, partly because it had circulated in manuscript for so many years, "Christabel" was already divided from itself, seen as more and less than it was – a constellation of projections, hopes, failures, misunderstandings, ambiguities, and suspensions.[2] If, on the one hand, the *Biographia*'s description of the "willing suspension of disbelief," as Elinor S. Shaffer argues, "summed up a complex movement of thought away from mimetic theory that had been taking place for half a century,"[3] in a more immediate sense, it provided an *ex post facto* apologia for "Christabel" and a thinly veiled condemnation of the readers who had, in Coleridge's mind, failed to appreciate properly the poem's "human interest and semblance of truth." Of course, the decision to suspend disbelief and enter productively into the generative play of illusions able to access "a human interest and a semblance of truth" (*BL* 2.6) assumes that the quality and boundaries of the illusion are clearly demarcated in advance. This may, in fact, be the case for a theatrical production, which contains the illusion on a proscenium stage, or a supernatural poem set in printer's type and fixed in a bound volume. In these cases, any disturbing after-effects pale in comparison to what has been left behind in a fixed location or material object. But not every illusion can be so effectively enclosed. Coleridge, as we have already seen, was fascinated by the capacity of the mind to generate phantoms in waking life as well as in dreams. Perception, that is, carries with it the irreducible trace of hallucination. The divided self experiences its identity as uncanny and undecidable. It must rely on a kind of faith – analogous to the "poetic faith" supposed to be the result of willingly suspended disbelief – as it makes judgments about the structure and the content of reality by discerning within it a "semblance of truth."

This chapter focuses on two of Coleridge's sustained meditations on the problem of a divided self in a contingent world: the supernatural, gothically inflected "Christabel" and the aphoristic devotional work *Aids to Reflection* (1825). Taken together, they provide a comprehensive look into what Coleridge, at the end of the "willing suspension of disbelief" passage in the *Biographia*, calls "poetic faith." Rather than seeing "poetic faith" as a limited imitation of some purer, more fully spiritualized faith, this chapter argues that the overlaying of these two texts presents a version of faith that is, irreducibly, a matter of poetics. Despite a handful of acknowledged echoes, "Christabel" and *Aids to Reflection* are not texts that are typically placed in conversation, particularly not in the way that I propose to do here. Yet they are both concerned with the integrity of the self and rely upon shared discourses of suspension. A consciousness that is constituted by its discontinuity with itself must remain perpetually vigilant as it moves through a complexly layered reality, whether that reality is structured by gothic tropes or the mysteries of Christian theology.

Coleridge delivered "Christabel" to the public as an avowedly unfinished product, the first instalment in a story that he would claim, for nearly the rest of his life, that he was on the verge of finishing. The preface to the poem in the 1816 volume includes Coleridge's admission that his "poetic powers have been, till very lately, in a state of suspended animation," alongside the assurance "that I shall be able to embody in verse the three parts yet to come, in the course of the present year" (*CPP* 161).[4] Coleridge's description of his poetic powers echoes the way that he describes his own embodiment in chapter 10 of the *Biographia*. In both cases, the image of suspended animation enables Coleridge to bridge the temporal and textual gap between the late 1790s and 1816–17, imposing a virtual stability on an unstable historical reality. As Tim Fulford has recently argued, the prefaces added to these older poems, particularly "Christabel" and "Kubla Khan," for the 1816 publication enabled Coleridge to invent "a persona that would stand between the author and a personality-addicted public, protecting himself from attack while, hopefully, enchanting readers with a mythologised poet-figure who was too other-worldly to appear either grasping and commercial, on the one hand, or rustic and jacobinical, on the other."[5] Where "Kubla Khan" was an elegy for inspiration that had fled never to return, Coleridge talked about "Christabel" as though it were to be continued – and finished – at some future date, depending, of course, on his ability to reclaim the proper state of suspended reverie.

A number of biographical explanations have been proposed to explain Coleridge's inability or unwillingness to finish "Christabel."[6] In this chapter, however, I am most interested in the structural and thematic difficulties he may have encountered. The forms of suspension he employed in "Christabel" – particularly those having to do with stifled speech, the discontinuity of the self, and, most importantly, the act of prayer – bring the poem to an impasse. However, although the poem as such was in essence left behind by its creator (much in the same way that its eponymous heroine is abandoned by her father at the end of part 2), Coleridge continued to explore its central themes in other ways and in other genres and texts – particularly *Aids to Reflection*. Written in an aphoristic form, *Aids to Reflection* presents both straightforward counsels to readers seeking guidance in their spiritual lives and an ambitious philosophical defence of Christianity as the highest object of human reason. The structure of the aphorism interrupts the logical flow of philosophical or theological argument with "deliberately discrete and disjointed reflections."[7] Much as the dissonant formal elements of "Christabel," such as the "lulling, almost lobotomized repetitions … its shifting narrative voices, and its metrical hesitations and forward rushes,"[8] inhibit the reader's progress through the poem, the aphorism holds a reader up, encouraging the practice of "*slowing* down and achieving a deliberate, ruminative frame of mind."[9] Granted, *Aids to Reflection* does not provide a map for emerging from the gloomy corridors of Sir Leoline's castle into the clear air of transcendental philosophy. Robert Mitchell characterizes it as a "life-manual," the kind of book that "sought to provide readers with a set of protocols that would allow for life experiences, which meant both an experience of the disorientating nature of life, and (as a consequence) an experience that altered one's life."[10] Part of that disorientation, as I will argue here, involves a return to spiritualized versions of the same gloomy, unsettling encounters that destabilize "Christabel." *Aids to Reflection* takes up the issues that "Christabel" raises, imagining ways to remain in the gothic cathedral of the mind, where "glimmer" and "gloom" are irreducible qualities of reality itself.

Spectral Selves

At one level, *Aids to Reflection* indicates, as John Beer notes, "an evident presumption on Coleridge's part that such work" – the work, that is, of deep thought and active reflection on the operations of one's own mind – "conscientiously and thoroughly undertaken, will eventually lead towards certain truths revealed by intuition," and that "those who commit themselves to the discovery of the inner light within will reach a position close to that of orthodox Anglican Christianity."[11] However, that capacity for reflection, so crucial to the intellectual and spiritual methods Coleridge developed in his later years, presupposes an essential disharmony in the self – a disharmony that has the capacity to generate images and delusions, spectra and hallucinations. The constitutive "disharmony" between the self and the self was a problem that conditioned much of Coleridge's writing. In the first issue of *The Friend* (1 June 1809), he writes:

> Among these universal persuasions we must place the sense of a self-contradicting principle in our nature, or a disharmony in the different impulses that constitute it – of a something which essentially distinguishes man both from all other animals, that are known to exist, and from the idea of his own nature, or conception of the original man. (*Friend* 2.7)

To be human is to be divided from oneself and also to be aware that such a division exists. The consciousness of that division – or, to put it more accurately, the consciousness that consciousness itself is a product of self-division – renders man something other than an animal, even as it also reinforces the gap between his discontinuous reality and an idealized originary wholeness. As David Vallins concludes from his survey of Coleridge's writings on "conviction" and "delusion," "it appears that distinguishing insightful from delusive states of feeling was a matter of personal, and not merely rhetorical, interest to Coleridge, underlying the very possibility of trusting his intuitions."[12] The final stanza of "Constancy to an Ideal Object," one of Coleridge's late poems, explores how an act of perception can become one of creation:

> And art thou nothing? Such thou art, as when
> The woodman winding westward up the glen
> At wintry dawn, where o'er the sheep-track's maze
> The viewless snow-mist weaves a glist'ning haze,
> Sees full before him, gliding without tread,
> And image with a glory round its head;
> The enamoured rustic worships its fair hues,
> Nor knows, he *makes*, the shadow, he pursues! (25–32)

Coleridge compares the "ideal object" of the poem's title to what is, essentially, an optical illusion. The Brocken Spectre (so named for the remote mountainous region in Germany famous for the phenomenon) throws the uncanny relation between the self and the world into relief. It is not a hallucination, for the image is produced by external conditions of light and atmosphere, as well as the presence of the spectator at the proper moment. It is, as Stephen Prickett writes, "a kind of experience where perception is in a peculiarly literal sense an act of creation" that "depends on a co-operative interplay of the perceiver and the perceived."[13] Though the Brocken Spectre can be said to be objectively real in the sense that it is an observable phenomenon, the full effect of the apparition will be visible only to a single person. Sebastian Mitchell explains that, "If two figures stand upon a hillside or mountain, then under the right conditions they will both see two shadows. But each person will see a glory only around him or herself, because the diffraction which creates the surrounding arcs of colour can only be viewed from the anti-solar point, the point from which one's own shadow is cast."[14] The division between creation and perception becomes blurred: the phenomenon arises as it is observed. The conditions for producing the angles of light and cloud necessary for the Brocken Spectre to appear are most readily found in the solitude of high mountains and usually at sunrise or sunset; all of these are, of course, conditions that are conventionally associated with the sublime.

The Brocken Spectre emblematizes for Coleridge the condition of a self that must respond not only to the discontinuities of an external reality, but also to the ways that the self differs from itself, sometimes in ways that appear uncanny, detached, and strange. While in Germany in 1799, Coleridge copied two accounts of the Brocken Spectre into his notebooks (*CN* 1.430). Prickett observes that "We can … even in these excerpts feel something of the almost eerie ambiguity of the Brocken-spectre which so appealed to Coleridge. It made such a lasting impression on him that he reverted to it as an image of a certain kind of ambiguity at intervals throughout the rest of his life. In particular, we find him associating it with creativity."[15] The amplified shadow that characterizes the Spectre is rendered uncanny partly because it appears to be so completely disconnected from the observer who casts it. Those who are unaware that it is a trick of the light may find themselves startled by the apparition or, like the "woodman" in Coleridge's poem, find in it something divine, especially when it is surrounded by a "glory" of diffracted light. But as Coleridge and his readers know, the Spectre is simply the man's own shadow caught by a particular angle of the sun at a remote altitude. The poet in "Constancy" does not share the woodman's delusion that the Spectre is an entirely separate entity; the awe that he experiences comes from the knowledge of the collaboration, as it were, between the human figure and the natural phenomena of light and clouds. Scientifically speaking, in fact, the Brocken Spectre was "created" by efforts to investigate it. Sebastian Mitchell notes that "there is no empirical evidence that the Spectre *was* observed prior to its scientific investigation in the eighteenth century. What evidence there is suggests the opposite: that the Brocken Spectre, unlike the rainbow, is an essentially modern phenomenon, and its divine and supernatural attributes only became apparent at the same time as its scientific observation."[16] Yet, as Morton Paley writes, "There remains a certain poignancy in [Coleridge's] knowledge that the image is self-generated. That self-knowledge brings freedom from illusion but not emotional fulfilment is a theme of the later poems."[17] Neither the poet nor his woodman, that is, can lay claim to having had the more "real" experience. Indeed, even the observer who, like Coleridge, understands the scientific explanation for the apparition may find himself startled, or even awed, by its appearance.

Unsettling as it may be at first glance, the Brocken Spectre at least has the virtue of amplifying a visible, physical form. Coleridge was also preoccupied with the way that inner visions take on an outward form. Ignorance leads the woodman of "Constancy" to mistake the Brocken

Spectre for a divine visitation, but some of the greatest thinkers in the world, Coleridge imagined, could find themselves worshipping or cowering before spectres of their own making. In *The Friend* (5 October 1809), Coleridge imagines how Martin Luther may have experienced his "nightly combats with evil Spirits" as an external reality:

> I see nothing improbable in the supposition, that in one of those unconscious half sleeps, or rather those rapid alternations of the sleeping with the half waking state, which is *the true witching-time* ... the fruitful matrix of Ghosts – I see nothing improbable, that in some one of those momentary Slumbers, into which the suspension of all Thought in the perplexity of intense thinking so often passes; Luther should have had a full view of the Room in which he was sitting, of his writing Table and all the Implements of Study, as they really existed, and at the same time a brain-image of the Devil, vivid enough to have acquired apparent *Outness*, and a distance regulated by the proportion of its distinctness to that of the objects really impressed on the outward senses. (*Friend* 2.116–17)

Here, Coleridge is less interested in dismissing these images as Luther's hallucinations than he is in speculating about the conditions under which they could achieve "*Outness*" – a kind of non-material existence similar to that which the Brocken Spectre can be said to possess. The "rapid alternations of the sleeping with the half waking state" and the interruption of consciousness by "the perplexity of intense thinking" (both phenomena with which Coleridge was himself well acquainted) facilitate the movement of Luther's "brain-image" into the physical space of his study. Luther, in Coleridge's account, has fallen into a sudden sleep while continuing to believe he is awake, a condition brought on, as Jennifer Ford puts it, by the combination of a "sedentary lifestyle," nervous ailments, and "theological training."[18] Gavin Budge contends that Coleridge's refusal to dismiss Luther's hallucinations as "mere mental illusion" departs from conventional medical accounts so as to suggest "the conception of metaphor as the product of the materially embodied condition of human thought."[19] As with the production of the Brocken Spectre, these apparitions emerge from a particular configuration of a body and mind in the world. It is impossible either to accept them as absolute realities or reject them as phantasms; from this perspective, the terror of the combat arises from this irreducible ambiguity – the presence of a "semblance of truth" that solicits appreciation while remaining elusive.

As both the image of the Brocken Spectre and the story of Luther demonstrate, diagnosing the "real" origins of supernatural delusion – a trick of the light, a disruption of digestion caused by overwork – cannot on its own rob an image of its outness or counteract the intensity of emotion contained in the initial encounter. As we have seen in the previous chapter, the concept of a "willing suspension of disbelief" that Coleridge introduced in volume 2 of the *Biographia Literaria* participates in a broad constellation of meanings and affordances that pervade his writing. To willingly suspend one's disbelief in order to, say, enter more fully into the emotional stakes of a theatrical production can also, as I argue in this chapter, be the first step in a much wider practice of both recognizing and responding to the presence of discontinuity in the world. It is a lesson in deferral – a training in aesthetic response and sober consideration – but also a call to attend to the conditions of a contingent reality, particularly when those contingencies are unveiled in moments of sublime suspension. Both "Christabel" and *Aids to Reflection* turn the gaze of the subject back upon himself, revealing not a stable soul but a constitutively divided self.

"Metaphysical suspense and theoretical imbecility"

Set in the "*true witching-time*" that had fostered the projection of Luther's "brain-image" into his study and preoccupied with the borders between sleeping and waking states, "Christabel" condenses Coleridge's varied interests in suspension into a single haunting and haunted poem. The poem's adventure takes place on an uncannily still night in "a Month before the Month of May" (21) – what David Ward characterizes as a "seasonal ambiguity that is neither a winter death nor renewal of life, an atmosphere in which one might imagine the emergence of a creature suspended between the inanimate and the living."[20] Alternating between disturbing noises and syncopated stillness, the opening lines of "Christabel" are immediately off balance. They offer possibilities only to withdraw or qualify them moments later: "Is the Night chilly and dark? / The Night is chilly but not dark" (14–15); "The Moon is behind, and at the Full; / And yet she looks both small and dull" (18–19). Christabel herself first appears on this not-yet-spring night as a quintessential gothic heroine, compelled by "Dreams, that made her moan and leap"[21] to seek a place deep in the "Midnight Wood" (29) to pray for her fiancé, "her own betrothed Knight" (28). Her sexual restlessness barely concealed by the assertion of pious intentions, Christabel moves quietly towards the oak tree, finding briefly the calm that had eluded her in her bedchamber. But the stillness of the wood is, like the setting of "Frost at Midnight," so excessive that it trembles in anticipation of its own rupture. Christabel's concentration is broken by a sound, registered first by the spasmodic movement of her body: "The Lady sprang up suddenly" (37). Christabel's "leaping" – a movement recorded before its provocation is revealed – recalls Coleridge's own "palsy" on Scafell and reinforces the ways that suspension may be ambiguously embodied. Her first mental response is confusion: "It moan'd as near, as near can be, / But what it is, She cannot tell – " (39–40). The phrase "cannot tell" will reappear throughout the poem to mark Christabel's inchoate confusion, a gothic suspension of speech that also echoes the construction of Coleridge's sublime, that is, the suspension of the comparing powers.[22] Rather than going on to identify the source of the disruption, however, the poem dilates and dawdles in its description of the eerie calm that has already been shattered, much like the tranced conditions that De Quincey had described in "On the Knocking at the Gate":

> Is it the Wind that moaneth bleak?
> There is not Wind enough in the Air
> To move away the ringlet Curl
> From the lovely Lady's Cheek –
> There is not Wind enough to twirl
> The One red Leaf, the last of its Clan,
> That dances as often as dance it can,
> Hanging so light and hanging so high
> On the topmost Twig that looks up at the Sky. (44–52)

The pause is minutely described, active, and crowded. The narrator's insistence on this stillness is itself excessive and, more importantly, mobile. It performs one of the most fundamental actions of suspension by calling attention to what is placed in abeyance. Verbs such as "move," "twirl," "dance," and "hang" are presented in order to indicate that these actions are *not* currently taking place. The result is a kind of speculative uncertainty – is it, or is it not, windy? What are we supposed to be listening for? The narrator commands, "Hush, beating Heart of Christabel!" (53), again calling attention to disorder and confusion: one deafening silence competes with another. These moments of interruption, not merely generic or descriptive but also formal, lay the groundwork for the work of reflective reading insofar as they "interrupt automaticity"[23] – holding up or suspending the reader's progress from the first moment that Christabel's mind goes blank.

"What sees She there?" (57). The poem pauses again before introducing the figure of Geraldine, who, with "Gems entangled in her Hair" (65), presents a figure of calm stability that exacerbates the disorder of Christabel's aberrant body. Where Christabel "sprang up" at the first sign of Geraldine's presence, the latter glides noiselessly into the scene. Though she has often been treated as an apparition or a projection of Christabel's repressed desires and fears,[24] Geraldine's appearance is described in comparatively referential terms, with her "silken Robe of White" (59) as well as her "Neck," "Arms," and "Feet," all of which are more readily visible than Christabel's beating heart. Christabel's own status as "a received representation – a feminine character who in turn raises the ghosts of different subtexts"[25] becomes more palpable even as her identity becomes more unstable. Where Christabel seems to get smaller – "She folded her Arms beneath her Cloak" (55) – Geraldine seems resplendent, "bright" (58), and larger than life, so that even the narrator exclaims, "I guess, 'twas frightful there to see / A Lady so richly clad as She, – / Beautiful exceedingly!" (66–8). In contrast to her appearance, however, the tale that Geraldine relates to Christabel is fractured and incomplete, involving a violent kidnapping – "They chok'd my Cries with Force and Fright" (83) – and an indeterminate period of suspended animation: "I have lain entranc'd" (92). About her captors she can only say, "Whither they went, I cannot tell – " (99), a line that reproduces the language and punctuation of Christabel's confusion around the site of unarticulated personal trauma.

Although her tale deals rather directly with gendered violence, Geraldine has remained a stubbornly unsympathetic figure, even as the poem's ambiguities have come to be celebrated. It is the self-division expressed in a line like "Me, even me, a Maid forlorn" (82) that foreshadows, in most interpretations of the poem, Geraldine's suspect illegibility. However, responding with sympathy and openheartedness, Christabel puts her faith in the authenticity of Geraldine's tale and invites this mysterious figure into her home. In so doing, she (at least in the eyes of the vast majority of the poem's readers) fails the most basic test presented to any reader of fantastic literature – telling the difference between fiction and fact. Walter Jackson Bate puts it bluntly: Geraldine's story, in his view, "would convince no one except an innocent and rather obtuse maid."[26] Christabel is, by extension, guilty of reading like a girl – or, to use Coleridge's image, she behaves like a patron of the circulating libraries engaged in mindless literary consumption. However, as Karen Swann argues, "Geraldine's tale" – unlike Christabel's – "presents sexual and moral categories as unambiguous and distinct: villainous male force appropriates and silences an innocent female victim." Swann goes on to characterize "sophisticated readers, who employ literary history to read Geraldine as a figure of untruth" as "the worst ruffians" when it comes to their refusal to take her story seriously.[27]

Christabel's reading – or misreading – of Geraldine parallels the predicament of a reader confronted with a poem that seemed just as dangerously unstable. Given the dangerous enthralments that result from her willingness to suspend her judgment and her disbelief when it comes to Geraldine, readers might be forgiven for their reluctance to suspend their own disbelief in turn, particularly as Christabel's seemingly voluntary suspension gives way to a deepened enchantment. Similarly, Swann points out that the generic instability of "Christabel" and the signifiers that may or may not mean anything seem to have been uniquely poised to provoke readerly paranoia: "Coleridge's contemporaries recognized that jokes and dreams demand different attitudes: if one responds to 'Christabel' as though it were just a wild weird tale, and it turns out to be a joke, then the joke is on oneself. 'Christabel' frightened its reviewers, not because it was such a successful tale of terror, but because they couldn't decide what sort of tale it was."[28] Reviewers responded to this collection with concern, consternation, and even horror.[29] In the same *Examiner* essay where he criticized Coleridge as an indolent, suspended genius, William Hazlitt singled out the "dim, obscure, and visionary" "Christabel" for censure as being not only offensive but downright dangerous: "The faculties are thrown into a state of metaphysical suspense and theoretical imbecility" (*CCH* 207). Unwary readers of Coleridge's poem, Hazlitt warned, risk being taken in only to be left stranded in confusion – or, worse, left prey to the kind of mental paralysis that afflicts the heroine throughout the poem. This attitude also colours more recent critical readings. Mary Favret, for instance, makes an argument similar to Hazlitt's when she points out that the suspension of disbelief, when taken as an authorial mandate, may leave a reader unable to avail herself of the tools of critical analysis. "Coleridge's push for 'poetic faith,'" writes Favret, "the 'willing suspension of disbelief' ... especially in 'Christabel,' leaves readers scratching their heads in perplexity and submitting, gratefully or begrudgingly, to the inscrutable genius of the poet."[30] By identifying suspension as the proper mental state for appreciating his poem, Coleridge could not help but imply that wanting to know (for instance) whether Geraldine was a lamia, a man, or a maiden in distress was little more than realist pedantry and a kind of bad faith that wilfully ignored the poem's larger project – even though what that larger project was remained unclear. From this perspective, the best description of how it feels to read "Christabel" may be Christabel herself.

At any rate, Geraldine's behaviour becomes increasingly illegible and unsettling. She faints "belike thro' Pain" (129) as they cross the threshold of the castle and pointedly fails to affirm Christabel's praise for the "Virgin all divine / Who hath rescued thee from thy Distress!" (139–40). The "angry moan" (148) of Sir Leoline's dog echoes strangely in the background, for "Never till now she utter'd Yell / Beneath the eye of Christabel" (150–1). Inside Christabel's bedchamber Geraldine's erratic behaviour continues: she speaks cryptically, claims to see the ghost of Christabel's mother, faints again, and then almost immediately revives, as her "fair large Eyes 'gan glitter bright" (221). In what is perhaps the poem's most notorious instance of authorial misdirection, the narrator goes out of his way to call readers' attention the body of Geraldine – "Behold! her Bosom and half her Side" – only immediately to block the view: "A Sight to dream of, not to tell!" (252, 253). Hazlitt objected to these lines as an obscene gesture masquerading as "an exquisite refinement in efficiency" (*CCH* 207), suggesting that the interests of propriety would have been better served in this situation by a more explicit "telling" – that is, by a description specific enough to limit the number of constructions that could be put on Geraldine's identity. An empty space at such a crucial moment does seem to attract the most perverse (if also perversely banal) interpretations. Thus unusual pressure is brought to bear on what might be thought of as the difference between delusion and perception. If what we see suspends our comparing powers to the extent that we can no longer speak, how can we be sure of what we have seen?

This ambiguous suspension is reinforced by Geraldine's address to her companion:

> In the Touch of this Bosom there worketh a Spell,
> Which is Lord of thy Utterance, Christabel!
> Thou knowest to night, and wilt know tomorrow
> This Mark of my Shame, this Seal of my Sorrow;
>   But vainly thou warrest,
>   For this is alone in
>   Thy Power to declare,
>   That in the dim Forest
>   Thou heard'st a low Moaning,
> And found'st a bright Lady, surpassingly fair.

And didst bring her home with thee in Love and in Charity
To shield her and shelter her from the damp Air. (267–78)

The touch of the unspeakable crosses the aporia between the world as it is and the world as it is represented. Its most immediate effect is the superimposition of a compellingly (and provocatively) simple story on the first two hundred lines of the poem. Gone are the chattering questions, the howling mastiff bitch, and Christabel's panic. All markers of interruption and inarticulate speech are effaced. Even the poem's metre becomes smoother and more conventional, the better to mesmerize a reader, like "a medicated atmosphere, or as wine during animated conversation" (*BL* 2.66). The poem no longer registers the aberrantly "beating Heart" of Christabel; the life, it seems, has gone out of her. Geraldine, who had initially attested to her "Distress" and stumbled over her words "for Weariness" (73, 74), now becomes a composed "bright Lady" who does not need to speak at all because there is no longer anything to "tell." The more elegant version of the first part of "Christabel" emphasizes Geraldine's physical attractiveness over her status as the victim of a violent crime and represents Christabel as being motivated by hospitality, rather than whatever obscure recklessness had brought her to the woods. By limiting Christabel's "Power to declare" to that which is straightforward, the spell generates a narrative that, ironically, makes fewer demands on an audience's willingness to suspend disbelief – or on a father's indulgence in a wayward, night-wandering daughter. In many ways, then, Geraldine's "spell" performs the same kind of revisionary work discussed in the previous chapter: the transformation of the Scafell letter into the "Hymn before Sun-rise" or the foregrounding of suspension, rather than politics, in the *Biographia*'s account of the *Watchman* subscription tour. Each of these cases involves a confrontation with discontinuity and contingency – the fear of falling, a past that can neither be embraced nor rejected, a meeting with a mysterious figure in a place where you aren't supposed to be – and each is revised in ways that foreground the contingencies they are trying to conceal. In "Christabel," however, the simplification fails to take, for the revision takes place within the same text as the original encounter. The uneasy equilibrium of the story told in the spell is frankly presented as an enchantment that opens an abyss between what Christabel knows and what she can tell.

The unfolding of the spell closes the first part of the poem. Before the story continues, however, the poem's narrator dilates upon the image of the sleeping women. The conclusion to part 1 offers a troubling glimpse of Christabel

> Asleep, and dreaming fearfully,
> Fearfully dreaming, yet, I wis,
> Dreaming that alone, which is – (293–5)

This unrestful sleep seems less like a reprieve from reality than a perilous encounter with it. The structure of chiasmus – "dreaming fearfully / Fearfully dreaming" – re-emphasizes Christabel's powerlessness in the grasp of a paralysis that threatens to collapse any meaningful distinction between sleeping and waking states, between dreams and reality. Chiasmus, like the impasses discussed earlier, provides Coleridge with a way to foreground rhetorically the dissonance in assertions of self-identity. As Deborah Channick notes, Coleridge's use of the figure here is somewhat idiosyncratic: "Classic poetic theory defines chiasmus as a structuring device that creates harmony by bringing together oppositions in a unified form, whereas in 'Christabel' Coleridge uses it to emphasize disharmony."[31] Coleridge, furthermore, imposes his particular version of chiasmus on the "somnial space" of dreams capable, as Jennifer Ford argues, of suspending time and other laws. "This suspension," she writes, "fundamentally alters other properties usually taken as unalterable,"[32] rendering the world radically contingent. Indeed, within "Christabel," "[T]hat alone, which is" occupies the absent centre of this suspensive space, a site roughly equivalent to the interval that produced the "glimmer," "gloom," and the abandonment of philosophy in the *Biographia Literaria*. As a result, it is impossible fully to determine the referent of "that alone, which is." This phrase can only point back to a series of other abysses and suspensions, not the least of which is Geraldine's unspeakable body. That mark was described as "a Sight to *dream of*, not to tell," and, for this reason, it remains indefinitely productive of terror. Christabel's dream, in other words, is the obverse of Coleridge's experience on Scafell, where the transcendence of terror was achieved by the realization that the experience, however frightening, was not a dream. Geraldine's touch continues to work its paralysing psychosomatic terror in these lines, a terror, that, as David Ward writes, "remains locked in the inarticulate self and is composed of inextricable complexities of pain and captive pleasure."[33] By the time Christabel faces her father the next morning, she will not be able to tell even the simplest story about the night before.

"Forc'd unconscious Sympathy"

In the final chapter of the *Biographia Literaria*, Coleridge presents the publication of "Christabel" as an attempt to, in a sense, set the record straight about what the poem actually was. Though it had been excluded from *Lyrical Ballads* on the grounds that it constituted "an interpolation of heterogeneous matter" (*BL* 2.8) when placed alongside the fruits of William Wordsworth's greater poetic industry, "Christabel," as Coleridge claims, "became almost as well known among literary men as if it had been on common sale, the same references were made to it, and the same liberties taken with it, even to the very names of the imaginary persons in the poem" (*BL* 2.238). As the author of this somewhat promiscuous – though highly praised – literary property, Coleridge had no choice but to reassert its propriety by offering an official version. He claims to have been taken aback when the published "Christabel" was met with "nothing but abuse ... in a spirit of bitterness at least as disproportionate to the pretensions of the poem, had it been the most pitiably below mediocrity, as the previous eulogies, and far more inexplicable" (*BL* 2.238–9). He blames personal enmity on the part of his anonymous reviewers, again implying that they were incapable of suspending their disbelief and could not, as a result, understand the "human interest and semblance of truth" that had been intended.

But these reviewers may have understood the truths of "Christabel" all too well. The events that unfold in part 2, including the domestic set-piece in the conclusion, testify to the impossibility of setting the record straight. Instead, readers encounter the suspension of reference and of referentiality in its most extreme form. Geraldine proves herself simultaneously capable of torturing Christabel with meaningful glances and of seducing Sir Leoline with a more detailed version of the kidnapping tale that she had related the night before. She now claims to be the daughter of Lord Roland de Vaux of Tryermaine, a former friend of Sir Leoline's, and his enthusiastically chivalric response to this story is punctuated only by his increasing irritation at his daughter's strange behaviour. Bard Bracy's dream of a dove crushed by a snake would appear to be a straightforward allegory of Christabel's enchantment the night before. Sir Leoline, however, interprets it as referring to Geraldine's kidnapping – a sign, perhaps, that Christabel's reading practices are hereditary – and rebukes his daughter for her strange and hostile behaviour towards their guest. By the end of this section, Christabel lies "wan and wild" (621) – and, more importantly, silent – at her father's feet. Sir Leoline smarts at the insult he has received from his daughter and sends Bard Bracy away to Tryermaine. In the final lines of part 2, he himself "Led forth the Lady, Geraldine!" (655). In "Dejection: An Ode," Coleridge had attempted to banish the "viper thoughts, that coil around my mind, / Reality's dark dream!" (94–5). "Christabel" leaves its readers with the uneasy sense that the dream related by Bard Bracy is itself "that which is": the "bright green Snake" remains "Coil'd around" the helpless bird (549–50) – a relatively straightforward image which, in the poem, is misread with violent consequences.

At first, when she enters the presence of her father near the beginning of part 2, Christabel's outward signs of filial piety are swiftly contradicted by the effects of "The Vision of Fear, the Touch and Pain!" (453):

> Again she saw that Bosom old,
> Again she felt that Bosom cold,
> And drew in her Breath with a hissing Sound:
> Whereat the Knight turn'd wildly round,
> And nothing saw but his own sweet Maid
> With Eyes uprais'd, as one that pray'd. (457–62)

Before any explanations can be offered, Christabel provokes her father's ire with odd behaviours that appear to satirize the very complaisance that had made her a dutiful daughter. Christabel's identity, like Geraldine's, is revealed to be a moving target, receding into a seemingly perpetual suspension. After all, dutiful daughters very rarely need to pray in the woods at midnight, and transcendence is also a form of transgression. By the end of this section, she has been reduced to a mere copy of Geraldine, and an inferior one at that:

> all her Features were resign'd
> To this sole Image in her Mind:
> And passively did imitate
> That Look of dull and treacherous Hate.
> And thus she stood in dizzy Trance,
> Still picturing that Look askance
> With forc'd unconscious Sympathy
> Full before her Father's View – (603–10)

This passage initially suggests a surprising degree of correlation between Christabel's mind and body, to the extent that she becomes the image of the thing that she sees "in her mind." At the same time, however, the condition of "dizzy Trance" – applied to Christabel at two separate moments in this section – places both her mental and physical will under the direction of another, more powerful force. "Askance" can refer to either the direction of a gaze (a sidelong or oblique glance) or its affective content (disapproval or suspicion).[34] We can presume that Geraldine's "Look askance" partakes of both meanings, but the poem offers few other concrete descriptions, in favour of a triple repetition of this construction that has the ultimate effect of dissipating whatever information it was supposed to contain. Geraldine "look'd askance at Christabel" (581) after Sir Leoline pledges to avenge her honour, and, a few lines later, the narrator relates again: "with somewhat of Malice and more of Dread / At Christabel she look'd askance!" (586–7), leaving some doubt as to whether the gesture has been repeated or simply prolonged. When Christabel is described as "still picturing" Geraldine's "Look askance," it remains similarly ambiguous whether the picturing is taking place in her mind, on her body, or both. Christabel herself seems to disappear under this ambiguity. Her situation is made more perilous at this moment because Geraldine directs the "Look askance" towards her alone. Sir Leoline sees only Geraldine's "large bright Eyes divine" (595) and grows increasingly impatient with his own daughter as a result. Cut off from its source or "original" version, Christabel's distorted appearance near the end of the poem is at best a parody of sublimity and at worst a grotesquerie capable of turning a father against his daughter.

Much of the language that the narrator uses to describe the manipulation of Christabel – "The Maid, alas! her thoughts are gone / She nothing sees – no sight but one!" (597–8) – explicitly invokes Edmund Burke's language of sublime "astonishment": "that state of the soul, in which all its motions are suspended, with some degree of horror. In this case the mind is so entirely filled with its object, that it cannot entertain any other, nor by consequence reason on that object which employs it."[35] Christabel's "dizzy Trance," for instance, suggests the vertigo of looking down from a great height – the opposite, perhaps, of Coleridge's own "prophetic Trance & Delight" that he experienced on Scafell. These aesthetic resonances were not lost on Coleridge's contemporary readers. Josiah Conder, reviewing the 1816 volume, observed that, "Horror is the prevailing sentiment excited by 'Christabel': not that mixture of terror and disgust with which we listen to details of crime and bloodshed, but the purely imaginative feeling, the breathless thrill of indefinite emotion of which we are conscious when in the supposed presence of an unknown being, or acted upon by some influence mysteriously transcending the notice of the senses" (*CCH* 210). As discussed in the previous chapter, Coleridge's version of sublime experience also draws upon a language of suspension – specifically, the "suspension of the comparing powers." Christabel is repeatedly described in this section as one who cannot "tell." To explain Christabel's inability to answer her father's apparently sympathetic query, for instance, the narrator remarks, "I ween, She had no Power to tell / Aught else: so mighty was the Spell" (473–4). Near the end of the scene, this connection is made even more explicit: "For what she knew, she could not tell, / O'er-master'd by the mighty Spell" (619–20). Although this construction rather oversimplifies both Christabel's speechlessness and the spell that ostensibly produced it, it does strengthen the connection between parts 1 and 2 of the poem by reinforcing the connection between suspension and the sublime. After all, another way to say, "my comparing powers have been suspended" is, "I cannot tell."

Thus, the suspension of Christabel's cognitive and verbal faculties at this key moment enable her to communicate, however partially, a "semblance of truth." Rather than repeat the simplistic narrative that had been imposed on her the night before, Christabel, at some level at least, chooses a more complicated, disjunctive silence that mirrors the critical situation of the poem as a whole: the "difficulty of speaking properly in or about 'Christabel'" that Susan Eilenberg characterizes as "essential rather than accidental." Christabel's suspension, which, in the end, is neither the consumerist delusion of (female) circulating library patrons nor a measured critical indulgence, constitutes an eminently Coleridgean response to the reality of her situation. As Eilenberg concludes, "there can be no language proper to an undefinable subject."[36] By placing Christabel's powers of speech in suspension at this key moment, Coleridge invites his readers to perceive one version of "human interest and semblance of truth" structured by the supernatural. It adumbrates the consequences of suspension when it is no longer possible reliably to distinguish between the effects of a voluntary decision to believe in the fantastic and the duress of "forc'd unconscious Sympathy" (609). From this perspective, the spell which governs Christabel's speech in defiance of what she "knows" is nothing more – or less – than the narrative demands placed on the subjected, speaking self who attempts to testify to an unspeakable reality.

The Pains of Prayer

"To pray," writes the theologian Michael F. Andrews, "means always to pray to God, to pray with the passion of the infinite, to pray for the possibility of givenness *without condition*, to pray for the impossible."[37] To pray for the impossible is a form of "willing suspension" – a giving-over of oneself to an absolute experience of reality, beyond words, beyond knowledge, and, moreover, beyond cause and effect. The Apostle Paul writes in the letter to the Romans that "the Spirit also helpeth our infirmities: for we know not what we should pray for as we ought; but the Spirit itself maketh intercession for us with groanings which cannot be uttered."[38] Prayer, that is, achieves the most when the animating intention of the supplicant is least articulated. It is something of a paradigmatic speech act for Christabel, who finds herself particularly ill served by the maxim, "Saints will aid if Men will call" (330). Transcending the inability of human language fully to express the human desire for the divine, prayer as described by Paul takes on a radical dimension that removes it from the economies of narrative and representation and enables the subject, paradoxically, to will that his will conforms to God's. The demands of this kind of faith are rigorous, requiring not merely adherence to a law but also a conscious choice to abandon the self to the sublimity of a faith without seeing, without touching, without sensibility. The spiritual subject, like "Christabel" itself, must remain poised in a state of actively suspended animation.

Prayer – or, more specifically, the act or appearance of being at prayer – is a central motif in "Christabel." It is, after all, the intention to "pray / For the Weal of her Lover, that's far away" (29–30) that first drives Christabel from unrestful sleep into the "Midnight Wood" and thus into the poem itself; it is this activity that is interrupted by Geraldine's appearance. The narrator finds this image so compelling that he returns to it in the conclusion to part 1 in order to impress upon his readers a greater sense of Christabel's piety and innocence:

> It was a lovely Sight to see
> The Lady Christabel, when She
> Was praying at the old Oak Tree. (279–81)

Recasting Christabel as "a lovely Sight to see" interposes another layer of mediation between the reader and the events narrated earlier in the poem. Previously, the emphasis had been on her actions: "She kneels beneath the huge Oak Tree, / And in Silence prayeth She" (35–6). Relocated and fixed in a suspended past, Christabel becomes less a subject than an object of a controlling gaze, anticipating the more explicit representations of suspended will in part 2. So too does the narrator's comparison of Christabel to "a youthful Hermitess, / Beauteous in a Wilderness / Who, praying always, prays in Sleep" (320–2) have the effect of naturalizing Christabel's silence as a function of both her piety and her gender. The opacity of these scenes, not to mention the intrinsic mystery of prayer itself, makes these moments – and, by extension, Christabel's motivations – radically ambiguous. Thus, on the one hand, it is possible, as J. Robert Barth argues, that Christabel's prayers "spring from a desire to reach beyond oneself: to love and embrace the other – as Christabel longs for her lover, for her departed mother, for her father, even for Geraldine – and ultimately to reach beyond one's own weakness to a transcendent meaning or reality."[39] Barth, that is, presumes that Christabel's posture offers a clear indication of her spiritual intentions and desire for a truth that is larger than herself. Andrew Cooper, on the other hand, weighs more or less the same evidence and concludes that Christabel's piety is, at best, superficial: "it appears the girl has composed herself according to the moral chiaroscuro typical of Ann Radcliffe, where the heroine's unspotted purity is always set off by its dangerous proximity to darkness."[40] Far from placing her piety and purity beyond debate, Cooper reads these references to Christabel's prayers as a set of clichés that obscure the heroine's true nature, a performance in which she is centrally complicit. The narrator equivocates.

The insistence that Christabel is a "lovely Sight" when she prays at the oak tree omits any specific reference to the purpose of those prayers that had been foregrounded at the beginning of the poem. When she begins to writhe under Geraldine's influence in part 2, moreover, Christabel initially appears to her father "With Eyes uprais'd, *as* one that pray'd" (462, italics mine) – a construction that emphasizes the potential emptiness of this posture. In this moment, she resembles the "hypocrites" condemned by Christ for praying while "standing in the synagogues and in the corners of the streets, that they may be seen of men."[41] To be seen at prayer, then, is already to have the efficacy of one's supplication undermined and one's motives questioned. Yet, even private prayers seem to fail her. During a temporary suspension of the "Trance" that has overtaken her, "the Maid / Paus'd awhile, and inly pray'd" (613–14) – presumably for sufficient strength to make her final utterance. But Sir Leoline ignores Christabel's plea (her last spoken words in the poem) to send Geraldine away. Her powers of supplication seem particularly ineffectual, to the point that it is often impossible to "tell" for what or to whom she is praying. Yet, prayer, as Coleridge understands it, demands a willingness to divide and suspend the self and, moreover, to "affirm what it cannot understand (i.e., God and a personal relation to him) in order to understand itself."[42] Operating in close proximity to the avowals of her inability to "tell," Christabel's prayers disclose the radical discontinuity that is the enabling condition for the spiritual self. Far from achieving transcendence, they appear to trap her more fully within herself.

The images of Christabel at prayer are further complicated by the ways that the language of the poem parallels the agonized scenes of "The Pains of Sleep." This poem, the final text in the 1816 volume, opens with two competing scenes of spiritual meditation. Coleridge first recounts his habitual mode of praying:

> silently by slow degrees,
> My spirit I to Love compose,
> In humble Trust mine eye-lids close,
> With reverential resignation,
> No wish conceived, no thought expressed!
> Only a *sense* of supplication ... (4–9)

Prayer appears here as a salutary practice of willing suspension – a suspension not simply of bodily animation and perception, but of the workings of a language-bound mind that quiets itself into a non-specific "*sense* of supplication." Yet, like Christabel's increasingly troubled sleep, Coleridge's prayers take on a disturbingly unwilled dimension:

> But yester-night I pray'd aloud
> In anguish and in agony,
> Up-starting from the fiendish crowd
> Of shapes and thoughts that tortured me ... (14–17)

These lines connect spoken prayers to the machinations of a "fiendish crowd" that emerges from the projections of his own mind. They take on a now-unwelcome "outness" that deconstructs the boundary between the will and its suspension. Coleridge encounters not one stranger or one "bright Lady," but a multitude of disturbing images and thoughts that have seemingly been unleashed in this act of reflection.

His description of "the powerless will / Still baffled, and yet burning still" (21–2) evokes Christabel's vulnerability to her own nightmares, along with the disturbing possibility that these visions and terrors might, in fact, comprise the whole of "that which is." What is perhaps even more painful about these lines, especially when read alongside "Christabel," is that they mark the disarticulation of knowledge from the ability to speak about or act on that knowledge; essentially, they formalize the inability to "tell." The version of suspension that is represented in "The Pains of Sleep" is closer to the double bind that arises upon viewing the Brocken Spectre that is described in "Constancy to an Ideal Object" than it is to, say, the visionary height of the Scafell letter. The message of "Constancy," as Sebastian Mitchell argues, is that "your understanding of the causes of the ideal object will not stop you yearning for it. The glory's fair hues are not dispelled by the knowledge of how these images are produced, just as a grasp of the psychology of idealisation does not dissolve the emotional substance which such ideal thinking produces."[43] Knowing the dream *as* dream – or, as in Christabel's case, knowing the spell *as* spell – does not make Coleridge any less subject to it. Indeed, while the representation of nightmares in "The Pains of Sleep" may have been to some extent politically expedient, as Fulford and others have suggested, it also – and perhaps more emphatically – draws attention to what Ford calls "a self which is perceived as fundamentally dislodged and disrupted."[44]

At the beginning of part 2, Christabel wakes from her own dreams into Geraldine's disruptive presence, and experiences a sense of obscure, transpersonal guilt – "Sure I have sinn'd!" (381) – that leads her to pray "That He, who on the Cross did groan, / Might wash away her Sins unknown" (389–90). There is a sense in these lines that Christabel is, as it were, attempting to cover all her bases by seeking forgiveness for unacknowledged crimes: is it the pious suspension of the self that constitutes (poetic) faith, or simply a wilful suspension of accountability that evades responsibility? The lines evoke the by now familiar "theme of not knowing why the sinful feeling arises, of being spellbound and unable to articulate why the guilt is felt" that Ford characterizes as "a recurrent feature of Coleridge's quest to comprehend his dreams."[45] Similarly, the Coleridge of "The Pains of Sleep" is jarred into consciousness by his "own loud scream" (37) on the third night of protracted sufferings. His prayers thus appear to make him more vulnerable to contingency – including the contingency generated by his own conflicted, discontinuous self. The "shame and terror" (26) of the opium dreamer consists in the confused proximity to horrible sins that makes it impossible to tell "Whether I suffered, or I did" (29). This is a particularly damning comment for Coleridge to make about himself, for, as Alexander Schlutz has argued, the "dual condemnation of the self as both the perpetrator and the victim of a crime in a universe that provides no readable signs of a moral order and the existence of a benevolent God, is, needless to say, precisely *not* the religious framework Coleridge sought to secure in his attempts to establish a complete philosophical system."[46] At the same time, however, the structure of division proliferates in Coleridge's own spiritual experiences to the extent that they reveal themselves to be constitutive of the undivided system he seeks. Thus, though Coleridge, in "The Pains of Sleep" and elsewhere, seeks to let go of his sinful selfhood in order to find himself regenerated through the influence of the Holy Spirit, he finds that all of the paradoxes and discontinuities that he harbours are heightened rather than effaced.

Both "Christabel" and "The Pains of Sleep" were composed prior to 1813–14, one of Coleridge's worst periods for opium use and spiritual doubt.[47] Yet, in many ways, they seem to anticipate this crisis. A December 1813 letter describes Coleridge's mental state in painfully vivid terms:

> O I have seen far, far deeper and clearer than I ever saw before the ground of pernicious errors! O I have seen, I have felt that the worst offences are those against our own souls! That our souls are infinite in depth, and therefore our sins are infinite, and redeemable only by an infinitely higher infinity; that of the Love of God in Christ Jesus. I have called my soul infinite, but O infinite in the depth of darkness, an infinite craving, an infinite capacity of pain and weakness, and excellent only as being passively capacious of the light from above. Should I recover I will – no – no may God grant me power to struggle to become *not another* but a *better man* – . (*CL* 3.463)

Coleridge has a reputation for being hyperbolic when in pain. Nevertheless, his letters from these months testify to both a profound despair and an at least intermittently courageous determination to confront his deeply troubled self. It is one thing to encounter the sublime through the mediation of some natural, external force such as a mountain or high cliff. It is quite another, as Coleridge recognizes, to discover within oneself an infinity that seems constituted by the "darkness" and "craving," "pain and weakness" that one had hoped to escape. Coleridge nonetheless affirms the very discontinuity of his broken selfhood. To the extent that this letter suggests any kind of transcendence, it is not the "rising above" of the conventional sublime but a recommitment to the act of reflection: his determination to "become *not another* but a *better man*" – sadder and wiser, perhaps, but also more attuned to the constitutive discontinuity of the self. If the "willing suspension of disbelief for the moment" was, in Coleridge's mind, the thing that "constitutes poetic faith," then something like a self in suspension – a self *as* suspension – became increasingly necessary for religious faith and, for that matter, personal survival.

Meeting the Secret Lodger: From "Christabel" to *Aids to Reflection*

In an 1814 letter to his erstwhile publisher, Joseph Cottle, Coleridge concluded that

> Christians expect no outward or sensible Miracles from Prayer – it's effects and it's fruitions are spiritual, and accompanied (to use the words of that true *Divine*, Archbishop Leighton) "not by Reasons and Arguments; but by an inexpressible Kind of Evidence, which they only know who have it." (*CL* 3.478–9)

Coleridge's understanding of prayer as that which can never raise the expectation of outward effects – at least not in the mind of a true Christian – helps explain why the presence of so many conflicting scenes of prayer and supplication in "Christabel" inhibits narrative closure. To take the poem to a tragic conclusion (or to call the final scene of paternal rejection an ending) would be intolerable, amounting to an abandonment of both spiritual and poetic faith. But a more conventionally "happy" ending, one perhaps closing with the long-wished-for marriage to the faraway lover and the defeat of Geraldine, would risk presenting prayer as one among many mechanistic exercises designed to produce a predetermined "outward or sensible" result: a speech that more closely resembles a hypnotic incantation or a paralysing spell.

In a note he appended to this letter to Cottle, Coleridge remarks that "If there could be an intermediate Space between inspired & uninspired Writings, that Space would be occupied by Leighton" (*CL* 3.479). Leighton's writings provide a similar "intermediate space" for Coleridge.

Just as Coleridge turned briefly to Leighton in his letter to Cottle, it was partly through his longer imagined conversation with the seventeenth-century archbishop that Coleridge was able to return to the spiritual issues raised by "Christabel."[48] A decade before the publication of the result – that is, before the publication of *Aids to Reflection* – Coleridge was already engaged in using Leighton as a theological sounding-board as he undertakes the process of reading and reflection in the hopes of regaining a sense of "intellectual stability"[49] grounded in something other than mechanistic necessity. *Aids to Reflection*, begun as a series of commentaries on excerpts from the work of Archbishop Robert Leighton, seems at first glance to represent a rather different Coleridge from the one who composed *Christabel: Kubla Khan, A Vision; The Pains of Sleep*. The task that Coleridge set himself in *Aids to Reflection* was partly an intellectual defence of Christianity, largely through the elaboration of a definitive distinction between reason and understanding, and partly through the development of a method for reflection which others could adopt in their own spiritual negotiations. Alan Vardy captures both these dimensions in his characterization of *Aids to Reflection* as "a Kantian reflection on Leighton's aphorisms" and a work whose "true significance ... was not to be found in *what* to think, but rather in *how* to think."[50] Coleridge remains attuned to the multiplicity of meanings and associations attached to the notion of reflection. John Beer, who devotes an entire section of his editorial introduction to *Aids* to the topic, points out that reflection "could be used both as an abstract word to describe a mental process and as an image invoking metaphors of religious and moral illumination" and traces this "double sense" back to writers such as Plato and Thomas Aquinas (*AR* lxxxix). Reflection thus remains mobile, its referential status suspended and uncertain.

Near the beginning of *Aids*, Coleridge assures his reader, "[B]y reflection you may draw from the fleeting facts of your worldly trade, art, or profession, a science permanent as your immortal soul; and make even these subsidiary and preparative to the reception of spiritual truth" (*AR* 10). This "reflection" consists in an active, creative responsiveness to paradox and discontinuity, a practice of faith that consistently recognizes the essential non-coincidence of the human soul with itself. The nature of Coleridge's project – his intention to demonstrate that, as Douglas Hedley writes, "Language is ... *a living power which enables men to improve their vision of the truth*"[51] – means that it cannot be otherwise. Through its recognition of contingency and its reliance on suspension as form and method, *Aids to Reflection* enacts a movement beyond associationist determination into an unknown, uncharted future. For Coleridge, I argue, this movement held the possibility of an alternative to feeling that was not merely thinking. Recovering the shared discourse of uncanny suspension in "Christabel" and *Aids to Reflection* demonstrates that the seemingly circumscribed aesthetic claims of the "willing suspension of disbelief" are, indeed, at the very centre of Coleridge's spiritual and philosophical practices. The resonances between "Christabel" and *Aids* suggest the extent to which the experience of sublimity provides the groundless ground of Coleridgean faith – much more than it does, for that matter, in Kant. A recent essay by Murray J. Evans analyses the sublime language of *Aids* in terms of the "crossing or moving of boundaries," such as those between "unbelief and belief – and between either of these and the possibility of faith."[52] Building on Evans's general contention about the sublimity of religion in *Aids to Reflection*, I will offer a deeper understanding of the ultimately aesthetic investments of this late religious text, paying particular attention to the way that Coleridge, echoing the language of "Christabel," constructs reflection as a practice of suspension.

In the *Biographia Literaria*, Coleridge criticized the associationist thinking of David Hartley because it held that "the will, and with the will all acts of thought and attention, are parts and products of this blind mechanism, instead of being distinct powers, whose function it is to controul, determine, and modify the phantasmal chaos of association" (*BL* 1.116). He again alludes to these conventions in *Aids to Reflection*:

> If you have resolved that all belief of a divine Comforter present to our inmost Being and aiding our infirmities, is fond and fanatical – if the Scriptures promising and asserting such communion are to be explained away into the action of circumstances, and the necessary movements of the vast machine, in one of the circulating chains of which the human Will is a petty Link – in what better light can Prayer appear to you, than the groans of a wounded Lion in his solitary Den, or the howl of a Dog with his eyes on the Moon? (*AR* 86)

The "sixteen short Howls" of Sir Leoline's "toothless mastiff Bitch" (12, 7) that rattle the opening lines of "Christabel" are, in *Aids to Reflection*, transformed into the futile cacophony of associationist dogma.[53] The "vast machine" of determinism obscures and threatens the practice of faith. One of the ways that Coleridge works against the associationist machine in *Aids to Reflection* is through his use of the aphorism. Suspension is central to the genre of aphoristic writing. The aphorism's disjointed formal qualities enable Coleridge to nudge his reader towards the discovery of truth, a discovery at once spontaneous and orthodox, capable of resisting both the flight into dogmatic certainty and the collapse into mechanistic necessity. In fact, the very first aphorism of *Aids* acknowledges the shared function of poetry and philosophy in awakening the otherwise insensible soul to active, participatory thought through a process of what is, essentially, defamiliarization:

> Extremes meet. Truths, of all others the most awful and interesting, are too often considered as *so* true, that they lose all the power of truth, and lie bed-ridden in the dormitory of the soul, side by side with the most despised and exploded errors. (*AR* 11)

To put it another way, the subject must pass from one form of suspension (the paralysed slumber in the "dormitory of the soul") to another (a suspension of judgment that persists throughout the duration of the act of reflection). And so, too, must the subject continually suspend the assumptions, even those seemingly based on experience, that separate reason and mystery and confuse facts with truth. Coleridge thereby appeals to a reader's "gratuitous and (as it were) *experimentative* faith in the Writer" (*AR* 9). To understand fully the method the book lays out, the reader must in a sense pay her faith forward, without condition or expectation. This mental movement resembles the "poetic faith" of which Coleridge had written in the *Biographia Literaria*, a faith constituted through a willing suspension of disbelief. And just as the willing suspension of disbelief places a reader at the risk of excusing lapses that should not be excused, this "experimentative faith," a giving-over of oneself to the thought processes of another, has the potential to be dangerous – not least because, once undertaken, the practice of reflection has the ability to confront a reader with an inner and outer world far more discontinuous, and far more strange, than she had expected.

The reader who wishes to embark on the work of reflection will, Coleridge grants, experience opposition from other people. But the most important battles are to be fought against one's own fears and inhibitions. The pain of reflection – of seeing the self in all its strangeness, discontinuity, and vulnerability to contingency – is greater, Coleridge contends, than any physical mortifications carried out in the name of spiritual enlightenment. Most people, he suggests, would prefer literally to walk through hot coals than contend with what they find within themselves:

> In countries enlightened by the gospel ... the most formidable and (it is to be feared) the most frequent impediment to men's turning the mind inward upon themselves, is that they are afraid of what they shall find there. There is an aching hollowness in the bosom, a dark cold speck at the heart, an obscure and boding sense of a somewhat, that must be kept *out of sight* of the conscience; some secret lodger, whom they can neither resolve to eject or retain. (*AR* 24)

As he had elsewhere, particularly in the anecdote of Luther's dreams, Coleridge accords a certain "outness" to the unspeakable forebodings raised by the encounter with what is at once wholly unexpected, radically contingent, and irreducibly personal. The capacity for reflection that separates man from animals becomes, in this version of the situation, "an obscure and boding sense of a somewhat." Scholars have tended to read the "secret lodger" as an embodiment of something unmistakably evil, a characterization that, as we have seen, has also been applied to Geraldine. Michael S. Macovski, for instance, links the figure to "what Coleridge had earlier described as 'some hidden vice' that continually threatens him, an undisclosed evil," while Anya Taylor notes that it allows Coleridge to "acknowledge the dark self he might find" when he reflects upon his own nature.[54] To some extent, these interpretations are authorized by Coleridge's note on the passage, which includes a sonnet by George Herbert, "Graces vouchsafed in a Christian land." Essentially, this poem bemoans the power of a single "BOSOM-SIN" to destroy the spiritual fruits that are cultivated by nearly every part of society, from parents and teachers to laws and "Bibles laid open" (*AR* 24n). Yet read from another perspective, the "BOSOM-SIN," however deplorable, nonetheless offers a singular point of resistance to an admittedly overwhelming ideological complex that encompasses not only social life but also what Herbert calls "Angels and grace; eternal hopes and fears!" Obviously, Coleridge is not endorsing the practice of holding on to one's sense of guilt or secret sin in order to achieve some modicum of breathing space in a culture choked by the determinations of Christianity. But something like the confrontation with this spectral self is an essential step in the process of more trenchant and salutary reflections that no longer rely on their cultural reinforcement; in other words, these practices keep the truths from becoming too true. Coleridge specifically does not mandate a reflex action that would purge the mind of anything that does not fit in with its best version of itself. Rather, as Christopher Stokes points out, "Coleridge considers it imperative to stare this secret lodger in the face, this impurity or stain on the *tabula rasa*."[55]

The uncanny encounter with the "secret lodger" – this strangely familiar stranger whose presence confuses and even paralyses the will – seems clearly to evoke the meeting of Christabel and Geraldine, as well as, more implicitly, the gothic cathedral erected in the empty space at the centre of the *Biographia Literaria* where Coleridge had interrupted himself. There, too, his invented correspondent had reported that his reading had been accompanied by a "*chilly sensation of terror*" (*BL* 1.301, italics in original). *Aids to Reflection*'s sense of a "dark cold speck at the heart" further recalls the "chilly but not dark" weather in "Christabel" and suggests failed projects of self-consolidation – how do you protect yourself from the cold that comes from within? Although it is tempting to think of "Christabel" as the supernatural nightmare from which the philosophical rigour of *Aids to Reflection* enables us to awake, the relationship between these two texts is not simply progressive; one does not supersede the other, and their meanings are mutually informing. Thus, I read the confrontation with the secret lodger as both necessary and, in a certain sense, neutral. The decision to "eject" or "retain" this avatar of a self that fails to coincide with itself, of a division internal to the subject and perhaps even constitutive of it, is presented here as a genuine occasion for a pause or hesitation. Indeed, in order for the "uneasy heart" to serve as "the ignition and driving force behind rational inquiry,"[56] there must first be a pause in order to register that such unease exists. Coleridge thus affirms that to know the self – a crucial step in the work of reflection – requires exploring its construction. It is not a matter of wholesale self-annihilation so much as of recognizing how the experience of discontinuity becomes constitutive of a spiritual self that achieves both its apotheosis and its annihilation in a work of reflection that is simultaneously process and event.

Coleridge's conception of the self as infinitely dark as well as infinitely strange provides a significant point of connection between the otherwise distant worlds of his supernatural poetry and his religious philosophy. Common to both spheres of thought is the critical necessity of a willing suspension of certainty, even at the moments of greatest vulnerability. The paralysing, psychoanalytically overdetermined encounter between Christabel and Geraldine at the beginning of "Christabel" – an encounter marked by the suspension of the ability to "tell" on the part of both women – is thus repeated, in *Aids to Reflection*, as the sublime suspension of certainty that radically reorients an individual life in ways that cannot be determined in advance. Seen from the vantage point of this later prose work, the meeting of Christabel and Geraldine becomes newly strange, but also newly legible in its openness to a reality of contingency. Reading Geraldine as an early iteration of the secret lodger allows Christabel's response, maligned as it has been, to appear as valid and courageous as any other. To criticize Christabel for a failure in judgment necessarily presupposes that we, as readers, have a firmer grasp on the situation – that we can see clearly (or clearly enough) the normative reality that eludes the poem's eponymous heroine. Yet, the textual clues usually invoked to demonstrate Geraldine's evil – the hostile response of Sir Leoline's dog, Geraldine's strange behaviour at the threshold of the castle, her preternatural beauty ultimately belied by a hideous body – are only revealed after the initial confrontation, and many of them could be read as possessing a more equivocal valence. Recognizing the essential undecidability of the encounter, Christabel opens herself to the possibility that this reality may not be reducible to the binary separation of fact and fiction; she meets her "secret lodger" and, in a radical gesture of poetic faith, extends hospitality before she knows who she has invited in. Evans observes that, in *Aids*, "Coleridge's techniques combine negative definition with recurring trenchant imperatives to act: Reflect. Reflect again. It's not what you think. It's not this, or this, or this."[57] Truths that sleep in the soul are predictable and static: the awakened mind finds itself unsettled to the very core, unhomed, as it were, in the search for its true self. If this awakened soul took on an embodied form, it might look something like Christabel, who awakes the morning after her encounter with Geraldine to "such Perplexity of Mind / As Dreams too lively leave behind" (385–6). She, too, finds herself to be a stranger at home, and perhaps even a stranger to herself. What Coleridge considers to be absolute, incontrovertible truth can never, in the strict sense, approach the level of fact. It must remain just groundless enough, just far enough beyond the reach of human understanding, to necessitate an intentional act of faith that, at some level, must always remain intellectually impossible.

Similarly, writing of the doctrine of election, Coleridge explains, "In relation to the Believer it is a *Hope*, which if it spring out of Christian Principles, be examined by the tests and nourished by the means prescribed in Scripture, will become a *lively*, an *assured* Hope, but which cannot in this life pass into *knowledge*, much less certainty of fore-knowledge" (*AR* 173). The language echoes that of the letter to Cottle written more than a decade earlier, when Coleridge was already negotiating the problem of faith without outward signs. What makes this act of reflection so radical is the way that Coleridge opens himself to the process without trying to determine, control, or predict what will happen – without fully knowing that it is happening, or how it will turn out; the assurance he offers can be nothing more than a lively hope that does not harden into knowledge – either of a future or present state. Coleridge attempts to chart a middle way between absolute determinism and absolute contingency. All possibilities (including that of deleterious influence and misapprehension) are radically open:

> It will suffice to satisfy a reflecting mind, that even at the porch and threshold of Revealed Truth there is a great and worthy sense in which we may believe the Apostle's assurance, that not only doth "the Spirit aid our infirmities"; that is, *act on* the Will by a predisposing influence from without, as it were, though in a spiritual manner, and without suspending or destroying its freedom ... but that *in* regenerate souls it may act in the will; that uniting and becoming one with our will and spirit, it may "make intercession for us"; nay, in this intimate union taking upon itself the form of our infirmities, may intercede for us "with groanings that cannot be uttered." (*AR* 78)

The influence of the Holy Spirit can never be conflated with compulsion; it acts upon the soul "without suspending or destroying its freedom." This is an important point, one that reaches back to Coleridge's earlier commitment, forged from the depths of his own despairing encounters with himself, that he seek something other than self-annihilation. Prayer as described in Romans 8:26 – the "groanings which cannot be uttered" – here becomes the form for all interactions with the divine, a means through which infinite brokenness and infinite darkness can encounter infinite goodness.

Glory Around, Darkness Within

Speculating in *Susperia De Profundis* (1845) about why death seems more "profoundly affecting" in the summer than in the winter, Thomas De Quincey proposes that "The summer we see, the grave we haunt with our thoughts; the glory is around us, the darkness is within us. And the two coming into collision, each exalts the other into stronger relief."[58] De Quincey's figure collapses the Brocken Spectre with the one who perceives/creates it, producing an image that implies that the constitutive discontinuity of the self is, to a certain extent, the full realization of Coleridgean reflection. One cannot, in the end, flee from the Spectre any more than Geraldine can be prevented from entering Christabel's bedchamber. The Brocken Spectre, the shadow surrounded by glory and visible only to the figure who casts the shadow, makes a brief appearance in a long note to *Aids to Reflection* that consciously interrupts a discussion of reason and understanding. The Spectre is summoned during a long disquisition on the resistance that most people have to the work of thinking and to those who engage in it: "It is an old Complaint, that a man of Genius no sooner appears, but the Host of Dunces are up in arms to repel the invading Alien" (*AR* 226). Coleridge divides the world into "Busy-indolent and Lazy-indolent" people and observes that "To both alike all Thinking is painful, and all attempts to rouse them to think, whether in the re-examination of their existing Convictions, or for the reception of new light, are irritating" (*AR* 228). In all cases, Coleridge argues, the underlying desire has to do with avoiding the confrontation with the true self, whether the "secret lodger" or some other "invading Alien," that would be the inevitable result of intellectual labour. In the encounter with Genius, Coleridge remarks, "as many as are not delighted by it are disturbed, perplexed, irritated. The Beholder either recognizes it as a projected Form of his own Being, that moves before him with a Glory round its head, or recoils from it as from a Spectre" (*AR* 227). It is easy enough to understand the problem with the latter response – the recoil – as being a result of delusion, a mind that terrifies itself because of its ignorance of the natural processes that generate the phenomenon. He, at least, is a version of the woodman at the end of "Constancy to an Ideal Object," who lacks the scientific training to know that what he is seeing is an illusion. He cannot suspend his disbelief, because there was no disbelief to suspend. But what of the other possible "Beholder," the one who appears to understand the Spectre and the glory for the optical effects that they are? Stephen Prickett remarks that "the ambiguity … is the point of the image. Does deep call to deep so that the genius of, say, Shakespeare strikes us as if it were a projection of our own selves writ large, and endowed with a universal significance; or does it seem a spectre: gigantic, alien, and too self-revealing to leave us comfortable? The point is that the phenomenon allows both these possibilities."[59] What this implies is that the role of a philosophical genius may, in part, consist in provoking in the minds of others a certain suspension of disbelief in ways that are strikingly congruent with the stated goals of Coleridge's supernatural poetry. The beholder who understands the Brocken Spectre as projection of his own shadow (rather than as a supernatural phenomenon) will be prompted to seek in this vision the contours of his true self, despite – or, perhaps, because of – the ways that his image has been enlarged and distorted. Nearly all of his surface qualities (the characteristics that would be visible in a conventional mirror) have been erased.

Despite the cynicism Coleridge professes about the resistance to reflection on the part of his countrymen, the later reception of *Aids to Reflection*, particularly in America and among Victorian readers, suggests that not everyone deserved his disapproval. In the early 1840s, Frederick Denison Maurice, the Cambridge Apostle, friend of Tennyson, and the closest thing Coleridge ever had to a disciple,[60] observed that

> … I have heard [*Aids to Reflection*] generally denounced as unintelligible by persons whom I had the greatest difficulty in understanding, who were continually perplexing me with hard words to which I could find nothing answering among actual things, and with the strangest attempts to explain mysteries by those events and circumstances which were to me most mysterious, and which, as they lay nearest to me, it was most important for my practical life that I should know the meaning of. On the other hand, I have heard the simplest, most childlike men and women express an almost rapturous thankfulness for having been permitted to read this book, and so to understand their own hearts and their Bibles, and the connexion between the one and the other, more clearly.[61]

Though couched in the language of Victorian class paternalism, Maurice's description of the "practical" character of *Aids to Reflection* affirms that its greatest importance lies not in its specific metaphysical claims but in its recognition that it can help its readers understand themselves on some fundamental level by facing the discontinuity that runs through claims of identity. *Aids*, at any rate, does not condescend to its readers by presenting a simplified version of a fully coherent reality; it takes seriously – and encourages its readers to take seriously – the moments of doubt and division, the uncertain "somethings" that haunt the edges of the sublime. In Coleridge's vision of "allness," hierarchies have no place, differentiation is meaningless, and the suspension of judgment comes as kind of a release from the imposition of differentials. But in reality, where moments of sublimity are always necessarily incomplete, suspension means giving oneself over to a potentially violent or exploitative force, and decisions are pressed upon us. "Poetic faith" ultimately has less to do with giving oneself over to illusion and much more to do with suspending the delusions that prevent us from interacting with the world as it is. "Christabel" became unfinishable because Coleridge was essentially writing his own life. He can only continue these lines of thought by transmigrating them to an entirely different genre: creating an open-ended methodology rather than seeking narrative closure. In this way, Coleridge is able to offer hospitality to that secret lodger. While he was deeply invested in unity, in allness, and in an ultimate – if not fully perceptible – coherence to the world, his writing is continuously jolted by encounters with non-coincidence, non-identity, breaches of logic, and ruptures in time and space.

"There are indeed," Coleridge writes, "Mysteries, in evidence of which no reasons can be *brought*. But it has been my endeavor to show, that the true solution of this problem is, that these Mysteries *are* Reason, Reason in its highest form of Self-affirmation" (*AR* 9). "Mystery" names the moment where dogma gives way to method, content to form, stability to contingency. Life as a mystery is also life experienced through successive, open-ended acts of willing suspension. Taken together, "Christabel" and *Aids to Reflection* represent a way of confronting and, more importantly, living through a reality experienced as a crisis of failed expectation. Perhaps more than any major Romantic-era writer, Coleridge remains attuned to the ambivalent concatenation of emotion that underlies the experience of sublime transcendence. To recognize infinitude is always to recognize the possibility of infinite darkness. His legacy to writers such as Percy Bysshe Shelley, Alfred Tennyson, and Christina Rossetti was the understanding that suspension – understood in its most capacious, but also its most complex sense – was the necessary precondition of poetic (and religious) faith, independent of all dogmas and fixed meanings in ways that were at once enabling and perilous. The following chapter explores the implications of that suspension for the work of Percy Shelley, who was able to embrace the lessons of discontinuity and contingency in a more straightforward way than Coleridge, who remained to the end committed to the possibility – however slim, however distant – of "allness." For Shelley, a world whose only rule is contingency – a world capable of radical, unexpected change – becomes both the challenge and the ecstasy of suspension.

Chapter Three

Ecstatic Suspension in Shelley's "Universe of Things"

Percy Bysshe Shelley tried – and failed – to meet Coleridge in 1811. Having recently been expelled from Oxford and married to Harriet Westbrook, the young poet travelled to Keswick, but found only Robert Southey.[1] This missed encounter appears to have haunted Coleridge well into his "Sage of Highgate" years. Thomas Allsop records the following comment, probably from 1822 or 1823:

> I was told by one who was with Shelley shortly before his death, that he had, in those moments, when his spirit was left to prey inwards, expressed a wish, amounting to anxiety, to commune with me, as the one only being who could resolve or allay the doubts and anxieties that pressed upon his mind.[2]

Imagining the desires of Shelley's last days, Coleridge mourns the loss of the opportunity to have been to Shelley something like what Leighton had been to him: a catalyst for working through the impasse of self-reflection, a means of recovering from the paralysis of the encounter with the "secret lodger" of the hidden self. Shelley's longing to speak with Coleridge, whether or not it has a basis in historical fact, at least seems plausible. Allsop does not record whether Coleridge had a source for this information about the younger poet, though the accounts of Edward Trelawny and others do affirm – in a general sense – Shelley's restlessness of mind in those final months at the Villa Magni, as evidenced in sleepwalking and waking dreams, which are themselves forms of suspended existence.[3] Arising from the airy, speculative, and ephemeral context of conversation at Highgate and filtered through the memories of others, Shelley's rumoured desire for Coleridge as the "one only being" with whom he yearned to "commune" in those last days in Italy discloses both more and less than what is captured by traditional notions of literary influence, something that reveals itself only in modes of (willing and willed) suspension. Preserved in an eternal youth by his early death, Shelley's image becomes for Coleridge a kind of spectral lodger, an ideal avatar of unrealized, yet still potentially powerful, possibility.

In many ways, Shelley's interest in suspension is much more concentrated and visible than it is in the work of his predecessor. Coleridge relied on forms, practices, and figures of suspension in order to come to terms, often reluctantly, with the constitutive discontinuity of reality. Shelley, on the other hand, finds in suspension a means of creative transformation and a source of ecstasy. For instance, in a footnote to *Queen Mab* (1813), Shelley declares that

> Time is our consciousness of the succession of ideas in our mind. Vivid sensation, of either pain or pleasure, makes the time seem long, as the common phrase is, because it renders us more acutely conscious of our ideas ... If, therefore, the human mind, by any future improvement of its sensibility, should become conscious of an infinite number of ideas in a minute, that minute would be eternity. I do not hence infer that the actual space between the birth and death of a man will ever be prolonged; but that his sensibility is perfectible, and that the number of ideas which his mind is capable of receiving is infinite ... Thus, the life of a man of virtue and talent, who should die in his thirtieth year, is, with regard to his own feelings, longer than that of a miserable priest-ridden slave, who dreams out a century of dulness.[4]

In this passage, Shelley imagines a consciousness capacious enough to arrest time by heightening perception. The description echoes certain Coleridgean structures: the dilation of a poem like "The Nightingale," the visionary paralysis of Scafell, the suspension of the comparing powers that comes to characterize Coleridge's understanding of the sublime. At the same time, however, Shelley's conception of suspension departs from that of Coleridge in both intensity and affect. The younger poet is, by and large, less troubled by the distinction between willing and unwilling suspensions; paralysis is not necessarily an occasion for panic – at least not until the final months of his life. Suspension, for Shelley, is not simply the interruption of habitual processes of perception, but becomes the central movement of perception itself, the realization of an infinite capacity for experience.

In this chapter, I am mainly interested in Shelley's rendering of suspension as an ecstatic mode in a poem that has often been read as the apotheosis of the Romantic sublime: "Mont Blanc: Lines Written in the Vale of Chamouni" (1817). However, suspension appears throughout Shelley's poetry as a figure of receptivity and possibility. In *Alastor* (1816), the figure of suspension marks the narrator's deliberate openness to inspiration and his readiness for the task of creation:

> serenely now
> And moveless, as a long-forgotten lyre
> Suspended in the solitary dome
> Of some mysterious and deserted fane,
> I wait thy breath, Great Parent … (41–5)[5]

The suspended lyre is an Aeolian harp, that quintessentially "Romantic" image of poetic genius as receptivity that always hovers on the edge of passivity. Shelley returns to this image in the opening lines of *Epipsychidion* (1821), again using an act of deliberate suspension to invoke a friendly spirit: "In my heart's temple I suspend to thee / These votive wreaths of withered memory" (3–4). More complexly, in *Prometheus Unbound* (1820), the Titan first appears in his agony of suspension on the side of a cliff: "a writhing shade / 'Mid whirlwind-peopled mountains" (1.203–4), yet the revolution is already pending: "what an awful whisper rises up! / 'Tis scarce like sound, it tingles through the frame / As lightning tingles, hovering ere it strike" (1.132–4). The suffering of the suspended Prometheus is situated within a scene pervaded by energy that trembles and "tingles." Shelley's representations of the natural world are also frequently structured by forms of suspension and hovering. *Alastor* takes place under overhanging skies, in view of trees that "frame / Most solemn domes within" while others appear "Like clouds suspended in an emerald sky" (434–5, 436). And, in at least one moment in that same poem, suspension manages to suggest both stillness and implacable forward motion:

> The boat fled on, – the boiling torrent drove, –
> The crags closed round with black and jagged arms,
> The shattered mountain overhung the sea,
> And faster still, beyond all human speed,
> Suspended on the sweep of the smooth wave,
> The little boat was driven. (358–63)

Thus suspension for Shelley involves both holding and being held. Read as part of a network of images of lingering, overhanging skies and "solitary domes," it suggests worlds of potentiality and possibility – something different from simple passivity, but also something that foregrounds lyric suspension as one mode among others for arresting time by expanding perception. It is a deliberate ecstasy, yet also an ecstasy that ends by placing in abeyance the possibility of deliberation itself.

Composed during the dark, cold summer of 1816, "Mont Blanc" first appeared as the final section of the *History of a Six Weeks' Tour*, an anonymously published text whose arrangement and much of its composition is generally attributed to Mary Shelley. The poem's central drama lies in Shelley's contemplation of the ravine in section 2, where he suspends binary thinking and enters fully into a relation with a contingent, unconditioned "universe of things" (1). He nearly loses himself in gazing on the vertiginous depths of the Ravine of Arve, experiencing a "trance sublime and strange" through which he comes to view "my own, my human mind" as if from the outside (35, 37). This "trance sublime and strange" deliberately suspends thought, referentiality, and subjectivity. In other words, it suspends all those categories that typically condition the experience of the self in the world, along with the categories of "self" and "world." Shelley allows his separate self to exist alongside the radically undefined, uncontrollable "vacancy" of the mountain and the unstable plenitude of the ravine. Locating himself within the "unremitting interchange / With the clear universe of things around" (39–40) – a universe which includes the mindlessly destructive power emblematized by Mont Blanc, the rolling waters of the River Arve, and the "wild thoughts" (41) of human projection – Shelley realizes a sublime that foregrounds the suspension of conceptual thought, a more capacious version of the suspension that Coleridge had placed at the centre of the sublime. Opening itself to radical suspension in the world of mutability, "Mont Blanc" is a poem about the process through which we learn how to live in a world governed by contingency. As the poet's awareness and perception become more acute, more focused, the gaps and discontinuities become impossible to ignore. It is a meditation on what it might mean to give up the search for an underlying reason. Suspended within a "now-ness" of poetic temporality through an apostrophic invocation that is first addressed to the Ravine of Arve, the sublime of "Mont Blanc" is constituted, ultimately, by Shelley's experience of radical discontinuity. Rather than transcendence and mastery, its *telos* is contingency: the suspension and undoing of *telos*.

Like the longer text in which it appears, "Mont Blanc" draws heavily upon the recognized tropes of early nineteenth-century travel writing. Yet, the poem is generally considered as single text, separate from the collaborative *History*, and, as such, it is recognized as paradigmatic, offering what Christoph Bode characterizes as a representation of the sublime "unique in British Romanticism."[6] Strikingly, however, it has been difficult for scholars to agree on what that representation is. An influential line of criticism by scholars such as Frances Ferguson and, earlier, Earl Wasserman reads "Mont Blanc" as a celebration of the transcendent power of the human mind. Wasserman finds in the poem the mandate to resist the confusion of "the discontinuous external world" emblematized by the ravine in favour of the elevated view represented by the mountain's summit: "Meaning lies in the mind's visionary apprehension of a single, eternal, immutable, and amoral Power which lies behind the seemingly absurd mutability and recurrent emptiness, and of whose necessary laws the activities of the world are a manifestation."[7] Ferguson, too, sees the poem as a project of transcendence, writing that Shelley "identifies the sublime as the aesthetic operation through which one makes an implicit argument for the transcendent existence of man – not because man is able to survive the threat posed by the power of the material world but because he is able to domesticate the material world for the purposes of aesthetics," a realization that she sees as essentially Kantian.[8] David Miall, on the other hand, emphasizes the ways that "Mont Blanc" presents "a conception of the sublime at odds with some standard accounts," including that of Kant, partly because the poem seeks to "explore what the sublime landscape can teach about the common basis of the mind and nature" – rather than establishing the superiority of the one over the other.[9]

Bode, who emphasizes the Kantian overtones of "Mont Blanc," argues that the poem "presents a view of nature, of creation, in which man holds no privileged status but is brutally and helplessly exposed to the rage of its elements."[10] However, for all of the parallels with Kant that have been both identified and disputed in "Mont Blanc," I argue that the poem may be more effectively read in conversation with Coleridge's rereading of the Kantian sublime as the suspension of the comparing powers. This is not to say that Shelley had access to the marginalia and fragments in which Coleridge sketched out his aesthetics – he obviously did not. As Bode points out, it is unlikely that Shelley was more than passingly familiar with Kant.[11] He was, however, familiar with Coleridge's poetry and was reading "Christabel" during the Geneva summer. Critical tradition, moreover, considers "Mont Blanc" to be, in part, a deliberate rejoinder to the religious effusions of Coleridge's "Hymn before Sun-rise."[12] Shelley, of course, was not privy to the epistolary account of the experience that preceded the poem – the Scafell letter of 1802 discussed in chapter 1. Yet, the similarities between that letter and the experience recounted in "Mont Blanc" are striking, from the sense of physical peril to the realization of a visionary paralysis. Both writers, in fact, use the word "trance" to describe this feeling: Shelley is held rapt in a "trance sublime and strange" (35) while Coleridge reports "a state of almost prophetic Trance & Delight" (*CL* 2.842). One of the main differences in these two situations is that Coleridge obscures the relationship between suspension and contingency in his published poem, while Shelley foregrounds suspension as the central term – and the very condition of possibility – of sublimity itself.

Shelley embraces the "suspension of the comparing powers" that constitutes Coleridge's rereading of Kant, and goes further in realizing a fully relational sublime capable of suspending, at least, temporarily, notions of dominance. According to Kant, the things we call sublime "raise the soul's fortitude above its usual middle range and allow us to discover in ourselves an ability to resist which is of a quite different kind, and which gives us the courage [to believe] that we could be a match for nature's seeming omnipotence." The superiority that Kant describes as the compensatory gesture of the sublime – what is gained as recompense for the terror of incomprehension – has often been stereotyped as mastery or domination. The experience that Shelley realizes in "Mont Blanc," by contrast, imagines a "superiority" that is independent of external forces not because it is stronger or ignores them, but simply because it is able to respond to them, without the kinds of non-aesthetic judgments that we are otherwise accustomed to make. Shelley's ecstatic embrace of suspension enables him to explore more fully than was possible for Coleridge the sublime consideration of nature as, in Kant's terms, "a might that has no dominance over us."[13] This elevation may be more like dangling by a thread, standing on the edge of a precipice, or simply hovering. This version of the sublime does not culminate in a feeling of mastery (at least not as the word is usually understood), nor does it consist in finding the powers of the human mind reflected back in nature. Both ethical and non-coercive, it does not exchange the power of nature for the power of man, but rather points to a momentary suspension of dominance itself: not the negation of power, but the suspension of the very structures of reference and conceptual thought that make it possible to distinguish the dominant from the dominated.

I argue that the Ravine of Arve as Shelley depicts it in the first three sections of the poem is ultimately the more significant site of contemplation than the mountain, as the ravine is the place where he most fully realizes his ecstatic mode of suspension. Of course, the vast majority of readings of the poem take for granted that the mountain is the culmination of Shelley's poetic efforts. Nigel Leask elaborates a trajectory where Shelley's attention "mov[es] upward rapidly from contemplation of the ravine of Arve with a singular lack of humility," and "rises above the crowded and commercial viewing-platform of the tourists, above the platitudes of conventional sublime piety." In Leask's estimation, "Shelley suggests that a correct understanding of the mountain's catastrophic agency is contingent upon an elite sensibility which, rejecting the valley view, seeks the view from the top."[14] "Remote, serene, and inaccessible" (97), the mountain has long been considered the privileged site of material, geologic, temporal, and discursive otherness in the poem, the thing that challenges Shelley's "human mind" to negotiate a meaningful space for consciousness in its shadow. However, though indirectly present through the manifestations of power, the mountain does not explicitly "appear" until line 61 – almost halfway through the poem – halting the meandering syntax of the first two sections in favour of more discrete units of meaning that characterize the poem from that point on. The first sixty lines of "Mont Blanc" are, by contrast, focused on Shelley's immediate surroundings in the Vale of Chamounix and on the "commotion" (30) caused by the river as it rolls through the jagged, cavernous ravine. Shelley, indeed, signals his embeddedness in the "everlasting universe of things" in the poem's very first line. As a result, he takes the Ravine of Arve – not Mont Blanc – as his figure for the relationship between mind and world, a move that, as Steven Shaviro has observed, subverts the instantiation of the subject-object binary on which so many of the mountain-oriented readings of the poem depend.[15]

Most discussions of "Mont Blanc" similarly elide its initial publication, treating it as an entity independent of the prose writing that comes before it. In the handful of discussions that resist this temptation, it is generally assumed that "Mont Blanc" is the *telos* of the *History*, much in the same way that Mont Blanc is assumed to be the *telos* of the poem. Donald Reiman, for instance, characterizes the *History* as "a fully collaborative effort, carefully conceived to culminate in Shelley's 'Mont Blanc.'"[16] The sections that come before it, he suggests, provide context for the poem, much in the same way that the early sections of "Mont Blanc" provide a kind of "context" for the mountain. Mont Blanc – and "Mont Blanc" – stand alone in a way that their surroundings do not. Both the mountain and the poem, that is, function as the unquestioned, stable centre of the contingent ecological and textual systems that surround them – exemplary emblems of sublime transcendence and the consolidation of the lyric subject. Jeanne Moskal, however, observes that this "constructed ascent" reinscribes "both a traditional hierarchy of genres ([Mary Shelley's] diary, her letters; his letters, his lyric poem) and a conventional hierarchy of gender (writings by a woman superseded by those of a man)."[17] To read "Mont Blanc" (the poem) as part of the *History* is, then, already to de-emphasize Mont Blanc (the mountain) in favour of the contingencies that attend the movements of bodies and texts alike. So, too, does such a reading trouble the assumption that "the separate elements of *History* can be read as the distinct products of single authorship,"[18] revealing instead the traces of collaborative authorship that cannot be fully separated into individual contributions any more than the essence of the Ravine of Arve can be fixed in any specific quality – or even on the mountain itself.

A "trance sublime and strange"

The first section of "Mont Blanc" plunges the reader into a sublime that is already in progress, where the comparing powers have already been suspended:

> The everlasting universe of things
> Flows through the mind, and rolls its rapid waves,
> Now dark – now glittering – now reflecting gloom –
> Now lending splendour, where from the secret springs
> The source of human thought its tribute brings
> Of waters, – with a sound but half its own,
> Such as a feeble brook will oft assume
> In the wild woods, among the mountains lone,
> Where waterfalls around it leap for ever,
> Where woods and winds contend, and a vast river
> Over its rocks ceaselessly bursts and raves. (1–11)

The "rapid waves" that characterize the "universe of things" take on, temporarily, the qualities of light and darkness. In lines 3 and 4, Shelley describes the movement as a succession of evanescent "now"s connected by dashes that serve to highlight the absence of causal connection. The words he uses to describe the flow – "dark," "glittering," "reflecting gloom," and "lending splendour" – are all suggestive of surface qualities: brief, perhaps even illusory, impressions created by the water's interaction with wind and light. Everything is in motion, and the desire to maintain any specific state of mind will be as unsuccessful as attempts to capture the glitter and gloom – echoes, perhaps, of "Christabel" – of Shelley's waters. Arising in a moment, gone in an instant, these qualities of the "universe of things" draw attention to how discontinuity and unpredictability constitute reality. Lines 6 and 7 liken the human mind, previously identified with the ravine as a conduit for the "flow" of "things," to a "feeble brook" and tributary to the same river, amplified by the echoes of distant "waterfalls" in mountain forests. Everything is already happening, and happening simultaneously. This passage undermines the ability to distinguish between subject and object, creating an undetermined relation that will continue to inform the following sections. The "universe of things" may achieve a provisional priority over the "mind" through which it "rolls," but the terms are mutually constitutive; it is never precisely clear where one ends and the other begins. Like a Möbius strip, which transforms two sides into an object with one continuous surface, Shelley effects a connection between mind and world in the middle of the passage, holding them both in suspension. The perceiving subject is also already suspended, immersed in the scene that unfolds. The exchange imagined here is unequal because the "feeble brook" of human thought can never resist the "rapid waves" of the universe of things, yet it is not fully determined and lacks a clear regulating principle other than contingency. In addition to the complexity of Shelley's figuration and grammatical constructions, what makes this passage so challenging is that it describes a relation to the world that is difficult for a human subject to realize in a single instant, let alone maintain as an ongoing practice of perception. A mind conditioned by binary thought may be incapable of allowing the universe to "flow" through it unhindered: the tendency is towards grasping and attachment, towards imposing the very structures of separation that the section resists. It is difficult, in fact, to summarize this section of "Mont Blanc" without reinstantiating these structures and thereby oversimplifying the scene. In the following section, this state coalesces into the "trance sublime and strange" that enables Shelley to participate more fully in the movement he lays out in "Mont Blanc"'s opening lines.

In the *History*'s prose account of the Chamounix excursion, the description of the mountain, ravine, and sky is punctuated with a reminder that this narrative structure is a concession to the limits of language and perception: "this was all one scene, it all pressed home to our regard and our imagination" (*HSWT* 152). It is only the limited, human perspective that reads the coursing of the river as an unfolding narrative; in the time-space produced by the ravine, these events are simultaneous and precariously interdependent. The apostrophic address to the Ravine of Arve in the second section of "Mont Blanc" allows Shelley more closely to approximate this feeling of eternity by instantiating what Jonathan Culler calls "a fictional time in which nothing happens but which is the essence of happening."[19] Grammatically a single sentence, section 2 hovers in a holding pattern, promising an ending that never arrives, and spinning itself into a moment of prolonged suspension and incomprehension – an approximation of the Kantian "inhibition" that precedes the sublime "outpouring of the vital forces." The layout of the poem in the 1817 *History* visually reinforces this lyric suspension of narrative time. The second section of the poem occupies two facing pages, enabling a reader to dwell with Shelley in this space of suspension as long as he or she can stand it, offering no particular incitement to turn to the next page.

The section begins with the apostrophic address, "Thus, thou, Ravine of Arve" (12) and ends with the deictic assertion, "thou art there!" (48). Shelley renders the ravine in images of plenitude and multiplicity: it is "many-coloured, many-voiced," with "pines, and crags, and caverns" sprawling underneath "Fast cloud shadows and sunbeams" (13, 14, 15). The dashes and semicolons both connect and separate, holding different images in an indeterminate relation with each other. A number of rhymes and near-rhymes – "Arve's commotion/ceaseless motion," "sound/around," and "eternity/gaze on thee/phantasy" – intensify the interplay of cacophony and stillness. The river cascades through the ravine "like the flame / Of lightning through the tempest" (18–19) – no longer simply "reflecting" or "glittering" but electrifying and transforming the landscape with intermittent bursts of light. The ravine is "passive," yet it channels and focuses a seemingly uncontrollable "Power." The caverns along the sides of the Ravine, "echoing to the Arve's commotion" (30), amplify the noise of the waterfalls and river into "A loud, lone sound no other sound can tame" (31) – a sound capable of absorbing all the other "voices" in this vast wilderness. "[C]ommotion" signifies not confused or disruptive activity but rather a mode of contingent relationality: a co-motion that draws attention to the undetermined interaction of incommensurate elements in a limited space. Thus poetic form does not mask contingency; it serves as an aid to suspended (i.e., active and ungrounded) receptivity rather than providing a fixed rule.

Frances Ferguson finds within this "cluster of images that are continually put into relation with one another, an elaborate schema of reciprocity" that regulates the exchange of attributes among different natural objects.[20] It is a textbook example of what Jerrod E. Hogle describes as "transference" in Shelley's poetry: "the transfer of elements through other elements, onto further elements, or back to themselves [that] inaugurates a double drive in the spectator: a desire to penetrate every complex to 'something' deeper or higher and a need to divert every glance at every target (outward or inward) toward some different point, some resemblance, where that something might possibly lie."[21] However, within this enclosed space – a space that also, inexorably, resists its own closure – Shelley encounters a deeper, more constitutive rift. Alongside the "giant brood of pines" (20) and the "earthly rainbows stretched across the sweep / Of the etherial waterfall" (25–6), he perceives

> the strange sleep
> Which when the voices of the desart fail
> Wraps all in its own deep eternity; – ... (27–9)

This abstraction occupies the same grammatical register as the pines and waterfalls and rainbows – that is, the same level as phenomena immediately accessible to the senses, even when they remain figuratively "etherial." The combination of the "earthly rainbows" and "etherial waterfall" is the paradigmatic example of a "transfer of attributes" that, as Ferguson argues, renders "the phenomena ... palpably more than themselves,"[22] while still preserving some level of difference, to the extent that these objects remain distinguishable from each other. By contrast, the "deep eternity" absorbs all these different qualities. No longer the ceaselessness of motion or the everlastingness of things, this eternity of silence suggests deep geological time, inaccessible to human perception and indifferent to human history. This blank power resides not on the summit, but rather subtends the surface ceaselessness of the natural world. No law obtains here except that of contingency. This realization jolts Shelley into an encounter with his own vulnerability that manifests itself as the paralysis of "the strange sleep." Coupled with "deep eternity," the language of "strange sleep" – a form of particularly illegible suspension – registers the ungraspability of the "universe of things around" (40). The "deep eternity" of this "strange sleep" suggests a form of infinity that exceeds whatever the mountain can offer, even as the image hovers between the connotations of sleep and those of death, blurring the lines between the two.

Queen Mab had opened with an encomium to the shared qualities of sleep and death – "both so passing wonderful!" (1.8). "Wonderful" here suggests a form of sublimity without the promise of mastery.[23] It is a position entirely appropriate to a poem that dramatizes the physical suspension of Ianthe's body and conscious cognitive faculties in sleep in order to enable her soul – "The perfect semblance of its bodily frame, / Instinct with inexpressible beauty and grace" (1.133–4) – to accompany the fairy queen on her visionary journey. Only by temporarily separating soul and body, and by holding the latter in abeyance, can Ianthe be allowed to experience the possibility of a freedom from the "desolating pestilence" of power that "Makes slaves of men, and, of the human frame, / A mechanized automaton" (3.176, 179–80). "Mont Blanc" similarly stages suspension as an enabling posture that does not permit a simple binary of activity and passivity; unlike *Queen Mab* it does so in the first person. Shelley enters fully into the "unremitting interchange" with the "universe of things," that reiterates the terms of the general relationship between mind and world of section 1 at a level that is at once more personal and more dangerous:

> Thou art the path of that unresting sound –
> Dizzy Ravine! and when I gaze on thee
> I seem as in a trance sublime and strange
> To muse on my own separate phantasy,
> My own, my human mind, which passively
> Now renders and receives fast influencings,
> Holding an unremitting interchange
> With the clear universe of things around … (33–40)

The "strange sleep" of the trance effects an awakening into the "unresting" sublime of the ravine. This trance becomes sublime insofar as it suspends or brackets the expectations, desires, perceptions, fears, and conditioning that create the "separate phantasy" of individuated subjectivity as independent from the contingent, external reality constituted by "the clear universe of things." It enables Shelley to both know and not know what he is experiencing; he may reflect upon "My own, my human mind," neither judging it nor identifying with it. This is, in fact, the only passage in "Mont Blanc" where Shelley speaks of "my own, my human mind" instead of "the mind" or the "human mind," making explicit the extent to which he is implicated in and affected by what he experiences in the Vale of Chamounix. This is also the first moment in the poem where the lyric "I" emerges. That it is placed in suspension almost as soon as it does appear speaks to an experience of discontinuity in the constitution of Shelley's own subjectivity: he both is and is not himself. The self of the "separate phantasy" arises first as a visual phenomenon, as if to suggest that the act of looking (or, at least the kind of looking that introduces the individual's "point of view") inhibits the more expansive feelings triggered by the sublime. The mind that "passively / Now renders and receives fast influencings" is, paradoxically, a mind that at some level actively constitutes and maintains its own suspension. It allows the trance to remain "sublime and strange," that is, at least partially untheorized and uncontrolled, even as the possibility of response remains open. In this way, the trance marks the site of Shelley's confrontation with a world of contingency that is at best indirectly framed by the regulating power associated with the mountain.

The remainder of section 2 offers a brief glimpse of what that interchange might look like, how Shelley's mind can "rende[r] and receiv[e] fast influencings" when the difference between the dominant and the dominated has been suspended. Significantly, the "human mind" is not absent from the scene, but it is resituated as one term, one element among many: a "legion of wild thoughts" (41) that floats above the "darkness" of the ravine. Though these thoughts may seem insubstantial compared to the jagged physicality of the rocks and raging river, they subtly alter and interact with those more solid-seeming natural objects. The structure of their movement – "whose wandering wings / Now float above thy darkness, and now rest" (41–2) – recalls the flow of the "universe of things" in the first section, particularly in the repetition of the word "now" that reinforces the passage's lyric suspension. Wasserman has claimed that this passage indicates an abhorrence of darkness and vacancy and a transcendence thereof: "thought is seen not only to constitute the universe for man but also to have the power to transcend that universe, to 'float above' the 'darkness' of the ravine that represents the boundaries of the human universe."[24] But Shelley has not retreated from reality into "the still cave of the witch Poesy" (44) any more than he has acheived the kind of transcendence that would place him above it all. Continuing to address the ravine, Shelley names the cave as a location where "that [the ravine's darkness] or thou [the ravine itself] art no unbidden guest" (43), invoking a discourse of hospitality that makes it more difficult to assent to the interpretation that the image represents the "primitive, superstitious enclosure of the mind's cave" opposed to the the "sceptical truth which an unflinching and reflective scrutiny of the mountain's naked ice-plains and remote summit can teach."[25] Although this interchange does not take place between two human-seeming subjects (or between the subject and himself), it resembles Coleridge's encounters with the "secret lodger" – or even Geraldine – discussed in the previous chapter. Even "shadows" and "Ghosts" and the "faint image" of the ravine that haunts the caverns (45, 46, 47) may participate in this world, for they, like the "strange sleep," reflect the constitutive discontinuity – even the potential nothingness – of reality itself, apprehended through a posture of suspension.

"Some unknown omnipotence"

The last line of section 2 brings the apostrophic address to the ravine to a close and seems, at least temporarily, to return the poem to narrative, rather than lyric, time. However, the influence of the ravine's "strange sleep" continues to be felt, as the poet moves from description to investigation, from an ecstatic suspension of self to an epistemological suspension of judgment. Pausing in his description of the ravine, Shelley considers the conditions under which his consciousness becomes possible. He revises his perceptions as he goes along, unwilling to rest on a specific interpretation when reality is always in motion. He first surmises that "Some" – though not necessarily he himself –

> say that gleams of a remoter world
> Visit the soul in sleep, – that death is slumber,
> And that its shapes the busy thoughts outnumber
> Of those who wake and live. – I look on high;
> Has some unknown omnipotence unfurled

The veil of life and death? or do I lie
In dream, and does the mightier world of sleep
Spread far around and inaccessibly
In circles? (49–57)

Here again, it is possible to detect parallels with the language of both the Scafell letter and the "Hymn before Sun-rise." The "gleams of the remoter world" and the rolling out of the "veil of life and death" suggest the visionary insights of Coleridge's letter. At the same time, Shelley, like Coleridge in the "Hymn," must look "on high" to the mountain; he does not climb to the summit. Yet, where Coleridge had drawn confidence and calm from the assured knowledge that he was not dreaming on Scafell, Shelley suspends his judgment even on this seemingly crucial point. Of course, these questions are to some extent meant rhetorically. In this, they anticipate the final lines of John Keats's "Ode to a Nightingale" (1819): "Was it a vision, or a waking dream? / Fled is that music – Do I wake or sleep?" (79–80).[26] Here, however, the rhetorical questions are posed at the very centre of the poem, destabilizing the binaries upon which they rely with consequences that reverberate through the rest of the text. Life and death, dreaming and waking, immediacy and inaccessibility are all happening simultaneously in the eternal now of the "unremitting interchange." In other words, where the "strange sleep" of the previous section had offered an image of irreducible silence among the roar of waters, that same geological space now becomes the site where life and death are no longer mutually exclusive.

However, these meditations are almost immediately interrupted by Shelley's upward-looking gaze, no longer focused on the ravine, but not yet fixed upon the mountain. In this interval, which acts as a hinge (or another twist of the Möbius strip) between the sublime of the ravine and that of the mountain, he looks but does not see, sensing only the potentially oppressive authority of an "unknown omnipotence" that strategically veils its workings from mankind.[27] It is into this scene that

piercing the infinite sky,
Mont Blanc appears, – still, snowy, and serene –
Its subject mountains their unearthly forms
Pile around it, ice and rock; broad vales between
Of frozen floods, unfathomable deeps,

Blue as the overhanging heaven, that spread
And wind among the accumulated steeps ... (60–6)

The advent of the mountain is equivocal at best. Mont Blanc flashes into view and then disappears again, obscured by the clouds it penetrates. Shelley's gaze does not travel upwards indefinitely but comes to rest on the "broad vales," an aural pun on those "veils" that conceal and reveal, and the "unfathomable deeps" – the sites, perhaps, of the "deep eternity" evoked a few lines earlier – that have more in common with the Ravine of Arve than with the summit of Mont Blanc. The prose account hints at an even more ambivalent experience: "Mont Blanc was before us, but it was covered with cloud; its base, furrowed with dreadful gaps, was seen above" (*HSWT* 151). The "dreadful gaps" visible from below – expanded, in the poem, to the "rude, bare, and high, / Ghastly, and scarred, and riven" (70–1) landscape – provoke Shelley's awareness of gaps in his knowledge of the mythological and geological past. Here, another set of rhetorical questions arises – this time as an attempt to think a world prior to human consciousness itself. Musing upon this inhuman landscape, Shelley is prompted to wonder:

Is this the scene
Where the old Earthquake-daemon taught her young
Ruin? Were these their toys? or did a sea
Of fire, envelope once this silent snow? (71–4)

Drawing upon a language at once mythological and scientific, Shelley imagines a catastrophic geological past. Although he briefly anthropomorphizes Earthquake and her children (an echo of the "giant brood of pines" of section 2), he also, as Leask has comprehensively demonstrated, shows himself to be cognizant of the scientific debates of the day, in which naturalists and geologists such as James Hutton and George-Louis Buffon were asking many similar questions about the origin of the earth.[28]

Shelley's questions, however, do not yield any answer, nor are they posed in a "scientific" form. They are turned back on themselves and silenced: "None can reply – all seems eternal now" (75). This is the only line in the poem that is also a complete, end-stopped sentence. As such it carries with it the force of finality – even though the poem is far from over. The pronouncement marks the end of the interval between apostrophes and the resumption of poetic time that knows neither past nor future. Partial as human imagination may be in both its mythological and scientific dimensions, it is not for that reason fully powerless. The suspension of reference enacted in this passage creates a reflective space within the catastrophe itself. Here Shelley confronts the vision of a world without him, a world that has no ultimate reason to be the way it is and that could, therefore, be otherwise.

Faced with the overwhelming force of nature, Shelley becomes aware of his own insignificance, but this awareness – as in the conventional understanding of the Kantian sublime – points to the higher significance of his own reason. The lines that immediately follow this pause resemble a retreat back into something like orthodoxy:

> The wilderness has a mysterious tongue
> Which teaches awful doubt, or faith so mild,
> So solemn, so serene, that man may be
> But for such faith with nature reconciled;
> Thou hast a voice, great Mountain, to repeal
> Large codes of fraud and woe; not understood
> By all, but which the wise, and great, and good
> Interpret, or make felt, or deeply feel. (76–83)

This passage grounds many of the influential readings of "Mont Blanc" such as Ferguson's that argue that Shelley, through his apostrophic relationship with the mountain, "creates an image of sublimity that continually hypostatizes an eternity of human consciousness. Because even the ideas of the destructiveness of nature and the annihilation of mankind require human consciousness to give them their force, they thus are testimony to the necessity of the continuation of the human."[29] The wilderness, in this reading, is endowed with a voice only insofar as it is able to be heard by the "wise, and great, and good." Nature becomes the Great Pedagogue – all that remains for the human seeker is to pay attention and to trust in a higher order whose outlines are already apparent from the structure of her own mind. However, thanks to the cryptic nature of the phrase "But for such faith," it is not immediately apparent whether Shelley finds this faith to be essential to the process of reconciliation or antithetical to it.[30] There is a version of faith that constructs its objects in its own image. True "reconciliation," however, begins with seeing things as they are, including the ways they are difficult, uncomfortable, and unexpected. All codes, insofar as they are codes, are potentially generative of "fraud and woe." Anything else is simply superstition: an ideological fiction that perpetuates the belief that there is some other explanation that exists just beyond the reach of human exploration.

The prose sections of the *History* that precede the poem draw attention to the ways that "codes of fraud and woe" are far from being repealed. The destructive (and seductive) potentials of power are built in to the "universe of things" from the very beginning and cannot be excluded. The terms of that critique become more explicit when "Mont Blanc" is read against earlier passages of the *History*, such as Shelley's prose account of the visit he and Byron paid to the Castle of Chillon. Both poets were deeply affected by this visit, for Chillon had served for much of its history as a prison for those accused of theological crimes. Byron used the dungeon as the setting for his meditation on repression, "The Prisoner of Chillon." Shelley, for his part, remarks upon the myriad instruments of death and torture that remained on display, calling to mind "that cold and inhuman tyranny, which it has been the delight of man to exercise over man." One of the most troubling of these instruments is, at least according to legend, part of the castle's deliberate design: "an opening to the lake, by means of a secret spring, connected with which the whole dungeon might be filled with water before the prisoners could possibly escape!" (*HSWT* 130). Although the existence of such a spring is historically unlikely, Shelley seems to believe what his guide tells him. His description of Chillon breaks off at this thought, and the letter resumes – at a different part of the excursion – on the following page. The concealed machinery of terror and death by drowning haunts the seemingly different "springs" in "Mont Blanc" – springs that, there, are the "source of human thought." At the very least, this resonance suggests the facticity of the distinction that Shelley makes in his prose, drawing attention back to the contradictory construction that makes "inhuman tyranny" the "delight of man." It registers on a species-wide scale the capability for "infinite darkness" that Coleridge had discovered in himself during his spiritual crises: the kind of darkness, that is, capable of creating the "codes" that make thinkable the cruel refinements of the Chillon dungeon and that would decree that certain kinds of speculation constitute punishable acts.

Matthew Borushko has recently contended that "Mont Blanc" offers a critique of "the violence inherent in sublimity: violence that, in both its dynamic of power and domination and its necessary concealment of its own means, provides a model for the institutionalization of repressive political authority."[31] The concealment of the deadly spring mechanism in the castle of Chillon presents a rather striking example of the power dynamic that Borushko identifies. Other parts of the *History* contain their own examples of the ravages that result from the assent to "codes of fraud and woe." During the initial "six weeks' tour" – the elopement tour of 1814 – Percy, Mary, and Mary's stepsister Claire Clairmont passed through a number of French towns that bore the marks of wartime devastation. In Nogent, Mary Shelley records that "the distress of the inhabitants, whose houses had been burned, their cattle killed, and all their wealth destroyed, has given a sting to my detestation of war, which none can feel who have not travelled through a country pillaged and wasted by this plague, which, in his pride, man inflicts upon his fellow" (*HSWT* 19). Not long after, the travellers discover a "wretched" village:

> It had been once large and populous, but now the houses were roofless, and the ruins that lay scattered about, the gardens covered with the white dust of the torn cottages, the black burnt beams, and squalid looks of the inhabitants, presented in every direction the melancholy aspect of devastation. (*HSWT* 22–3)

The residents of this village are so cut off from the rest of the world that they have not repaired their homes for fear that they will simply be destroyed again. The juxtaposition of the prose accounts of war's aftermath with the "natural" (yet also poetic) violence of "Mont Blanc" inhibits any efforts to rest in the seeming necessity of destruction of one for the benefit of the other, evading questions of responsibility by referring them to a higher power.

This, in fact, is the world that the poem begins to call into being in section 4. Whatever gains may be said to accrue from this reorientation of poetic energies nevertheless remain fragile and perhaps even more explicitly threatened by contingency. Section 4 begins with detailed invocation of the "universe of things" in a form that echoes the grammatical holding pattern of section 2, as if attempting to cast a hypnotic spell:[32]

> The fields, the lakes, the forests, and the streams,
> Ocean, and all the living things that dwell
> Within the daedal earth; lightning, and rain,
> Earthquake, and fiery flood, and hurricane,

> The torpor of the year when feeble dreams
> Visit the hidden buds, or dreamless sleep
> Holds every future leaf and flower; – the bound
> With which from that detested trance they leap;
> The works and ways of man, their death and birth,
> And that of him and all that his may be;
> All things that move and breathe with toil and sound
> Are born and die; revolve, subside, and swell. (84–95)

These lines proceed from one another with an almost mechanistic regularity, emphasized by images of changing seasons (the "torpor of the year" and its aftermath) and the circular patterning of the last two lines. Change is naturalized as part of an ongoing, totalizing cycle that claims to be capable of containing catastrophe. A number of the images of the natural world appear elsewhere in the poem: the forests and streams in section 1, the flashes of lightning in section 2 (and again in section 5). However, what had, in the opening sections of the poem, arisen as if under their own power now reappear as parts of a "daedal earth" of human creation. Its forces are tamed by Shelley's iambic pentameter and an unusual clustering of end-rhymed lines, "one of the resources," as William Keach has argued, "with which the poet verbally counters as well as encounters an experience of threatening power and sublimity."[33] The artifice of rhyme reinforces the artifice of the Labyrinth, constructed by the mythological Daedalus to seem infinite and to overwhelm those who find themselves inside it, unaware that any exit, any beyond, exists. It is possible to become lost in a maze of one's own making, mistaking the concealment of artifice – the "secret springs" – for the absoluteness of power. The danger lies not in the construction itself, but in the founding ideological gesture that forgets and conceals the constructedness of the construction. The images of "dreams" and "trance" – even though the one is "feeble" and the other "detested" – nevertheless resist and suspend these demands for a "daedal" calculation, for the sealing of the Labyrinth. As such, they are implicitly aligned with "Power," which otherwise "dwells apart in its tranquillity / Remote, serene, and inaccessible" (96–7). Shelley cannot help but intuit the facticity of that separation. He may apply his "adverting mind" (100) to learn the lessons of the landscape, but he seems to know in advance that such teaching will not be forthcoming. The glaciers that loom above the valley take on a malevolent cast that explicitly evokes the Garden of Eden: they "creep / Like snakes that watch their prey" (100–1). Where the mountain had once been able to pierce the atmosphere of Shelley's imagination, it now appears as the source of a greater-than-human woe, repealing human institutions and, indeed, life itself through brute force. The glaciers, as if "in scorn of mortal power" (103), descend from Mont Blanc as a massive "flood of ruin" (107):

> ... that from the boundaries of the sky
> Rolls its perpetual stream; vast pines are strewing
> Its destined path, or in the mangled soil
> Branchless and shattered stand: the rocks, drawn down
> From yon remotest waste, have overthrown
> The limits of the dead and living world,
> Never to be reclaimed. (107–14)

Undoing the very distinction between life and death, the glaciers' disastrous force exposes a rupture within reality itself. Even the syntax of these lines is "overthrown" and distended, a clear contrast with the incantatory regularity that had characterized the first half of this section. The implacable, slow-moving glaciers contain within them a seemingly unlimited power to destroy whatever lies in their path, whether the works of man or those of nature. In section 3, Shelley had looked up and wondered, "Has some unknown omnipotence unfurled / The veil of life and death?" (53–4). In the catastrophic ecosystem of section 4, that omnipotence appears all too present, all too knowable – if not, for that reason, any more legible than it had been. Neither does it affirm traditional accounts of transcendence – the challenge here is precisely not to rise above images of suffering, whatever their cause, but to dwell with them without looking away.

A voice capable of repealing "large codes of fraud and woe" is ultimately a voice that heralds the absoluteness of contingency. Explanations do not collapse because they fail to capture the absolute truth of the universe; the truth can be apprehended only through its own collapse. Shelley does not assume that transcendence is a foregone conclusion or the only way of understanding a sublime that recognizes, to once again invoke the Kantian phrase, "a might that has no dominance over us." Much like Coleridge, Shelley envisions a sublime that does not seek to stand alone, like the mountain. He looks rather to repeal an attachment to the conditioning that afflicts the human mind, the fictions that place human consciousness alone at the centre of the universe. Yet Shelley's sublime, for all its unbridled force and ability to destroy human categories of speech and thought, does not ultimately compel belief in anything – about God, nature, science, or the self. No one has to engage in a process of reconciliation. Not everyone can or will choose to hear the mountain's voice. This element of choice and non-coercion is what, paradoxically, makes those "large codes of fraud and woe" – emblematized by the "secret spring" of tyranny in the Chillon dungeon – so difficult to repeal.

Strictly speaking, the disaster represented in the second half of section 4 is of Shelley's own making; it is a projection of his imagination rather than an event to which he bears witness. Yet, much as the "secret springs" of section 1 whisper of the "secret spring" of concealed tyranny at Chillon, the *History* registers the aftermath of disasters that have their causes in nature as well as in human action. The weather of the Shelleys' 1816 journey to Geneva, described in letter 1, is a marked departure from the sweltering summer they had encountered in 1814: "The spring, as the inhabitants informed us, was unusually late, and indeed the cold was excessive; as we ascended the mountains, the same clouds which rained on us in the vallies poured forth large flakes of snow thick and fast" (*HSWT* 90). Although the Shelleys would not have known this, the "unusually late" spring of 1816 is now understood as one of the after-effects of the eruption of Mount Tambora in Indonesia the year before, which disrupted global weather patterns and caused profound humanitarian crises.[34] The traces of the globally devastating "Year without a Summer" haunt the circular impulse of "Mont Blanc," particularly once the poem attempts to return to where it began:

> Below, vast caves
> Shine in the rushing torrents' restless gleam,
> Which from those secret chasms in tumult welling
> Meet in the vale, and one majestic River,
> The breath and blood of distant lands, for ever
> Rolls its loud waters to the ocean waves,
> Breathes its swift vapours to the circling air. (120–6)

The caves and river, torrents and valley are all images familiar from earlier in the poem. Discursive thought remains suspended – just as the "swift vapours" hover in the "circling air," mimicking the forms that previously had been associated with the "mightier world of sleep" that figured the world's constitutive discontinuity. Shelley amplifies this point by using the word "Rolls" to describe the movement of the glacial "flood of ruin," thus recalling the poem's first two lines – "The everlasting universe of things / Rolls through the mind" – in a way that underlines the precariousness of that situation. At the same time, the menacing-glacier-turned-life-giving-river also "rolls" through distant lands, a reminder, perhaps, that the deep causes of these local disruptions were not fully identified until much later.

The Secret Strength of Subreption

The concluding section of "Mont Blanc" presents an image of imagined transcendence and detachment that remains poetically appealing, though arguably ethically and philosophically dubious. The mountain "yet gleams on high" (127), the "still and solemn" (128) location of ultimate meaning:

> In the calm darkness of the moonless nights,
> In the lone glare of day, the snows descend
> Upon that Mountain; none beholds them there,
> Nor when the flakes burn in the sinking sun,
> Or the star-beams dart through them … (130–4)

There is, of course, an inherent contradiction in the effort to imagine something as existing independently of human imagination. Yet these lines do make an effort to see contingency, rather than the human mind, as the most important force. Shelley holds his own effort to think not-thinking (or to imagine not-imagining) in suspension. The poem's final lines –

> And what were thou, and earth, and stars, and sea,
> If to the human mind's imaginings
> Silence and solitude were vacancy? (142–4)

– are often read as an assertion of the power of imagination: the glacier may annihilate, the river may both destroy and give life, the mountain may endure, but all these scenes gain importance only because of the "human mind's imaginings." Nevertheless, they do leave open the possibility of an independently subsisting universe, pointing Shelley and his readers towards a more complete engagement with a "universe of things" that no longer places its faith in a "secret strength," at least not one that operates according to a rule other than contingency.

Kant insists that "true sublimity must be sought only in the mind of the judging person, not in the natural object the judging of which prompts this mental attunement." This sublime resists representation and externalization, even in its use of natural objects to illustrate the kinds of things that might provoke a sublime feeling. "Indeed," Kant asks, "who would want to call sublime such things as shapeless mountain masses piled on one another in wild disarray, with their pyramids of ice, or the gloomy raging sea?" The question, like many of those in "Mont Blanc," is rhetorical, yet it draws attention to a popular discourse of sublimity – one that, to some extent, persists today – that fails to draw the necessary distinction between mind and object upon which Kant insists. Even those who possess the most refined mental attunements perpetually fall into what Kant calls the error of "subreption," a catachresis through which "respect for the object is substituted for respect for the idea of humanity within our[selves, as] subject[s]."[35] In simpler terms, subreption occurs any time an external object is called sublime. Subreption, this "set of possible confusions concerning the distinction between subjective and objective conditions of knowledge,"[36] seems – at least in the case of the sublime – to be something of a design flaw. For even to name an *experience* as sublime risks reactivating the error. Coleridge's emphasis on the sublime as the suspension of comparing powers amplifies this Kantian point. The sublime moment takes the subject by surprise as being "beyond all comparison" not merely in its presentation of absolute magnitude or force, but also in that it cannot be compared to *other* feelings that might also be called sublime. Even if a hundred people experience a feeling of the sublime at the sight of the same "threatening rocks, thunderclouds piling up in the sky ... volcanoes with all their destructive power," the sublime remains, in a certain sense, unpredictable and unique, happening for the first time each time it happens.[37]

"Mont Blanc" extends this point, emphasizing the fact that subreption is not something that "happens" to the "pure" concept of the sublime at some time after it first takes place; rather, the inevitability of the confusion between subject and object is part of what characterizes sublime experience itself. Suspension of reference, this constitutive difference between what we call sublime and what is sublime, is, in "Mont Blanc," figured not as a problem to be overcome but as part of the enabling conditions of sublimity: the "trance sublime and strange," the "vacancy" that must remain radically open. Shelley's use of rhetorical questions, including the one posed in the poem's last three lines, grammatically reenacts the play of representation and withdrawal. In this way, Shelley both acknowledges the inadequacies and emptiness of representational language and also suggests that sublime experience is made possible by those gaps, by its own impossibility. For even as the poem attempts to represent the scene, it is simultaneously engaged in a disavowal of representation, which is, of course, predicated on the ability to make comparisons – the faculty held in abeyance by the sublime. What is suspended is not only the powers of comparison, but expectations of referentiality. Understood as a form of constitutive discontinuity, the "vacancy" of the poem's final line can be seen as the essential enabling condition of the poem's experience of the sublime. The final question thus acknowledges all the ways things could have been otherwise, registering a condition of contingency and fragility that penetrates the world from top to bottom, linking the travel narrative, the biographical exigencies, the Romantic poem, and the mountain itself that appears both monolithically stable and strikingly fragile. What remains at the end of "Mont Blanc," then, is a profound sense of wonder, a sublime feeling that contemplates both the scale of the mountain landscape (i.e., the traditional subject of the sublime) and its very existence in this form, at this moment, in this poem.

Seeking the sublime in "Mont Blanc" reveals a "vacancy." The vacancy is not what is discovered "instead of" the sublime – or, for that matter, in the place of some "secret strength" that remains inaccessible; this suspension is the condition under which the sublime may arise. The question of vacancy is a serious one – in some ways more serious for Shelley than it was for Coleridge, for Shelley has refused in advance many of the consolations of Christianity as well as the Coleridgean faith in reflection. For Shelley, seeing the sublime in terms of suspension – the suspension of the comparing powers, the suspension of reference, and suspension as a more broadly available set of practices and forms – reveals that uncertainty is not a negative form of knowing or a lack of knowledge, but is instead a discourse and a posture in its own right. The "vacancy" associated with "silence and solitude" echoes the "trance sublime and strange" that Shelley had first experienced in the ravine; so, too, does the reference to "the human mind" echo Shelley's examination of "my own, my human mind" in that same passage. This was the place where the human had been revealed in its essential interconnection with the "universe of things," and this allusion at the end of the poem sets forth suspension as an essential posture through which to mediate relations between the "human mind's imaginings" and the "universe of things."

"Nought may endure"

The more things change, the more they stay the same. This, at least, appears to be the message of the short lyric "Mutability," which appeared in the same volume as *Alastor* in 1816. "We are as clouds that veil the midnight moon," Shelley declares in the poem's opening line. The apparent conventionality of this statement on change belies a world view both attentive to the instability of identity and willing to understand that instability as something that cannot be definitively effaced. Both "Mutability" and "Mont Blanc" invite their readers to look critically at notions of identity and the value judgments attached to claims of constancy, reflecting the development of Shelley's "persistently ambiguous attitude toward personal identity"[38] and a certain scepticism about the coherence of the world itself. The acceptance of change on a broad scale exists in tension with the impossibility of imagining a "tomorrow" that radically breaks from "yesterday" in a way that is not (or not merely) catastrophic. And yet, the life that Percy and Mary Shelley shared with each other – the life that was, in many ways, initiated by the journey that became the "six weeks' tour" – is a life that, in retrospect, can be viewed as a series of catastrophes that were hinted at even in 1816.

After its first appearance at the end of the *History of a Six Weeks' Tour*, "Mont Blanc" was not published again until the *Posthumous Poems* of 1824, edited by Mary Shelley.[39] Following an introduction that constructs Shelley as a philosophically minded lover of nature (while making scant reference to his political commitments), "Mont Blanc" joins a small group of other poems (including "Julian and Maddalo," "The Witch of Atlas," and the unfinished "Triumph of Life") that are set off from the mostly shorter "Miscellaneous Poems."[40] Once detached from the prose of the *History*, the poem gains an ersatz lyric stability, as if it has entirely cast off the problem of mutability and become what it is assumed to have been all along: a celebration of the eternal cooperation between the human mind and the natural world.

"Mutability" appears in the table of contents under "Miscellaneous Poems," but the lyric that bears that title in 1824 is not the poem of the *Alastor* volume, but a meditation that begins, "The flower that smiles to-day / To-morrow dies."[41] These sentiments are far less ambiguous than those of the earlier poem, and far more melancholy in their conventionality. The condition of change is rooted firmly in the human world ("Virtue, how frail it is! / Friendship, too rare!"). The forward movement of time is to be mourned even as the present moment should be celebrated. It is, for all intents and purposes, a conventional "carpe diem" poem that tells us what we already know in forms that are themselves familiar.[42]

However, the 1816 "Mutability" does surface at a crucial moment in Mary Shelley's *Frankenstein* (1818). Oppressed by the knowledge that his monstrous creation has begun to destroy the lives of those he holds most dear, Victor Frankenstein seeks consolation in a rainy-day climb to the glacial heights of Montanvert, in the Alpine region of Chamounix – the site, that is, of "Mont Blanc." Moving from the contemplation of the river valleys and mist-covered mountaintops to a broader reflection on the human condition, his thoughts trace a familiar path towards transcendence. Yet, this normally reliable source of mental elevation and sublimity fails to produce its intended effect. Victor's attention is drawn to images of desolation – paths of broken trees caused by avalanches – and to the sound of distant falling rocks that remind him of fragility and danger: "the slightest sound, such as even speaking in a loud voice, produces a concussion of air sufficient to draw destruction upon the head of the speaker."[43] As much as he wishes to rise above his own base sensibilities, like the mists rise from the rivers below, Victor finds that his worries pull him back down, rendering him helplessly distracted by every passing impression:

> Alas! why does man boast of sensibilities superior to those apparent in the brute; it only renders them more necessary beings. If our impulses were confined to hunger, thirst, and desire, we might be nearly free; but now we are moved by every wind that blows, and a chance word or scene that that word may convey to us.
>
> We rest; a dream has power to poison sleep.
> We rise; one wand'ring thought pollutes the day.
> We feel, conceive, or reason; laugh, or weep,
> Embrace fond woe, or cast our cares away;

It is the same: for, be it joy or sorrow,
  The path of its departure still is free.
Man's yesterday may ne'er be like his morrow;
  Nought may endure but mutability![44]

Despite their best efforts, humans are the playthings of chance and easy prey for their own weaknesses – a far cry from the disciplined perception of the "man of virtue and talent" envisioned in *Queen Mab*. This scene is often read as a critique or parody of a conventional Romantic nature-sublime.[45] Though the quotation of the poem is an anachronism,[46] Mary Shelley's invocation of it appears to perform a critical revision of the openness of "Mont Blanc." It replaces the liberating play of the "trance sublime and strange" with a declaration of helplessness before external stimuli that masks an ultimately futile attempt on Victor's part to evade the monstrous consequences of his own actions. He doubly evades responsibility by breaking off his personal thoughts in favour of a quotation that, understood as a conventional statement about the constancy of change, would serve to distance him from the consequences of his actions – consequences that are, famously, just about to confront him in this landscape of ice: his creature lurks nearby and will soon reveal himself.

However, though these lines seem to reify an adversarial relationship between the human mind and the natural world, "Mutability" tells a different story. The apparent conventionality of this statement on change belies a world view both attentive to the instability of identity and willing to understand that instability as something that cannot be definitively effaced. The human mind experiences states of unrest, happiness, and sadness but is never wholly identified with any one of those states. Thus, we might twist like "forgotten lyres, whose dissonant strings / Give various response to each varying blast" (5–6) – an ironic revision of *Alastor*'s own "forgotten lyre" – but those states of unrest, happiness, sadness, and distraction, however overwhelming, do not constitute the whole of the human mind. "The path of its departure" – that is, the departure of a particular emotional state – "still is free" (14). Like wind through an Aeolian harp, impressions pass through the mind, and though they may have disruptive and unexpected effects, revealing discontinuities and sites of uncertainty, they are neither totalizing nor permanent. The creature also alludes to this line when he recalls how his reading made him aware of his own difference: "I sympathized with, and partly understood them, but I was unformed in mind; I was dependent on none, and related to none. 'The path of my departure was free'; and there was none to lament my annihilation."[47] The creature's understanding of the line seems at once more personal and more trenchant than his creator's.

Within this context, the concluding lines of the poem – "Man's yesterday may ne'er be like his morrow; / Nought may endure but Mutability" (15–16) – encapsulate what we might think of as Shelley's aesthetics of contingency that also underlies "Mont Blanc." While it is relatively easy to assent, in a general sense, to the nebulous thought of change in a hazy, distant future, Shelley asks his readers to think of change as a much more proximate phenomenon. The idea that Wednesday is (or could be) so radically different from Monday as to be unrecognizable is surprisingly frightening but also strangely exhilarating. It brings contingency into a lyric present, enabling the sorts of dilations capable of making a short life seem nearly infinite. When nothing persists except for mutability, then each moment offers the potential for unlikely miracles.

Thus, in the sublime setting of the Alps, linear time – the time of literary history and influence, as well as authorship and biography – is suspended in favour of an impossible simultaneity. In this expanded spot of unthinkable time, everything happens at once. The absence of the 1816 "Mutability" from the 1824 *Posthumous Poems* in effect makes *Frankenstein* the most definitive gloss on its meaning – at least until the publication of Percy Shelley's *Poetical Works* of 1839. The presence of these two stanzas, anachronistically detached from the full poem and the context of the *Alastor* volume, opens a site of suspension within *Frankenstein* itself, even as it places this text within a complex textual ecology that includes the *History* in general and "Mont Blanc" in particular. Surrounded by prose, the poetic statement about contingency is contained and at least partially neutralized. Reflecting a solecism on Victor's part, it allows him at least momentarily to evade the confrontation with the consequences of his own actions, as well as any insight that would arise from the sublimity of the scene, inserting in its place a performance of aesthetic response. In Coleridgean terms, it could be seen as a refusal to look the "secret lodger" in the face; in light of "Mont Blanc," Victor, who has himself engaged in work intended to overthrow the "limits of the dead and living world," appears to refuse the opportunity to "muse" on his "separate phantasy" – even when, in the following pages, that "phantasy" reveals its hideously embodied form. It is his creature, neither alive nor dead, who bears the weight of suspension into the later years of the nineteenth century. Descending from the spectral peaks of the Romantic sublime, the aesthetics of suspension in the 1830s and afterwards is more typically embodied in uncanny figures of suspended animation. No longer simply the ecstatic trance of reverie, these suspended bodies resist the most fundamental of medical inquiries: they appear dead, but may nonetheless contain a living, conscious, and possibly even feeling subject. It is suspension itself that endures as both an epistemological concern and an existential condition.

Chapter Four

Tennyson and the Rhetoric of Suspended Animation

In his discussion of the "Defects of Wordsworth's Poetry" in chapter 22 of the *Biographia Literaria*, Coleridge takes exception to the description of the child of nature in the Immortality Ode. He objects particularly to the characterization of the child as one

> To whom the grave
> Is but a lonely bed without the sense or sight
> Of day or the warm light,
> A place of thought where we in waiting lie ... (120–3)[1]

Coleridge sharply criticizes Wordsworth's "assertion, that a *child*, who by the bye at six years old would have been better instructed in most christian families, has no other notion of death than that of lying in a dark, cold place" (*BL* 2.141, italics in original). The image, for him, is both emotionally disturbing – the "frightful notion of lying *awake* in his grave" is too "horrid a belief" for a child to hold – and theologically aberrant in its improper literalization of the biblical analogy of sleep and death. Although Christian consolatory discourse to some extent authorizes the metaphorical substitution of sleep for death, Wordsworth's rendering, at least as far as Coleridge is concerned, upsets the delicate balance of these two ideas. It threatens to collapse the complex interplay of the religious idea into a "horrid belief" or gothic cliché. "Thus it is with splendid paradoxes in general," Coleridge continues:

> If the words are taken in the common sense, they convey an absurdity; and if, in contempt of dictionaries and custom, they are so interpreted as to avoid the absurdity, the meaning dwindles into some bald truism. Thus

> you must at once understand the words *contrary* to their common import, in order to arrive at any *sense;* and *according* to their common import, if you are to receive from them any feeling of *sublimity* or *admiration.* (*BL* 2.141, italics in original)

Sleep and death are not the same thing; to claim otherwise is an evident "absurdity." However, in Christian discourse, they are also not *not* the same thing. Neither the literal nor the figural meaning of the words is sufficient to express accurately the profound spiritual mystery to which they refer. Coleridge does not suggest that the sleep/death analogy should be abandoned, but rather that it must be understood in a way that preserves the mystery at its centre. Both meanings must be kept in tension with each other. To insist too much on the literal reading of this linguistic construction, that is, to envision the sleep of death taking place in the bed of the grave, disrupts the whole. In other words, an act of deliberate suspension is required: the association must be understood as simultaneously literal and figurative, at once affirming and contradicting its "common import." Wordsworth must have agreed, at least on some level, for the lines do not appear in later versions of the poem (*BL* 2.140n3).

Nearly forty years after the *Biographia Literaria* was published, the speaker of Alfred Tennyson's *Maud* (1855) stumbles into a similar confusion:

> I looked, and round, all round the house I beheld
> The death-white curtain drawn;
> Felt a horror over me creep,
> Prickle my skin and catch my breath,
> Knew that the death-white curtain meant but sleep,
> Yet I shuddered and thought like a fool of the sleep of death. (1.521–6)[2]

Outside of the constraints of Christian religious discourse, the analogy undergoes an absurd gothic reversal – just as Coleridge had feared. If the Immortality Ode had been guilty of overstating the way that death resembles sleep, *Maud* insists too much on the ways that sleep is like death. The sight of the white curtain becomes an occasion for visceral terror: the speaker's body reacts as if to a sign of death before his mind can assure him that it is only a sign that the inhabitants of the house have gone to sleep for the night. The protagonist checks his initial physical reaction, criticizing it as the mark of a "fool." But the problem faced by Tennyson's protagonist is not that he must decide between the false and the true, but rather that he is caught between two irreducible sources of information: on the one hand, his internal bodily experience and, on the other, the "objective" reality that lies, in more ways than one, behind the curtain. The delusion or error, that shuddering horror, remains in some ways more "true" to the speaker, directly experienced in the body. Rather than the triumph of the reasonable explanation over the unreasonable or excessive response, the *Maud* speaker's reaction to the "death-white curtain" remains suspended, exposing the contingent relations and permeable boundaries between sign and signification, death and life.

At its most basic level, *Maud* is a poem about a person who finds himself at the mercy of forces that lie outside of his control. He is marginalized by a corrupt society that values riches over all else, separated from the woman he loves by the prejudices of her brother, and keenly aware of how historical and geological time make an individual human life seem insignificant by comparison. Tossed about by the forces that surround him as well as the uncontrollable impulses of his own mind, the *Maud* speaker witnesses the convergence of external and internal discontinuities, ranging from his emotional imbalance to events of world-historical importance, without being able to mediate between them. Faced with a world that operates according to increasingly arbitrary laws, he attempts to forge a coherent sense of self and narrative. He does so, however, through obsessive questioning, superstitious logic, and frequent recourse to the subjunctive and conditional moods – the appropriate tonal signatures for a "morbid poetic soul, under the blighting influence of a recklessly speculative age."[3] Unable to trust his disordered perception, yet aware, however dimly, that his perception is disordered, the speaker comes to adopt an increasingly paranoid relationship to others.

However, although Tennyson's protagonist may chastise himself for his visceral response to the "death-white curtain," his response is hardly unique in the context of mid-nineteenth-century Britain. The aesthetics of the sublime upset the boundary between life and death, while religious and medical treatises raised questions about whether such a boundary even existed. Ruth Richardson's pathbreaking study, *Death, Dissection and the Destitute*, lays out the contradictory discourses surrounding the human corpse in early nineteenth-century Britain, all of which were "coloured by a prevailing belief in the existence of a strong tie between body and personality/soul for an undefined period of time after death," a belief that "underpinned the central role of the corpse in popular funerary ritual, and gained added power from confusion and ambiguity concerning both the definition of death and the spiritual status of the corpse."[4] Debates over the Anatomy Act, passed in 1832, only intensified the stakes of this confusion. Ostensibly aimed at discouraging grave robbery and worse by allowing anatomy schools legally to obtain "unclaimed" bodies from workhouses and hospitals for the purposes of dissection, the Act heightened fears among the poor that they might be peremptorily declared dead for the benefit of anatomists and reinforced a disgust with the idea of dissection that, Richardson observes, transcended class lines.[5] Historian George K. Behlmer traces the roots of Victorian live burial panics – which arose intermittently into the 1890s – to a range of sources, including the visionary religious discourses of the eighteenth and early nineteenth centuries, the translation and dissemination of medical treatises on live burial, the founding of the Royal Humane Society for restoring the victims of drowning in 1773, and scientific investigations of vitality that involved suspending the animation of animal bodies and re-animating the corpses of convicted criminals. All of these cultural factors, he contends, contributed to "the deep confusion over human physiology that persisted into the twentieth century" and provided the background that enabled gothic fiction by writers such as Matthew Lewis, Mary Shelley, and Edgar Allan Poe to tap into its readers' greatest fears.[6] Availing themselves of "an opulent if unstable vocabulary to designate bodily conditions that hovered between the fully animate and the irrecoverably dead,"[7] Victorian writers proved themselves to be adept at imagining configurations of paralysis and consciousness that could confound even the most assiduous attempts to ascertain the state of the suspended body – considerably multiplying the possibilities that Coleridge had found so abhorrent. Whether presented as case studies in medical treatises or as gothic fantasy, stories of suspended animation, apparent death, and premature burial had the effect of engendering considerable scepticism about the trustworthiness of other people – not simply medical professionals – even as they also reinforced a sense of absolute dependence on them.

Accordingly, the uncertainty prompted by the "death-white curtain" anticipates the poem's penultimate scene, where the speaker is afflicted by an all-consuming delusion that he has been buried alive. For most readers, *Maud*'s mad scene represents the final triumph of the insanity that the speaker has been trying to outrun throughout the poem: what the speaker experiences as a shallow grave is really a madhouse. After all, as E. Warwick Slinn observes, "according to the rules of normal existence, where dead men do not speak, this claim to literal burial must of course be figurative, shedding doubt on the speaker's sanity."[8] At best, then, the so-called madhouse canto provides an excess of evidence for a condition long established. At worst it suggests the indulgence of a self-enclosed poet insufficiently solicitous of his audience. Yet, however much the "burial" experienced by the *Maud* speaker reflects the disturbed reality of a deranged mind, the fact that this derangement takes the specific form of live burial is significant, in that it mobilizes the concerns of a mid-nineteenth-century cultural and scientific discourse about suspension – specifically, suspended animation – and its risks. Whatever clarity Coleridge had hoped to restore in his complaint about Wordsworth's representation of the grave as "a place of thought" was, even in the early nineteenth century, irrevocably muddled.

In this chapter, then, I argue that Tennyson's use of live burial as the organizing metaphor for his "most faithful representation of madness since Shakespeare"[9] reflects a preoccupation with what might be broadly termed insignificance: not only the lack of societal importance the speaker complains of across the poem, but also a textual condition in which one's very survival depends on other people's reading practices, which are themselves always open to dispute. The status of the insignificant or non-signifying individual within a social context remains undecidable even – or especially – when, as in *Maud*, the burial is figurative rather than literal. Through the *Maud* speaker, whose status is liminal and uncertain, Tennyson undercuts a significant portion of the ontological foundation of mid-Victorian literature and culture. Mad or not, this subject experiences himself as having been let down by an entire cultural and scientific complex entrusted with maintaining the border between life and death, not to mention by an elaborate mourning culture in which Tennyson's own poetry had played a paradigmatic role.

Furthermore, what separates Tennyson from many of his Victorian contemporaries is his treatment of suspended animation as something other than a riddle to be solved through increasingly refined processes of epistemological investigation. At a time when medical science was searching for an unequivocal sign that would enable even a layperson to make a reliable diagnosis of death, Tennyson takes unreliability and illegibility as fundamental conditions of social existence. His rhetoric of suspended animation in *Maud* and elsewhere registers the operations of irreducible contingency, drawing attention to what exceeds or falls beneath the limits of language and epistemology. Just as, for Coleridge, no one way of understanding the association of sleep and death would capture both the meaning and spiritual grandeur of the analogy, Tennyson's rhetoric of suspended animation responds to a world that is constituted by its own discontinuity with itself. *Maud* confuses the living and the dead in order to register the profound discontinuities of scientific and social reality in the High Victorian era. The poem reflects a deep anxiety about insignificance, understood in its broadest sense both as a lack of importance (in society, in one's personal relationships) and as a suspension of the powers of signification themselves (as when a living consciousness is trapped within an inert, seemingly dead body). More than that, Tennyson declares his sympathy with the illegible bodies and texts that fall through the cracks of the kinds of epistemologically driven narrative forms that were becoming increasingly dominant at midcentury.[10] Enacted through a frequently disjunctive poetics, Tennyson's rhetoric of suspended animation resists the ascendency of narrative suspense and the closure upon which that suspense depends – implying that such closure may always come too soon.

"Who knows if he be dead?"

Critics have typically taken "What is it, that has been done?" (2.7) as the overarching, if unanswerable, question of *Maud*, attempting to gain some sense of the reality outside the speaker's monodramatic perceptions.[11] To the extent that there is a "story," as Seamus Perry observes, it emerges through the poem's "sequence of dramatic lyrics, all uttered by the same speaker, diversely set in moments when action is imminent or its aftermath evident ... on the edge of events or just after."[12] In its immediate context, the question refers to events that take place in the interval between parts 1 and 2 of the poem, usually understood to be a duel fought between the speaker and Maud's brother. Having fled into exile, the speaker is attempting to reconstruct the circumstances that brought him to this point; readers, too, remain unaware of what has "been done." However, as Slinn contends, "to turn the poem into a narrative of external events" amounts to "ignoring the brilliance of Tennyson's dialectical and figurative ambiguity which shifts dramatic action away from external event towards signifying process."[13] *Maud*'s interests lie not only with its processes of signification but with the structures which produce insignificance. For all of these reasons the overarching question of the poem is most aptly expressed in the following terms:

"Who knows if he be dead?" (2.119). Like "What is it, that has been done?" "Who knows if he be dead?" refers most directly to the status of Maud's brother, for the speaker appears to have departed while the other was alive, though seriously wounded. Nevertheless, it functions more broadly as a rhetorical question in Paul de Man's sense of the term, that is, as an utterance that "engenders two meanings that are mutually exclusive: the literal meaning asks for the concept (difference) whose existence is denied by the figurative meaning."[14] The conjunction of meanings that are mutually exclusive and mutually dependent creates what de Man calls a referential aberration, an undecidable suspension of reference between literal and figural. The two meanings thus no longer "exist side by side" but "engage each other in direct confrontation, for the one reading is precisely the error denounced by the other and has to be undone by it."[15] Although the figural meaning is generally privileged over the literal – we understand that the speaker is not literally searching for a person who could report on the status of Maud's brother but is commenting on the impossibility of establishing that status – de Man considers that literal meaning to be equally urgent.

"Who knows if he be dead?" also speaks to a broader, and emphatically literal, cultural preoccupation. By the beginning of the nineteenth century an increasingly institutionalized medical profession knew that the cessation of breathing was not an irrefutable sign of death, but, save for putrefaction of the limbs after several days, no other infallible criterion had yet emerged. Cholera epidemics on both sides of the Atlantic considerably heightened fears of premature interment, for the disease's symptoms were often contradictory. Richardson summarizes some of the difficulties that attended a diagnosis of death from cholera:

> A victim could be dead within hours, after violent purgings and vomiting had caused rapid dehydration and loss of body salts, causing visible physical shrinking and rigid muscular cramps. These cramps, or spasms, often relaxed only after death, causing sudden convulsions which could be mistaken for signs of life. Signs of death could be equally deceptive, as in many cases the body was blue ... stiff from muscular spasm, "cold as marble" and with heart and breathing rates so low as to be imperceptible. Cases were reported of people who survived a medical diagnosis of death, and when we consider that the medical test for death was merely the holding of a mirror near the mouth to seek signs of breath, we need not disbelieve such reports, nor discredit as unreasonable the widespread fear of premature burial or of dissection taking place before life was extinct.[16]

The mirror test was, by the 1830s, widely understood to be inaccurate, but it would be several more decades before any other reliable method of determining death was agreed upon.[17] The preponderance of possible but ultimately unreliable signs of death is effectively illustrated by James Curry's *Observations on Apparent Death* (1792), a manual that delineates nine different categories of apparent death – including drowning, "suffocation by noxious vapours," and "intoxication" – and offers more than twice that number of case studies. Addressing a general audience, the treatise counsels its readers "to use every exertion, and not to cease from employing the several means recommended, until many hours have elapsed, nor ever abandon a case without trial, unless indubitable marks of complete and permanent death evidently appear." Curry's text, and others like it, thus attempt to navigate the difficult task of delineating potentially reversible symptoms without making too many promises about who could be rescued and under what conditions. Affirming what was, at the time, conventional wisdom that, "a beginning putrefaction of the body, is perhaps the only unequivocal proof of death we are yet acquainted with in such cases,"[18] Curry suggests that the layperson's job is always to hold out hope and insist on tests to verify the presence of death. It is up to a representative of the medical profession – itself an unstable and fraught category – to decide when it is appropriate to give up hope.

Nineteenth-century fears of live burial centred less on the convention of deliberate live interments than on the largely unmotivated – but not, for that reason, less terrifying – potential for live-burial-as-honest-mistake. Discussions of live burial panics in both British and American contexts often turn to Poe's short story "The Premature Burial" (1844) as an exemplary text. Though less well known than his more extravagant tales of live interment, such as "The Fall of the House of Usher" or "The Cask of Amontillado," "The Premature Burial" exemplifies the plight of the illegible body and the fear of medical and social insignificance. More than that, "The Premature Burial" situates itself firmly within the realm of reality, appealing to "the direct testimony of medical and ordinary experience."[19] The story opens with a series of anecdotes about suspended animation that mimic those found in newspapers and in medical journals. Poe's first anecdote concerns a respectable Baltimore matron who was "seized with a sudden and unaccountable illness" and buried in the family vault. Three years later, her husband opens the vault and is startled to discover his wife's skeleton in a position that reveals that she had woken up in her tomb:

> On the uppermost of the steps which led down into the dread chamber, was a large fragment of the coffin, with which it seemed that she had endeavored to arrest attention, by striking the iron door. While thus occupied, she probably swooned, or possibly died, through sheer terror; and, in falling, her shroud became entangled in some iron-work which projected interiorly. Thus she remained, and thus she rotted, erect.[20]

The tragic fate of this unfortunate matron bears a striking resemblance to that suffered by one Charlotte Clopton of Stratford-on-Avon in the mid-sixteenth century. Occasionally cited as a partial inspiration for Shakespeare's Juliet, Charlotte Clopton appears frequently in nineteenth-century medical journals alongside medieval peasants mistakenly buried during plague outbreaks and gentlemen who awaken during their own autopsies. Although the details of the story vary, the broad outline involves a hasty burial after an infectious disease, followed by the later discovery of the body out of its coffin and in a posture that suggests an attempt to escape this most horrible of horrors. In one of his "Lectures on Medical Jurisprudence," the physician Antony Todd Thomson characterizes the Clopton story as "One of the most heart-rending accounts of premature interments that I know," an emotional reminder of the importance of carefully diagnosing death.[21] Charlotte Clopton also makes an appearance in an 1840 essay by Elizabeth Gaskell, who recalls hearing the legend on a trip to Clopton House she made as a girl. Gaskell's account largely agrees with that of Thomson but includes the sort of gothic embellishments that would have pleased Poe. In this version of the story, family members discover "Charlotte Clopton in her grave-clothes leaning against the wall; and when they looked nearer, she was indeed dead, but not before, in the agonies of despair and hunger, she had bitten a piece from her white round shoulder! Of course, she had *walked* ever since."[22] Gaskell's tone implies a certain justified scepticism about the ghost story, but the account of Charlotte Clopton's live burial does possess a clear mobility. It "walks" through travelogues, medical journals, and fiction. And what is most terrifying about this story and those like it is captured by a remark that Poe makes about the woman from Baltimore: "No one suspected, indeed, or had reason to suspect, that she was not actually dead."[23] These are not unduly hasty burials, nor are they gruesome gothic punishments. However, even the best intentions and the most assiduous reading practices can fail when faced with a body that is constitutively resistant to signification.

The narrator of "The Premature Burial" has a personal stake in these stories: he suffers from catalepsy, a condition that causes him to fall into trancelike states. Some of these trances may appear relatively mild, like the intoxication that Coleridge had experienced in Birmingham. At other times, however, the cataleptic body can fall victim to a much longer trance, wherein, Poe's narrator claims, "the closest scrutiny, and the most rigorous medical tests, fail to establish any material distinction between the state of the sufferer and what we conceive of absolute death."[24] Ironically, the narrator's fear of being mistaken for dead while in one of these deep trances exacerbates his condition, making the trances longer and more intractable. Less fortunate is the first-person narrator of Horace Smith's three-part novella "Posthumous Memoir of Myself" (1849), who, after having been incompetently and incompletely poisoned by his half-mad son, finds himself in a state of deathlike suspended animation. To all those around him, he appears to be dead, yet he retains full consciousness and the powers of sight and hearing, though not of motion or speech. At the end of the first instalment of the "Posthumous Memoir," the paralysed narrator confronts the fears that arise during his first night as a dead man:

> Perhaps my mind was still too much agitated to settle into any sort of oblivion; perhaps it would never be otherwise, and my trance – existence – might be a perpetual consciousness, and consequently an unvaried misery. Such a state must soon lead to madness; but how could a man be mad and motionless, a maniac and a statue? What inconceivable misery, to feel your brain raving and raging with an insanity which can find no vent for its fury, either by the explosions of the voice or the convulsive violence of the limbs![25]

Perhaps the only thing worse than being buried alive is the knowledge that such burial is imminent – or the awareness that it is actually happening. Against the widespread cultural assumption that death represented a cessation of consciousness as well as of motion and sensation, the posthumous memoirist ponders the nightmarish possibility that he will remain conscious throughout his ordeal – and possibly indefinitely. With no ability to respond to those around him, he can see no other end but the insanity that comes from being unable to express himself in a legible way. The terror of the situation is amplified by his parallel descent into social insignificance: one moment, he is a prominent businessman and *paterfamilias*, while the next he is treated as an inert object.

A similar set of thoughts occurs to a fictional Captain Hurst, whose story of deathlike paralysis is recounted "Death-in-Life" (1847), an unsigned narrative attributed to George Henry Lewes. Recalling the "concomitance of keen sensibility, with a complete absence of all outward indications thereof,"[26] Hurst traces in detail the psychologically harrowing two days he spends as a sentient corpse that force him to reconsider everything he had previously believed to be true about his own body. After two days of hearing people describe him as dead, without being able to make a legible sign to the contrary, Hurst comes to consider the possibility that these others may in fact be correct:

> I began to ask myself, "Is this death? Am I really alive? Do the dead hear and feel?"
>
> I then thought of the imperishable nature of my soul. It, of course, preserves itself through all bodily decay. Is it imprisoned in the body as long as the body holds together? and shall I be liberated only on the utter falling away of these fleshly walls that encompass me? Am I to be buried, sensible of all that is going on around me?[27]

Hurst's experience is presented as an appropriate subject for dinner-party discussion among educated male company, a first-person testimony to the fact that contemporary medical practice was still at a loss when it came to differentiating the signs of death from those of suspended animation. That Hurst had been willing to entertain the possibility that he was, in fact, dead – and, in turn, the notion that death could signify the extinction of motion but not thought – reflects the pervasive scientific and spiritual uncertainties of the mid-nineteenth century and a desire for some kind of authoritative pronouncement on the matter. If Hurst is correct in his suppositions, then everyone is vulnerable to the terrors of a conscious interment – perhaps the dead do "hear and feel." Even though this combination of paralysis, consciousness, and sensibility seems medically unlikely,[28] it is interpretable within the bounds of a Victorian medical and social imagination preoccupied with the illegibility of the suspended body. "Death-in-Life" demonstrates just how easily bodies can elude definition, with potentially terrifying consequences. Death is a matter of signs like anything else. If dead men do not speak, that is partially because not being able to speak is a kind of death. In other words, if speaking is taken as representative of signification in general, it is not so much that dead men do not speak as that dead men no longer speak in a way that is intelligible to other people.

Stripped of explicit gothic trappings, these stories connect the fear of premature burial to the loss of signifying power that attends the suspension of animation: an insignificance that renders a subject uniquely vulnerable to the contingencies of reading.

Despite the range of fictional testimonies and speculative historical anecdotes, the fascination with and fear of premature burial can appear to be more than slightly disproportionate to the actual risks. Even when we account for the ad hoc nature of nineteenth-century medical practice and the pressures of dealing with corpses in the midst of widespread infection, it remains likely that the vast majority of people who are buried are dead beforehand, and that the risk of being buried alive was probably less for Victorians than for populations of earlier ages. Yet stories of premature interment, whether presented as fact, fiction, or something in between, were, as Carolyn J. Lawes contends, "not about the dead at all; their focus was the living."[29] Behlmer observes that in the Victorian era, "Readers of the popular press were familiar with anti-Catholic tales of innocent girls immured in nunneries; with the financially feckless entombed in debt; with pottery workers slowly suffocating in clay dust; and of course with coal miners and grave diggers who, on occasion, were literally buried alive. Where the trope ended and true vivisepulture began," he concludes, "could be nearly as hard to distinguish as the body's vital signs."[30] The figure of live burial could function as a metaphor for a range of "social" deaths connected to forms of confinement and slavery.[31] Lawes argues that the popularity of accounts of live burial among antebellum American reading audiences indexes "the fear that life in the expanding United States was being lived too fast," leaving citizens vulnerable to early death and abrupt financial reversals – fears that were also shared by British Victorians.[32] In fact, *Maud* opens with the insinuation that the speaker's father had been ruined by the failure of a "vast speculation" (1.9) that enriched the father of Maud and her brother, creating the financial inequities that prevent the joining of the two families – all the more reason to take seriously the rhetoric of suspended animation that pervades the poem.

Death in Life: "The Two Voices" and *The Princess*

Long before the *Maud* speaker plaintively asks, "To have no peace in the grave, is that not sad?" (2.254), Tennyson was engaged in exploring the ambiguous nature of death and suspended animation. "The Two Voices" (1842), for example, invokes the language of medical uncertainty to counteract the seductions of suicide. One "voice," drawing upon the conventional discourse that casts the grave as a place of rest and retreat, promises that death will bring about the cessation of emotional pain. Responding to the speaker's fear that his "anguish" may become "fixed and frozen to permanence" (235, 237), the voice conjures the image of a peacefully indifferent corpse:

> His palms are folded on his breast:
> There is no other thing expressed
> But long disquiet merged in rest.
> His lips are very mild and meek:
> Though one should smite him on the cheek,
> And on the mouth, he will not speak. (247–52)

The image that the "voice" aims to present here is of a dead man who is blissfully insensible to the incursions of the world of the living, one who has achieved a too-perfect version of Christian equanimity. In later lines, this dead man is depicted as equally free from the concerns of those he had cared for in life. What is it to him, now, if his daughter "Becomes dishonour to her race" (255) or if the fortunes of his sons are mixed? But the other voice, like the protagonists of the "Posthumous Memoir" and "Death-in-Life," has reason to be sceptical of this conclusion. Death may have robbed this hypothetical corpse of the ability to signal his "disquiet," but there is no way to tell from these "outward signs" (270) whether the loss of signifying power is concomitant with the loss of things to signify. Thus the other speaker rejects the promise of peaceful death, replying that: "These things are wrapt in doubt and dread, / Nor canst thou show the dead are dead" (266–7). Ultimately, this is the voice that wins out, as the one who debates these issues in his own mind decides that it is better not to take the risk.

"The Two Voices" dramatizes the uncertain status of individual consciousness after death and, implicitly, the inability of medical professionals (let alone the lay observer) to ascertain correctly the signs of death. The uncannily peaceful corpse remains a figure of speculation that the speaker uses to talk himself out of his own despair. *The Princess* (1847) offers a more extended consideration of the illegibly suspended body. Like the narrator of "The Premature Burial," the first-person speaker (who is also many speakers) of *The Princess* suffers from "weird seizures" (1.14) associated with catalepsy. Because of a mysterious family curse, the Prince is liable to experience periods in which "while I walked and talked as heretofore, / I seemed to move among a world of ghosts, / And feel myself the shadow of a dream" (1.16–18). The passages establishing the Prince's cataleptic condition were mostly added for the fourth edition of the poem in 1851 – just four years before the publication of *Maud* – and were generally met with confusion by contemporary critics who wondered why Tennyson would "superimpose the seizures upon the poem when they seemingly add nothing by way of elucidation of the Prince's character or of the action."[33] Scholars have since offered a range of readings of the seizures, many of which have to do with the insufficiently stable – or insufficiently masculine – character of the Prince himself. Barbara Herb Wright demonstrates that the seizures "reflect the truths, half-truths, and outright untruths about epilepsy that were common currency in the Victorian view of the disease," including those that saw the condition as a marker of weak or disordered will.[34] Eve Kosofsky Sedgwick speculates in *Between Men* that the Prince's seizures "are best described as a wearing-thin of the enabling veil of opacity that separates the seven male narrators from the one male speaker … Is the Prince a single person, or merely an arbitrarily chosen chord from the overarching, transhistorical, transindividual circuit of male entitlement and exchange? He himself is incapable of knowing."[35] Although Sedgwick's reading is best known for having shifted the emphasis of the poem from heterosexual to homosocial relations, it is also possible to detect in this approach an echo of Shelley's "trance sublime and strange," which enables a temporary suspension of the burdens of individual selfhood in "Mont Blanc." More recently, D.B. Ruderman has reinforced the connection between gender and genre, proposing a link between the seizures, which "point to the femininity and even maternal nature of the Prince/narrator," and the songs added to the poem in 1850: "The seizures give way (birth) to the interpolated ballad sections of the poem, suggesting that sensitivity and sensibility are still poetic prerequisites in Tennyson's schema."[36]

Indeed, the uncanny, illegible dimensions of the Prince's cataleptic body are hinted at by the inserted lyrics such as "Tears, Idle Tears" – particularly in the reference to "Death in Life, the days that are no more" (4.40). But the illegibility of the Prince's body is also of central importance to the plot. During the battle with Princess Ida's forces, the Prince suffers a cataleptic episode that leaves him "stark / Dishelmed and mute, and motionlessly pale" (6.84–5). Quite simply, he appears to be dead. The irony is particularly acute because this is the moment at which his physical condition best matches his existing diagnosis of catalepsy. In turn, catalepsy is revealed to be most itself when it looks like something else, namely, death. Unable to make any signs that he lives, the Prince finds himself at the mercy of those around him. This vulnerability is also a particular source of consternation for the narrator of Poe's "Premature Burial," who even doubts that those familiar with his condition will act in his best interest: "I doubted the care, the fidelity of my dearest friends. I dreaded that, in some trance of more than customary duration, they might be prevailed upon to regard me as irrecoverable."[37] Indeed, the Prince's father – who, given the family medical history, should know better – peremptorily declares his son to be dead. It is Princess Ida who rescues him from an untimely burial by crossing enemy lines to dispute the paternal pronouncement. Against the evidence of her senses, Ida, demonstrating, perhaps, her familiarity with popular medical manuals like James Curry's treatise on apparent death as well as the feminine intuition that cannot be taught in a university classroom, insists that the Prince may still live. The Prince as an object in suspended animation – "silent in the muffled cage of life" (7.32) – accomplishes what he otherwise could not: he becomes a fixed, stable entity. Although he remains in a coma for most of the next section of the poem, he no longer dresses in women's clothing (as he had to infiltrate Ida's all-female university) or interacts with others while in a trancelike stupor. Most importantly, he now is capable of attracting Princess Ida's interest by allowing her freely to imagine hidden depths in his character. His insensible body calls forth the best of her "feminine" sensibility that had been suppressed by an overemphasis on education. In the presence of the Prince's passive body, she feels emboldened to speak of love and even to express it in the form of a kiss. Eventually, the Prince does come back to life; like many other literary victims of suspended animation, he regains his faculties independently of any medical intervention.

In this case, consciousness returns prior to motion. The interval between the two is long enough to allow the Prince's thoughts to turn explicitly to the possibility of live burial:

> I could no more, but lay like one in trance,
> That hears his burial talked of by his friends,
> And cannot speak, nor move, nor make one sign,
> But lies and dreads his doom. (7.136–9)

These lines describe almost precisely what "taphephobics" – people afraid of live burial – "fear the most: awareness of imminent burial combined with an inability to avoid it ... a conflict between the wakefulness of the mind and the slumbers of the body."[38] Robert Browning makes use of this figure in "Childe Roland to the Dark Tower Came" (1855), where the speaker compares himself to "a sick man very near to death" who overhears his friends discussing plans for his funeral. Browning renders this confusion in a way that is bitterly ironic: "still the man hears all, and only craves / He may not shame such tender love and stay" (25, 35–6).[39] The hero of Smith's "Posthumous Memoir" overhears similar conversations among his family members and household attendants. In the case of Tennyson's poem, the figurative status of the Prince's speech is not in doubt, for he is no longer in imminent danger of being buried alive. Yet, it is a fragile figuration, given that he *has* been lying in a trance that very nearly could have ended with the "doom" he envisions in the final line but for Ida's timely intervention on the battlefield and continuing care. Indeed, the fact that he is an object of care and compassion rather than an inconvenience is essentially an accident, so far as he knows. Because he necessarily constructs this part of his story from accounts supplied by others, it is never completely clear whether the image of "one in trance" describes a thought that the Prince had at the moment he emerged from his coma (when he could not yet have known that he had already been saved from one premature burial) or a gloss added later. These reflections take place just after his first attempt to speak to Princess Ida, and he does not know whether his words of love have been heard. Doubtless, the image heightens the suspense, making the reception of his utterance of love a matter of life and death – though still, it must be observed, only on a figural register.

After all this, *The Princess* is a story of suspended animation with a happy ending – happy, at least, according to the generic and social landscape of the poem, but also happy because the Prince can draw upon the metaphorical resonances of live burial to heighten his emotional state without becoming directly threatened by its physical actuality. Live burial remains an abstraction, and the implication seems to be that marrying the reformed Princess Ida will lessen the frequency of the Prince's trances as he comes to inhabit a fully masculine social role. But the Prince is also a prototype for the *Maud* speaker, who similarly seeks salvation from his self-contradiction in fantasies of battle, heterosexual love, and inherited social position. Like the Prince, who initially infiltrates Princess Ida's all-female university to enforce an engagement that had been formalized when they were children, the *Maud* speaker believes that he has a "right" to the hand of his attractive neighbour because of a long-ago agreement negotiated between their two fathers

(1.720–6). But Maud is no Princess Ida, able or even willing to look beyond all external signs to intuit the life locked into a beloved, though disordered, body.

Maud and the Wilful Suspension of Disbelief

The Coleridgean suspension constructed around sleep and death – the careful balancing act that enables it to be both legible and sublime – had attempted to mark the discursive relationship of sleep and death as a site of constitutive discontinuity, but one with a clear religious meaning. By overthrowing whatever remained of the boundaries between literal and figural, *Maud* reveals the irreducible physical and material dimensions of this analogy. In so doing, it leaves behind much of the religious discourse that had characterized the poem that had made Tennyson Laureate: *In Memoriam* (1850). Comparisons between these two poems have long been a commonplace of Tennyson criticism, generally to the detriment of *Maud.* Though Tennyson possessed a greater "cultural training" by the time he wrote *Maud*, that knowledge, as Scott Dransfield argues, was far from comforting, encompassing "an awareness of the stresses and strains of living in an age of economic and political reform, growing secularism, and scientific rationalism, which was seen widely among the Victorian middle classes to produce nervous ailments, hypochondriasis, exhaustion, and a consciousness of a pressing need to maintain one's health."[40] The later poem undoes the certainties and hopes of the earlier, instantiating an aesthetics of contingency that, as Francis O'Gorman comments, "diversely parodied its predecessor's most precious concerns, upturning them by placing them in the mouth of a man of uncertain sanity."[41] Operating within a world where Christian discourse no longer secures the borders between life and death, the *Maud* speaker determines his identity largely through his opposition to shared reality and is left radically vulnerable to the consequences of his ultimate illegibility.

Maud presents a poetic version of Frankenstein's creation. The measured language and narcotic regularity of *In Memoriam* gives way to the maddening – and maddened – monodramatic irregularity of *Maud,* which angrily broods on the kinds of earthly disorders that the earlier poem had aimed to transcend. Linking together formally and metrically divergent sections, observes Dransfield, "the poem as a (fragmentary) whole constructs the speaker's consciousness not so much upon these lyric utterances as upon the gaps and shifts between them."[42] A reader can only guess at the action that happens – or fails to happen –

somewhere other than in the poem itself. What links the disparate sections of *Maud* to each other is a shared rhetoric of suspended animation that begins with a motif of failed burials. At the beginning of the poem, the protagonist imagines that the body of his father still lies in the "ghastly pit" where it had been found "Mangled, and flattened, and crushed, and dinted into the ground" (1.5, 1.7) – a clear breach of nearly every Victorian funerary convention. (Conversely, Maud's deceased mother is described later on as properly "mute in her grave as her image in marble above" [1.159].) Upon hearing the news that Maud will return to the Hall, the speaker, sensing danger, resolves that "I will bury myself in myself, and the Devil may pipe to his own" (1.76) – a resolution he abandons as soon as he sees his old neighbour and childhood friend. More portentously, his stated intention to put aside the enmity that has arisen between himself and Maud's brother is imagined as another peremptory interment:

So now I have sworn to bury
All this dead body of hate,
I feel so free and clear
By the loss of that dead weight,
That I should grow light-headed, I fear,
Fantastically merry;
But that her brother comes, like a blight
On my fresh hope, to the Hall tonight. (1.779–86)

The repetition of "dead" – the hatred is both a "dead body" and "dead weight" – calls attention to the almost immediate failure of this performative utterance, lending a material dimension to the emotion he wishes to discard. The condition of "light-headedness" that the speaker attributes to this cathartic action is also a well-known side-effect of a lack of oxygen and can lead, among other things, to a fainting fit that places the body in suspended animation and that, in turn, can result in a mistaken diagnosis of death. That the speaker cannot help but describe Maud's brother as a "blight" already signals the incompleteness of this attempted burial. So, too, does the stanza's rhyme scheme suggest its ineffectiveness: "bury/merry" encloses the "dead weight" of opposition and even contains the effects of the speaker's light-headedness, but the final couplet, "blight/tonight," escapes this structure and renders this hatred mobile once again, attached to the very much living (at least at this point in the poem) body of the brother.

The speaker's attempt to dispatch a hatred still very much alive by treating it as if it were dead represents what we might think of as a wilful suspension of disbelief – not an actively undertaken assertion of poetic faith, but a disingenuous shrug that allows him to justify his passivity. The *Maud* speaker elsewhere constructs his linguistic reality through speculative questions and conditional modes. Not only do these utterances contain the possibility of their own negation, they also mystify their relationship to an external narrative. It is often difficult to establish on the level of an individual line whether the speaker is genuinely seeking information, deploying the question as a rhetorical commentary, or engaging in some combination of these functions. "Who knows if he be dead?" is arguably the paradigmatic example of these speech patterns. The protagonist's preference for the interrogative is particularly marked at the beginning of the poem, where he ponders the stories told about his father's death and considers his own situation by posing a series of rhetorical questions:

For there in the ghastly pit long since a body was found,
His who had given me life – O father! O God! was it well? (1.5–6)

Did he fling himself down? who knows? for a vast speculation had failed ... (1.9)

Villainy somewhere! whose? One says, we are villains all. (1.17)

Why do they prate of the blessings of Peace? we have made them a curse,
Pickpockets, each hand lusting for all that is not its own;
And lust of gain, in the spirit of Cain, is it better or worse
Than the heart of the citizen hissing in war on his own hearthstone? (1.21–4)

[W]ho but a fool would have faith in a tradesman's ware or his word?
Is it peace or war? (1.26–7)

Sooner or later I too may passively take the print
Of the golden age – why not? I have neither hope nor trust;
Make my heart as a millstone, set my face as a flint,
Cheat and be cheated, and die – who knows? we are ashes and dust. (1.29–32)

All these examples appear in the first thirty-two lines of the poem and do much to set the tone for what follows. Moving from the feeling of personal loss to the beginnings of a jeremiad on the broader failings of Victorian society, Tennyson's rhetoric of suspension, reinforced by the interrogative mode of so many of his speaker's utterances, constructs connections among incommensurable situations. Juxtaposing his father's death with the corruption of the "golden age" allows the speaker to hint at the possibility of a causal relationship between the two or, at least, to memorialize them together in a way that gives this private tragedy public significance. At the same time, his palpable fatalism suspends the possibility of action, as when the speaker pauses in one of his rants against British society to remark:

> Who knows the ways of the world, how God will bring them about?
> Our planet is one, the suns are many, the world is wide.
> Shall I weep if a Poland fall? shall I shriek if a Hungary fail?
> Or an infant civilisation be ruled with rod or with knout?
> *I* have not made the world, and He that made it will guide.
> (1.145–9, italics in original)

Faced with the overwhelming scale of world-historical events and an incipient awareness of his own implication in the conditions of that world, the speaker responds again with a set of rhetorical questions. With the "who knows," the speaker pushes away his own agency. He reinforces the self-alienating passivity that is implicit in his reiterated desire for withdrawal from both the social and the ethical world. In this way, the speaker shows himself to have absorbed much of the speculative positioning that he so deplores in his society. Taken together, these questions reflect rhetorically on the impossibility of knowing anything for sure. Of course, they also reflect a false assumption about the way that ethical responsibility works. Much in the same way that Victor Frankenstein invokes clichés about change as a way to avoid the consequences of his scientific hubris, the *Maud* speaker defers any action on his part to a "God" who will "bring them about." He does not seek answers; rather, he distances himself from those around him – and, indeed, from his own internal contradictions:

> What! am I raging alone as my father raged in his mood?
> Must *I* too creep to the hollow and dash myself down and die
> Rather than hold by the law that I made, nevermore to brood
> On a horror of shattered limbs and a wretched swindler's lie? (1.53–6)

> Why should I stay? can a sweeter chance ever come to me here?
> O, having the nerves of motion as well as the nerves of pain,
> Were it not wise if I fled from the place and the pit and the fear? (1.62–4)

The answers are, of course, little more than foregone conclusions, nor do they really matter. We may surmise that the speaker's initial solitary ravings are similar to those of his father, that he has broken his personal prohibition on brooding as soon as he opened his mouth, and that he will not depart from his home until it is too late. These are not attempts to establish "what is it, that has been done?" Instead, they rhetorically constitute the poem's reality as volatile and discontinuous – a suspended textual body that eventually becomes as unreadable as that of a victim of live burial or a patient suffering from insanity.

The speaker's stated desire to find himself on "solid ground" (1.398), of which the poem's burial imagery represents an extreme iteration, is counteracted by equivocations in grammatical form that impose an ersatz equivalence on vastly different speech acts. One of the ironies of this circumstance is that the speaker also places a high value on his and other people's "word." On the one hand, he maps the decline of Victorian morality through the generalized rise of "babble" and the increasing distance between "a tradesman's ware and his word." His dream of a "passionless peace" consists largely in being "Far-off from the clamour of liars belied in the hubbub of lies" (1.151, 152). On the other, he believes that he holds himself and Maud to a higher standard. "Dare I bid her abide by her word?" (1.561), he asks, contemplating the possibility that she may have already agreed to marry a rival suitor. Her claims on his affections would diminish were she to break a promise to another, even to be with him:

> Shall I love her as well if she
> Can break her word were it even for me?
> I trust that it is not so. (1.564–6)

Tennyson's gloss on this section reads: "You see he is the most conscientious fellow – a perfect gentleman though semi-insane! he would not have been so, had he met with happiness."[43] Gentleman he may be, but the speaker never reaps the social or personal rewards of keeping his word. His path is, rather, made more difficult because of his reverence for the socially binding powers of language and his willingness to subordinate his happiness and well-being to them, while so much of his own speech is characterized by equivocation. His marked preference for the conditional and subjunctive moods further binds him to increasingly impossible promises.

Is Maud what the speaker says she is? Under the speaker's gaze, she often appears disembodied: a hand, a voice, an eye, a smile, and, in one particularly strange passage, a "cold and clear-cut face" (1.79) that haunts his dreams with its "Dead perfection" (1.83):

> Growing and fading and growing upon me without a sound,
> Luminous, gemlike, ghostlike, deathlike, half the night long
> Growing and fading and growing, till I could bear it no more ... (1.94–6)

But the actual qualities of Maud, and even her objective existence, are of course beside the point; O'Gorman comments that the speaker has a tendency to describe Maud as being dead long before she actually is: "Frigidly, coldly perfect, Maud is caught between existence as living alabaster and dead, chilly materiality."[44] "[G]hostlike, deathlike," Maud herself emblematizes the problem of constitutive discontinuity and the speaker's conditional existence:

> Ah well, well, well, I *may* be beguiled
> By some coquettish deceit.
>
> Yet, if she were not a cheat,
> If Maud were all that she seemed,
> And her smile had all that I dreamed,
> Then the world were not so bitter
> But a smile could make it sweet. (1.278–84)

Here, the happiness of the speaker's entire existence becomes contingent upon this increasingly distant possibility of transforming "cheat" into "sweet." For Maud is, after all, an impossible child, daughter of the "gray old wolf" (1.471) responsible for the ruin of the speaker's father. Thus the speaker, once he has fallen in love, must construct for her a spurious, alternative filiation:

> Scarcely, now, would I call him a cheat;
> For then, perhaps, as a child of deceit,
> She might by a true descent be untrue;
> And Maud is as true as Maud is sweet:
> Though I fancy her sweetness only due
> To the sweeter blood by the other side;
> Her mother has been a thing complete,

However she came to be so allied.
And fair without, faithful within,
Maud to him is nothing akin:
Some peculiar mystic grace
Made her only the child of her mother,
And heaped the whole inherited sin
On the huge scapegoat of the race,
All, all upon the brother. (1.472–86)

The hero suspends (albeit barely) his previous condemnation of Maud's father not because he has decided that the older man did not deserve it, but because he is anxious to contain the effects of that condemnation. He deliberately contradicts and consciously revises family history to justify his attachment. As in his earlier resolution simply to bury the "dead body of hate," the speaker makes no attempt at forgiveness, lasting reconciliation, or accuracy. The possibility that Maud's father may not be a cheat serves as a conveniently asserted linguistic fiction: another wilful suspension of disbelief. Tennyson's line breaks work against the speaker's attempt to assert the singularity of Maud's goodness, and thus they undermine his ability to believe in her strictly maternal inheritance. "Deceit" disrupts the repetition of the attempt to replace "cheat" with "sweet" – an effort that does not, it should be said, become more convincing in its reiteration. The line ending "untrue" only binds Maud more closely to her father than ever. When the hero does finally effect the separation, it is not by logic or argument, but through a bald assertion and nonsensical appeal to the workings of "some peculiar mystic grace" – a fanciful term for what is really the speaker's will to delusion, an act of language against fact by an heir who knows better than to think that this paternal legacy can be contained.[45] These sorts of utterances – rhetorical, interrogative, conditional – are prominently implicated in the process that leads, eventually, to the so-called madhouse canto that concludes part 2. But they are not reflections of the speaker's madness per se. Instead, they are instances of linguistic suspension. The confusion of the living and the dead, the evasive grammars, and the increasing sense of self-dividing paranoia are all symptoms of the speaker's preoccupation with suspension and contingency. The figural play that comes to the forefront in the madhouse canto enables Tennyson to exploit the tensions and suspensions of reference that underlie Victorian cultural attitudes towards death in such a way as to crystallize the speaker's fears of insignificance.

Put another way, these referential aberrations do not lead to the madhouse so much as they assure that, when the madhouse is reached, it will be experienced as a form of live burial.

"Ever so little deeper"

Tennyson famously dismissed his "mad scene." He claimed to have composed it in about twenty minutes early in 1855 – possibly under the influence of a recent reading of Poe – making it one of the last sections of the poem to have been written. By contrast, he had been revising the "O that 'twere possible" lyric, often called the "germ" of *Maud,* since the 1830s.[46] Perhaps following this emphasis, critics have given relatively little attention to the scene. If, as Aidan Day and many other scholars have argued, Tennyson's "representation of the condition of near madness ... gives the poem some of its peculiar force,"[47] then much of the interest is lost when near madness becomes, simply, madness. Thus, although the conceit of live burial renders this passage one of those rare moments in Tennyson's poetry where the representation of melancholia "attain[s] some of the more luridly gothic effects of Poe,"[48] the "madhouse canto" appears merely to confirm the complete insanity towards which the rest of the poem has been hinting. Yet, it is also the culmination of Tennyson's rhetoric of suspended animation that calls into question the existence of a reality against which madness could be judged.

In "O that 'twere possible," the speaker expresses a desire to retreat "Into some still cavern deep" where he will be able "to weep, and weep, and weep / My whole soul out to thee" (2.236, 237–8). This tenuous lyric hope is abruptly shattered by the opening lines of the madhouse canto:

> Dead, long dead,
> Long dead!
> And my heart is a handful of dust,
> And the wheels go over my head,
> And my bones are shaken with pain,
> For into a shallow grave they are thrust,
> Only a yard beneath the street,
> And the hoofs of the horses beat, beat,
> The hoofs of the horses beat,
> Beat into my scalp and my brain,
> With never an end to the stream of passing feet ... (2.239–49)

The transformation of that "still cavern deep" into the unpeaceful tomb that lies "Only a yard beneath the street" disrupts lyric topography and implies, by extension, that the speaker's "soul" may be as shallow as his ersatz grave. His horror at finding himself still conscious quickly gives way to a sense of disappointed expectations. The speaker complains not simply of having been buried alive but of having been buried alive in a shoddy and perfunctory manner. He discovers to his further disappointment that this "world of the dead" (2.278), in addition to providing little shelter from the shocks of the above-ground world, also replicates its worst features and excesses. "I thought the dead had peace," he complains, "but it is not so" (2.253). Thus the speaker's delusional self-burial, when it takes place, leaves him *more* vulnerable to the incursions of the outside world than ever before. His ability to respond is all that he has managed to foreclose; the "Clamour and rumble, and ringing and clatter" (2.251) persist. The speaker's disillusion stems from the sense that he has not just been let down by his personal delusion but has also been betrayed by an entire Victorian cultural and theological discourse that constructs the grave as a site of rest, security, and peaceful sleep.

The speaker's description of his shallow grave echoes the poetic interment that Tennyson, in his first (unsolicited) act as Laureate,[49] had performed in "Ode on the Death of the Duke of Wellington":

> Where shall we lay the man whom we deplore?
> Here, in streaming London's central roar.
> Let the sound of those he wrought for,
> And the feet of those he fought for,
> Echo round his bones for evermore. (8–12)

By imaginatively keeping Wellington's bones in close proximity to the surface of the London street, Tennyson comes close to denying him the peaceful rest he has earned. In reality, Wellington's body was placed inside not one but four coffins, the better to ensure the sanctity of the grave, and buried in the crypt at St Paul's Cathedral – at least a few hundred feet from the "central roar" of urban London.[50] Juxtaposed with the cacophonous graveyard of *Maud* (both poems appeared in Tennyson's 1855 volume, the first he published as Laureate), this proposed placement becomes exceedingly difficult to understand as an unambiguous honour, even at the outer limits of metaphor. For the *Maud* speaker, the echo can only be an insulting reminder of his own insignificance, reinforcing his own namelessness and dispossession and emptying the memorializing language of anything like meaning. From this perspective, the delusion of live burial reinforces the speaker's sense of his own isolation and social death – not to mention the horror of his own redundancy, which Eve Sedgwick links to the gothic convention of live interment.[51] The *Maud* speaker and those "dead men" around him are at the mercy of an outside world that remains ignorant of their plight, communicating brutally through the impersonal vibration of horses' hoofs and the movements of a society that can barely remember to care about its deceased national heroes, let alone those who find themselves on its fringes, non-entities long before they died:

And here beneath it is all as bad,
For I thought the dead had peace, but it is not so;
To have no peace in the grave, is that not sad?
But up and down and to and fro,
Ever about me the dead men go;
And then to hear a dead man chatter
Is enough to drive one mad. (2.252–8)

This unpeaceful grave raises the disturbing possibility that the seemingly essential difference between life and death is itself a kind of fiction, a matter of convention and signs – and, more than that, of the ability to signify, to make oneself matter in the broadest sense of the term.

In pursuit of the impossible stability that seemed to be held out by consolatory discourse and burial customs, the "madhouse canto" mixes the speaker's inconclusive personal reflections with further ranting against the greed, hypocrisy, and general decline of his era that recall the preoccupations he voiced in *Maud*'s opening stanzas. Nearly all of the canto's language, from the epithets he applies to Maud's father ("grey old wolf") and brother ("Sultan") to the speaker's attacks on national perfidy and the financial motives of Quaker pacifists, echoes previous passages. But these repetitions are closer to parodies than moments of clarity. One of the more unsettling possibilities that arises from *Maud*'s madhouse canto is that the power to rectify the kinds of reading disorders that lead to live burials may not lie within the official, social world, even if it could be cleansed of its babble, gabble, and sundry other "sins of linguistic deviancy."[52] It is precisely the possibility of being known that surfaces in the madhouse canto, not as an escape from the pressures of epistemological breakdown, but as the expression of a paranoid fear of exposure:

> I never whispered a private affair
> Within the hearing of cat or mouse,
> No, not to myself in the closet alone,
> But I heard it shouted at once from the top of the house;
> Everything came to be known. (2.285–9)

When uttered by a victim of live burial, "Everything came to be known" is both an equivocation and a provocation. For, as we have seen, the referentially aberrant body is a body about which everything cannot, in an absolute sense, be known. The *Maud* speaker's complaint comes just after his denunciation of the "idiot gabble" (2.279) that surrounds him, chatter that yields little in terms of useful information. The language of the madhouse is, in a sense, both too private and too public, and the disordered excess serves as a reminder that expression does not automatically lead to intersubjective understanding. The nightmare does not lie in the revelation of any specific secret that he had wanted to keep hidden, but rather in the impossible demands made on a body that is constitutionally resistant to signification.

The section's final stanza offers a counterpoint to the image of apocalyptic exposure that once again draws attention to the uncertain status of the suspended body, as well as to the more intractable problem of constitutive discontinuity:

> Maybe still I am but half-dead;
> Then I cannot be wholly dumb;
> I will cry to the steps above my head
> And somebody, surely, some kind heart will come
> To bury me, bury me
> Deeper, ever so little deeper. (2.337–42)

The desire for a more complete burial forecloses the possibility of recuperation through an encounter with one's authentic, grounded inner being. In fact, it calls into question the very existence of that inner being. Readers are left, as Warwick Slinn suggests, "with the unanswered question as to whether this cry for what appears to be a total loss of signifying power represents the ultimate insanity – or the ultimate understanding. The very indeterminacy of such a question adds a deeply disturbing undercurrent to the poem."[53] Of course, the most fundamental – one hesitates to say "deepest" in this context – anxiety expressed in this stanza is that there might be nothing worth burying at all. If true, the speaker's insignificance would not be the result of any societal oversight but simply a function of some fundamental rupture that leaves him stranded in this liminal space, neither dead nor alive, both too far from the surface and not quite deep enough to be one thing or another.

Tennyson's suspended speaker, whose social death is real even if the burial is not, poses a significant challenge to the foundational assumptions of the "signs of death" debate. A central theme of both the medical literature and popular stories is that official bodies need to prescribe more refined reading methods in order to reliably interpret individual bodies; this principle depends on a belief in the ultimate transparency and legibility of those individual bodies that can be exposed through official codes. Even if meaning comes tragically late, as it did for Charlotte Clopton and Poe's Baltimore matron, or if some confusion persists about the condition itself, as with Captain Hurst's mysterious paralysis, these circumstances, too, can be partially recuperated by being absorbed into an archive of anecdotal evidence that generates conversations and investigations that will allow such mistakes to be avoided in the future. Similarly, while living through his own interment and disinterment, the narrator of the "Posthumous Memoir" has ample time to reflect on the moral quality of his life, find it lacking, and resolve to change his ways upon his return to the world of the living. The framing of catalepsy in *The Princess* suggests that it, too, can be more or less subsumed into that archive, while any excesses may be accounted for by the fairy-tale frame. These kinds of scenarios function within a literary discourse that understands the "buried life" as a figure of authenticity. In "The Buried Life" (1852), arguably the paradigmatic Victorian articulation of the trope, Matthew Arnold mourns his estrangement from the deeply submerged sources of a personal identity untainted by the masks that society requires. Though the poem uses "the void within the breast [as] an established literary trope connected to heartsickness and the inability to feel,"[54] it nonetheless remains confident that such interiority exists apart from and prior to its enunciation. It is maintained as the object of "unspeakable desire / After the knowledge of our buried life" (47–8). Such authenticity is so powerful (but also so fragile) that it cannot be accessed under the conditions of normal life. Only a dangerous limit experience can bring us into contact with this unreachable selfhood.

The situation is far different in *Maud*'s underworld-madhouse, where the speaker's imagined interment offers a literalized commentary on the metaphor of the "buried life." Meaning is both too frequently on the surface and buried "ever so little deeper" beyond the reach of public circulation. While writing *In Memoriam*, Tennyson had gained poetic strength by, as Herbert Tucker suggests, "drawing (through the inexpressibility topos) on the soul-saving reserve of what he cannot say."[55] In other words, *In Memoriam* had still been able to express a faith in the "the soul within," even if the condition of language meant that it was always "half revealed" and "half concealed." *Maud* suggests something quite different – that the reserve implied by the inexpressibility topos cannot, ultimately, serve a redemptive function. Tennyson's rhetoric of suspended animation affirms instead the existence of certain conditions that cannot be "read," no matter how careful the investigative processes brought to bear on them. Moreover, the forms his speaker's madness takes reveal that interiority itself is not merely, as Matthew Rowlinson suggests, "without public consequence,"[56] but is a contingent feature of a system that continues to impose its own reading practices upon constitutionally illegible bodies.

"That old hysterical mock-disease"

There exists a critical tendency to see *Maud* as an aberrational poem, the Laureate's last dark, inward moment before he, like his speaker, goes on to confront his "purpose" in the collective, public sphere. The dialectic between inexpressible inwardness and the "matter-moulded forms of speech" (*In Memoriam* 95.45) in which that inwardness must be externalized is one of the defining thematic and biographical preoccupations of a figure who, as a number of studies have shown, self-consciously, though somewhat reluctantly, assumed the mantle of the public poet, even at the cost of his so-called "Romantic integrity."[57] That Tennyson has been criticized, at different times, for putting both too much and too little of himself into *Maud* is symptomatic of the poem's vexed relationship to constructions of identity that hide beneath the surface. George Eliot objected to *Maud* on the grounds that it contained "scarcely more than a residuum of Alfred Tennyson; the wide-sweeping intellect, the mild philosophy, the healthy pathos, the wondrous melody, have almost all vanished, and left little more than a narrow scorn which piques itself on its scorn of narrowness, and a passion which clothes itself in exaggerated conceits."[58] She concludes, somewhat counterintuitively, that the poem's failure is indicative of its author's greatness: "it, perhaps, speaks well for Tennyson's genius, that it has refused to aid him much on themes so little worthy of his greatest self."[59] Eliot gives us no less than three Tennysons: the "greatest self" to which he should aspire, the "genius" that animates his writing towards that goal, and this narrow-minded "him" that insists on writing on inferior themes. The discourse of poetic genius attaches an immortality to the poet's "greatest self," but the status of the "him" remains more uncertain. Though it is not necessary to retrace here Tennyson's transformation from the post-Romantic lyricist to the Victorian public poet, a story that has been told in *Maud*'s criticism as well as in more wide-ranging considerations of his career, the figure of a living dead man, helplessly resistant to every practice of reading his society has to offer, emblematizes that difficult transition.

If the speaker's madness were understood as only a manifestation of his isolation and his refusal to join the social world on the terms of that world, then we might agree with Samuel Schulman that "The experience forces him to see that there is no way to make language private, to use it to shut out a larger world from the lovers. Meaning cannot be made exclusive: other people will interpret our communications whether we will it or not, and our words have unavoidable social consequences."[60] But to the extent that this "madness" – that is, the structures of referential aberration that produce suspended bodies – constitutes an irreducible part of reality itself, then the speaker does not simply re-enter the world but remains in this uncertain relation to it. In part 3 of *Maud*, the speaker appears to abandon his self-reflexive madness in order to join the nationalistic drive towards war – the "purpose of God, and the doom assigned," as the final line has it (3.59). It is essentially an effort to break the suspension of the madhouse canto by abandoning a personal delusion for one that at least has the advantage of being widely shared. The five stanzas that comprise part 3 are uncannily straightforward, free of the aberrant speech and irregular metrical patterns that characterize the rest of the poem. The hero's "recovery" takes place as an act of deliberate and conscious surrender of his subjectivity to an all-consuming social and political authority. In a way, it is not that different from the beginning of the poem. But the more pressing question to ask about the ending is not whether Tennyson expects his readers to assent to the political sentiments of this final section (most have not), but rather whether we are meant to believe that the speaker is in any position to do what he says he is doing. His recovery, such as it is, is determined by his own fiat: "It is time, O passionate heart and morbid eye, / That old hysterical mock-disease should die" (3.32–3). The patient transforms into a soldier, not because he has been cured of his disease, but because he has decided the disease never existed. However, one of the main reasons why confinement in a mental institution was metaphorically associated with burial is that both of these places are difficult, if not impossible, to escape. The standards for leaving an asylum – particularly if one has been confined there against his or her will – were known to be stunningly high.[61] Most critics take for granted that the speaker eventually leaves the madhouse or whatever place of isolation he had been in at the end of the previous section. Yet, the speaker's dismissal of his own, very real suffering, and the claim that a vision of his dead lover has inspired him to join the war effort, are hardly going to achieve much traction with the authorities. If *Maud*'s ending fails to provide a satisfying resolution of parts 1 and 2 – and by nearly every artistic and ethical standard it does – it fails because cannot honestly do otherwise.

Tennyson's fascination with liminal states has long been noted by critics, appreciative and otherwise. Clyde de L. Ryals comments that "Tennyson's withdrawal from external reality into a tower of contemplation and self-absorption is well known and needs no documentation," going on to cite "The Lotos-Eaters," "The Palace of Art," and "The Lady of Shalott" as examples of this phenomenon.[62] In a famous anecdote from the *Memoir*, the poet recalls his childhood habit of putting himself into a visionary trance by repeating his own name, "till all at once … the individuality itself seemed to dissolve and fade away into boundless being, and this not a confused state, but the clearest of the clearest, the surest of the surest, the weirdest of the weirdest, utterly beyond words …"[63] Seamus Perry has written appreciatively and movingly about "the luxuriance of Tennysonian suspendedness." However, while "[b]eing neither one thing nor another is a recurrent Tennysonian state, sometimes a pleasure,"[64] Perry also reminds us that it is a dangerous, sometimes terrifying condition, often for the same reasons that anecdotes about accidental live burials had the power to terrify. As the case studies and fictions show, the body in suspended animation demands a kind of perpetual attention, resisting summary and resolution as it disrupts the border between life and death.

Tennyson, it is true, never wrote another poem like *Maud*, though he did return to the plot device of live burial in *The Golden Supper* (1879). However, he never seems to have fully relinquished his authorial stake in *Maud*, as his well-documented penchant for reading it aloud in company demonstrates. Hallam Tennyson recalls that even at his father's last reading of *Maud*, which took place in August 1892, only a few months before his death, "His voice, low and calm in everyday life, capable of delicate and manifold inflection, but with 'organ-tones' of great power and range, thoroughly brought out the drama of the poem. You were at once put in sympathy with the hero."[65] But to be "put in sympathy" with this hero is also to become implicated in his complex web of conditional and contingent utterances and, in essence, to take on the very structures of suspension and discontinuity (if not their full, specific content) that leave the speaker trapped in liminal space. Thus, while Tucker implies that Tennyson's "insatiable demand for social ratification of this work suggests that he, like the rest of us, found it impossible to endorse *Maud* wholeheartedly,"[66] it is possible as well to see in these oft-repeated performances the trace of an ongoing, revisionary relationship between the creator and his work – and between the creator and himself.

Ultimately, *Maud* offers a critique of a reading that depends on preexisting categories of the genius and the self, the public and the private, the interior and the exterior. The self-cancelling gesture of the madhouse canto and the seemingly aberrant desire to be buried more securely mean that this reserve, if it ever existed in the first place, has been emptied; it, too, is subject to a being-known that depends on the ability to signify in legible ways. This chapter has argued that Tennyson's declaration of sympathy with suspended, discontinuous bodies is not ultimately aberrant: it instead reflects an insight into a reality that persistently fails to follow the rules imposed by human expectations and binary thought. Like Coleridge and Shelley before him, Tennyson recognizes that there is no possibility of faith without the prior affirmation of contingency – without, that is, allowing that the unknown "purpose of God" may also be non-existent, that the workings of the world escape rationalization. That affirmation of contingency – an affirmation that can be traced back to Coleridge's conception of "poetic faith" as the "willing suspension of disbelief" – achieves its Victorian apotheosis in the poetry and devotional writing of Christina Rossetti, to which the final chapter turns.

Chapter Five

Christina Rossetti's Poetic Faith

"Suppose there is no secret after all" (8).[1] Thus speculates the flirtatious speaker of Christina Rossetti's "Winter: My Secret." She playfully rebuffs the inquiries of her silent interlocutor – "you're too curious: fie!" (4) – as she avails herself of "a shawl, / A veil, a cloak, and other wraps" (11–12) against the "nipping" weather (10). From the performance of speaking about not speaking to the final stanza's deferral of revelation to some impossibly "languid summer day," when "there's not too much sun nor too much cloud" (28, 31), the poem elevates suspension to a paradigmatic lyric practice that sparkles with kinetic energy and even joy in its withdrawal. The possibility that the secret is produced by its concealment, rather than the other way around – a possibility that had haunted the *Maud* speaker into his madhouse-grave – becomes, in Rossetti's poem, something like a cause for celebration, hinting as it does at an uncontainable selfhood that no longer needs to seek its authenticity in the rhetoric of a "buried life."

Christina Rossetti is, in many ways, the poet of suspension *par excellence*. Nearly all of the other images, pauses, and hesitations that have emerged in the texts I have already discussed are at work – often to contradictory or ambiguous effect – in Rossetti's poetry. To the extent that "Winter: My Secret" may be considered, as Isobel Armstrong contends, "almost a summa of [Rossetti's] work,"[2] it is so because that poem thematizes and celebrates the existential suspension that is the condition of much of that work. Many of Rossetti's most famous lyrics dramatize liminal positions and anticipatory states: waiting, wishing, hoping, dying. The speakers of her poems oscillate between desires to go and desires to stay, to be present and absent, to reveal and conceal. "Remember" evokes the time "When you can no more hold me by the hand, / Nor I half turn to go yet turning stay" (3–4). Its speaker looks forward and backwards at once, lingering on the threshold between life and death. Suspension manifests itself elsewhere in Rossetti's poetry as a form of illness whose symptoms include fixation, arrested development, and acts of renunciatory withdrawal that uncannily resemble live burial. The playful withholding of "Winter: My Secret" always threatens to turn, perhaps without even a moment's notice, into something fixed and frozen, a hysterical paralysis that strikes at the moment of disappointment and is doomed to repeat it. "I looked for that which is not, nor can be, / And hope deferred made my heart sick in truth" (1–2), reflects the speaker of "A Pause of Thought." For the most part, however, Rossetti's speakers are willing to embrace – or at least accept – the mental and emotional anguish that comes from their liminality: the pain of uncertainty, the agony of delay, the endless search for rest.

Suspension serves a crucial spiritual function as well as an aesthetic one for Rossetti. As Antony Harrison argues, her poems "speak the 'unutterable,' reveal knowledge of the unknowable, envision the unseen. In short, they realize the unattainable. Despite Rossetti's ubiquitous emphasis upon 'hope deferred,' her poems often palpably create the world they desire."[3] While her religious commitments have long been known to scholars of her poetry, recent work by critics such as Dinah Roe, Emma Mason, Andrew Armond, and Elizabeth Ludlow has more fully established the Tractarian underpinnings of Rossetti's thought.[4] Particularly significant for Rossetti is the doctrine of Reserve, as summarized by G.B. Tennyson:

> since God is ultimately incomprehensible, we can know Him only indirectly; His truth is hidden and given to us only in a manner suited to our capacities for apprehending it. Moreover, it is both unnecessary and undesirable that God and religious truth generally should be disclosed in their fullness at once to all regardless of the differing capacities of individuals to apprehend such things. God Himself in His economy has only gradually in time revealed such things as we know about Him. Both the sacredness and the complexity of the subject of religious truth are such that they require a holding back and a gradual revelation as the disposition and understanding of the recipient mature.[5]

Reserve operates through deferral; its symbols, typologies, and parables all point towards the incomprehensible deity in ways that allow them to be interpreted and reinterpreted according to the spiritual maturity of the reader. The structure that Tennyson outlines here bears more than a passing resemblance to Coleridge's discussion of the sleep/death association described in the previous chapter. Tractarian doctrines, such as that of Reserve, give Rossetti a way of "talking about the divine, while acknowledging that direct communication with, or complete understanding of divinity is impossible."[6] Even a poem that does not seem to possess explicitly religious content such as "Winter: My Secret" may be read as a "test and a parody" of these principles. Mason argues that "A reading of ["Winter: My Secret"] as compliant with reserve cannot fail to associate the narrator with God himself, taunting the believer with the idea that he may or may not have secrets to be revealed."[7] In this reading, the speaker's speculation about there being "no secret after all" is, essentially, turned back to the questioning addressee: if there is a secret, it is not for you to know – at least not yet. The danger, as it was for Coleridge, is that the words themselves will be taken as the truths they represent, so that unwary readers will mistake language about the truth for truth in itself. In many ways, the relationship between the discourse of Reserve and its objects thus parallels the discontinuity Kant interposed between the things we call sublime and the sublime itself – the discontinuity that gives rise to the error of subreption. In both cases, the "truths" must remain ungraspable and incomparable, separate from any particular discourse, subject, or context.

Poems composed to be read according to the principles of Reserve are not riddles with definitive answers, but texts that remain ambiguous, requiring interpretation and reinterpretation. Within the symbolic economy of Tractarianism, a sign may have multiple significations, can be used ironically, or can simply fail to be understood. Outside of the privileged – and itself intensely controversial – ceremony of the Eucharist, signs do not reliably transcend their temporary, gestural function in order to *become* the truth towards which they point. The very obscurity of some of Rossetti's images, their ability to fall out of use so as to appear positively esoteric today, testifies to their temporary, unstable quality, even as it does not a priori mean that the truths to which they refer are less true. Within Rossetti's poetry, uncertainty and a belief in absolute truth can coexist; more than that, uncertainty achieves the status of absolute truth. Practices of suspension help keep "the poet's meaning in motion"[8] by refusing to rest on one single idiom, one single representation. Even at its most withdrawn – "A fountain sealed thro' heat and cold" ("The Heart Knoweth Its Own Bitterness," 44) – Rossetti's suspension is active and energetic, enabling potentially endless revisions.

Moving beyond simple binaries, her poems use suspension to interrupt the forward movement of reading and continually undermine seemingly stable interpretations.[9] They create spaces for the contemplation of as well as for the confrontation with a world of potentially endless variety, a world that demands careful attention.

This chapter argues that Rossetti rewrites the central tropes of Romantic suspension – Coleridgean dilation, the Shelleyan sublime – in a fully "Victorian" register, drawing upon a Tennysonian rhetoric of suspended animation in order to navigate a world that is constitutively resistant to rule-bound reading practices. She does not so much "discover" the world of constitutive discontinuity in the way that Coleridge, Shelley, and even Tennyson do; for her, such fractures are part of the given conditions of existence. Thus, although her writing registers many of the same signs of ungroundedness that Tennyson and the *Maud* speaker take as a cause for panicked rumination, Rossetti views suspension as an ontological condition capable of both provoking agony and disclosing unexpected spaces of relative freedom. Because she does not see suspension as an epistemological problem in the way that Tennyson does, her poems do not need to ask "Who knows if [s]he be dead?" Rather, they respond to the recognized instability of the boundary between life and death and investigate the multiplicity of subject positions that become thinkable when the world is understood to be constitutively discontinuous. What could be called Rossetti's poetic faith, as a practice of suspension, is not directed towards the elimination of ambiguity, but rather the acceptance (and embrace) of a contingent reality that is not – or, at least, that may not be – exclusively a symptom of human frailty.

At first glance, Rossetti's long narrative poem *The Prince's Progress* (1866) seems rather distant from the playful suspensions that structure her lyric practice, as well as from the plenitude and excess associated with the vastly more popular *Goblin Market* (1862). One scholar, demonstrating admirable powers of understatement, characterizes the "inevitable comparison of the long title narratives" as "mildly unfortunate."[10] Even Christina Rossetti seems to have shared the view that *The Prince's Progress* was something of a pale younger sister to *Goblin Market*. Writing to her brother Dante Gabriel Rossetti in March 1865, she remarked, "I readily grant that my *Prince* lacks the special felicity (!) of my *Goblins*; yet I am glad to believe you consider with me that it is not unworthy of publication."[11] Similarly, when William Michael Rossetti put together a selected edition of his sister's poetry in 1904, he commented only that "*The Prince's Progress* is the only rather long narrative, besides *Goblin Market*, which my sister produced. She preferred *Goblin Market*, and the great majority of readers have, I think, concurred with her."[12] The plot is straightforward enough. A Prince, "Strong of limb if of purpose weak" (47), undertakes a journey to claim his bride at the urging of the disembodied "true voice of [his] doom" (19). Throughout much of the text, he trudges through a bleak landscape, wishing to be elsewhere and to be doing something else. The Prince journeys through a "Tedious land" (152), engages in at least one "tedious trial" (250), and travels a "tedious road" (392). True to his easily distracted nature and to the impatience with tedium shared by many of Rossetti's readers, the Prince succumbs to the earthly charms of a lamia-like milkmaid, participates in an alchemist's attempt to brew the elixir of life, and lingers in the gentle ministrations of the mysterious women who pull him from the waters of a flash flood. Each of these encounters slows the "progress" promised by the title and, despite good intentions and a belated renewal of purpose near the end of the poem, he arrives at his destination only to find that his bride has died waiting for him.

The poem has generally been read as an overt critique of certain forms of suspension: delay, paralysis, indecision, and sloth all come to index the Prince's poor interpretive practices. Following the hint provided by the poem's title – an allusion to John Bunyan's *The Pilgrim's Progress* (1678) – most scholars have also read the poem as an allegory of spiritual life that places reading and interpretation at its centre. The exemplary journey of Bunyan's protagonist sets a standard for spiritual pilgrimage against which the shortcomings of Rossetti's weak-willed Prince stand out in sharp relief. Mary Arseneau, for instance, observes that "Both Rossetti's Prince and Bunyan's pilgrim are seeking the reward promised to them in the Celestial City, and both must cross a landscape fraught with physical challenges and spiritual temptation; but the Prince seems to have little sense of himself as a pilgrim and does not make the 'progress' that Bunyan's pilgrim makes."[13] In her view, and that of many others, the quest fails because the Prince does not recognize the need to interpret carefully the signs around him in order to comprehend their correct significance.[14] Even a scholar such as Dawn Henwood, who holds that the poem "challenges our moral sense and our interpretive faculties by confronting us with ambiguous, even disturbing, situations and characters," more or less accepts the basic premise that the Prince "has access, naturally, to all the orienteering tools of the Christian context ... [A]long with his pilgrim staff, the Bridegroom has at least the proddings of his God-given conscience, even if explicit Biblical guidance has not reached his fairy-tale kingdom."[15] The pervasive assumption that the Prince has deviated from some evident line of proper interpretation undergirds a longstanding tradition in Rossetti scholarship that marks *The Prince's Progress* as a site of interpretive restriction: the poem that reins in the kinds of readerly excesses seemingly encouraged by *Goblin Market*. If *Goblin Market* seduces its readers with hints of unbridled female sexuality, luxuriant imagery, and a seemingly endless field for speculation, *The Prince's Progress* is the text that forces readers to get serious once again and to appreciate the "real" Christina Rossetti, whose "uncompromising orthodoxy strenuously resists deconstructionist approaches to her writing."[16] According to this logic, we must be the religiously and historically aware interpreters that the Prince fails to be or else risk falling into the perdition reserved for poor readers. The attempt to contain Rossetti criticism spinning dangerously out of control into fashionable methodologies is in some sense also an attempt to contain the experience of failure represented in the poem and thereby to interpose distance between the Prince and the reader. Arseneau contends that, when it comes to discerning the poem's true meaning, even the aesthetic elements of the poem may simply be a distraction: "In *The Prince's Progress* the protagonist never comprehends his responsibility to probe the moral and spiritual dimensions of his experience," she concludes. "But the lesson that the Prince does not learn is one that Rossetti's readers must, for it is only when we look beyond the beautiful and apparently simple surface of Rossetti's poems and become aware of the multiple layers of literary allusion and moral and spiritual signification that we begin fully to appreciate her art."[17] The implicit promise of this perspective is that as long as we read according to Rossetti's expectations and desires we will be safe from the kind of interpretive failures that the Prince enacts.

Read in the context of an aesthetics of suspension that goes back to Coleridge, however, *The Prince's Progress* reveals itself to be a critique of the very notion of progress and of attempts to establish a single rule according to which the poem must be read, even – perhaps especially – those attempts that rely on Christian typology. Blending a secular, fairy-tale quest narrative with a texture of biblical allusions, *The Prince's Progress* pointedly fails to be one thing or another. The poem frustrates its readers largely because it raises eminently reasonable generic, narrative, intertextual, and even metrical expectations and then – maddeningly – declines to fulfil them in favour of a perpetual suspension. Despite its seeming concern with illustrating the importance of right reading and interpretation, it is easier, as Henwood observes, to "poke fun at the hero's obtuseness" than it is to identify "a model of interpretive astuteness within the poem."[18] A reader risks not only disappointment and frustration but also a kind of "interpretive queasiness" caused by the poem's "subtle hints" and "promiscuous" intertextuality[19] – and a careful reader might find such queasiness intensified instead of alleviated. Surface readings of the poem lend themselves to easy binaries – male/female, bride/bridegroom, good/bad – that collapse upon closer examination. In this way, *The Prince's Progress* imposes clear limitations on the seemingly unimpeachable project of figuring out what the poem means, at least to the extent that such "figuring out" depends on grasping a certain straightforward reading or tracking down a specific set of intertextual references. It is not simply that *The Prince's Progress* is a "parabolic poem" – that is, a poem that contains ample evidence for at least two different interpretations, depending on the critical orientation of the reader.[20] Rather, *The Prince's Progress* presents a critique of expectation as such, demonstrating that even the most reasonable anticipations in life and literature are open to reversal and failure. Rossetti's figures of intractable disappointment, attachment, and frustration – the arid, lonely scenes of the Prince's wandering; the doomed alchemist; and, perhaps more unusually, the image of the Prince's drowned body, captured in a moment of suspended animation after a flash flood – adumbrate this broader critique of the very notion of a reasonable expectation. Rossetti's practices of suspension hold up the poem at crucial moments, transforming experiences of negative affect into sites for the contemplation of the meaning of faith in a constitutively discontinuous reality. Ultimately, Rossetti's text solicits an active poetic faith in response to a world whose only rule is that of contingency.

The Fairy Prince Who Always Already Arrived Too Late

The composition history of *The Prince's Progress* complicates efforts to identify a stable theme, for, as Kathy Psomiades observes, the Prince's failure is "not only the poem's climax but its origin."[21] Much as Tennyson's *Maud* was "written, as it were, backwards" from the "O that 'twere possible" lyric,[22] the final section of *The Prince's Progress* was the first to be composed. The idea of turning the lyric poem into a medieval quest epic was suggested by Dante Gabriel Rossetti in 1865, on the grounds that such a text might be "commercially viable" if marketed to a reading public eager for another volume from the author of *Goblin Market*.[23] The sixty-line funeral dirge that mourns the neglected Princess was written in 1861 and published as "The Fairy Prince Who Arrived Too Late" in the May 1863 issue of *Macmillan's Magazine*.[24] It rebukes the tardiness of the "Fairy Prince" and celebrates the positive qualities of the Princess who died waiting for him. Dispensing with any trace of narrative framing, the opening lines of "The Fairy Prince Who Arrived Too Late" interpellate the title character with the accusation: "Too late for love, too late for joy, / Too late, too late!" (481–2).[25] These voices excoriate him at some length for his procrastination: "You loitered on the road too long, / You trifled at the gate" (483–4). Significantly, though, the voices do not accuse the Prince of being a poor reader or link his procrastination to misinterpretation or shallowness, those charges that are usually laid against him by readers of the longer poem. Nor is the Prince allowed to speak. He is not able to defend himself or even acknowledge an awareness of having failed, if he indeed possesses such an awareness. Preceded by his reputation for belatedness – announced in the shorter poem's title – and convicted in advance by his late arrival, the Prince suffers in silence during the long enumeration of the admirable qualities of the "enchanted princess in her tower" (487) whose "heart was starving all this while / You made it wait" (489–90):

We never saw her with a smile
  Or with a frown;
Her bed seemed never soft to her,
  Tho' tossed of down;
She little heeded what she wore,
  Kirtle, or wreath, or gown;
We think her white brows often ached
  Beneath her crown,
Till silvery hairs showed in her locks
  That used to be so brown. (511–20)

The handmaidens' accusations against the Prince are based on external signs; in the end, they can only speculate about the Princess's inner state, whether or not her "brows often ached" as she awaited her bridegroom. The Princess, like the Prince, is thus silenced by the voices of her handmaidens. They claim that "We never heard her speak in haste" (521), but do not reveal what she said or even whether she had any interest in marrying a man who was having so much trouble showing up. Joan Rees observes that, "although we are aware of [the Princess's] suffering it is, so to speak, depersonalized."[26] The lyric's emphasis remains on external style rather than internal content: "Her tones were sweet, / And modulated just so much / As it was meet" (522–4). In life, as in death, "Her heart sat silent thro' the noise / And concourse of the street. / There was no hurry in her hands, / No hurry in her feet" (525–8). Her rectitude is so perfect that it appears to have killed her, leaving her serving women to do the complaining.

Although the symbolic scheme of the long poem has sometimes prompted speculation that the Prince is a failed Christ figure, his designation as a "Fairy Prince" in the 1861 title seems to foreclose that interpretation by expressing (among other things) a generic difference from the Son of God.[27] The dirge is relatively secular, making use of only subtle biblical images and avoiding, for instance, any references to the dead Princess's afterlife. The Prince's originary failure is thus not necessarily conditioned by the intertextual relations that would enable his failure to be understood as a lapse in reading practices and a lack of spiritual depth. None of these arguments necessarily negates the religious readings of *The Prince's Progress* as a whole. Nevertheless, they do suggest that the poem's Christian borrowings should be read as a supplement, rather than as the definitive key to interpretation. Indeed, the narrative sections added in 1865, as Harrison notes, "make far more obtrusive use of symbolism in order to evoke a dreamlike atmosphere."[28] Far from explaining the failures denounced in "The Fairy Prince Who Arrived Too Late," these sections amplify the Prince's belatedness and make it more illegible. What the dirge's exclamation of "too late" registers is thus at least partially a recognition of the impossibility of arriving on time. This fundamental failure is bracketed and suspended – not resolved or overcome. Although Dante Gabriel Rossetti, as editor of his sister's work, generally "forges simpler poetic forms out of [Christina's] more complicated, unsettling poems,"[29] it is not clear, at least in this case, that his intervention had the desired result. The complexity of the dirge does not dissolve in the solvent of medieval quest narrative; rather, the two sections are added together without fully mixing. *The Prince's Progress* is not one poem, but neither is it two.

At the most basic level, the narrative and the dirge cannot agree on what it means to be "too late." The handmaidens in "The Fairy Prince Who Arrived Too Late" are deceptively precise:

Ten years ago, five years ago,
  One year ago,
Even then you had arrived in time,
  Tho' somewhat slow ... (491–4)

As a rhetorical strategy, these lines draw attention to the enormity and the irrevocability of the Prince's tardiness and should not be understood as literal measurements of time. Still, the force of this critique is amplified by the fact that it draws upon the familiar unit of the calendar year. The handmaidens avoid more conventional markers of fairy-tale temporality, the "once upon a time" and the "ever after" that bookend stories like *Sleeping Beauty*. The longer version of the poem, by contrast, begins indeterminately in a moment that is already repeated and undifferentiated from those before and after it:

Till all sweet gums and juices flow,
Till the blossom of blossoms blow,
  The long hours go and come and go ... (1–3)

The timeless time of the first two lines dissolves the "hours" of the third line, making them seem not only "long" but also infinitely recurrent and profoundly disconnected. Set against the vague promises of the first two lines, these hours seem even more aimless and insignificant, not to mention ungrounded and incommensurate with linear time. At the very least, the description of hours as "long" refers to the way they are being experienced in the mind of a single subject, a quality that also shapes the Prince's experience of his journey. Although the passing of specific days and hours is marked in the narrative, the measurements of time as a whole are so inconsistent in their referentiality that it is impossible to tell how long his pilgrimage takes. A reader can only surmise that the journey lasts somewhere between several days and "Till the blossom of blossoms blow."

In the first two stanzas of the full version of *The Prince's Progress*, the Princess "sleepeth, waketh, sleepeth, / Waiting for one whose coming is slow" (4–5). Her handmaidens quickly intervene to interrupt the cycle of sorrow and urge her simply to sleep: "we've muffled the chime, / Better dream than weep" (11–12). Before entering into this "Spell-bound"

(23) suspension, the Princess has only one question for her attendants: "How long shall I wait, come heat come rime?" (7). It is the only time her speech is rendered directly in the poem. Although ostensibly a metonym for the seasonal cycle and the rime – frost – of winter, "rime" also suggests "rhyme" and, by extension, the self-enclosed, suspended temporality of the rest of the poem. The answer the Princess receives to her question is appropriately tautological: "Till the strong Prince comes, who must come in time" (8). The circularity of this response limns the broader difficulty in telling time. Moreover, the poem's "spinning in time, its scrambling of temporal terms, and its verbal dallying"[30] provide the conditions for what looks suspiciously like a live burial. The injunction to "Sleep, dream and sleep: / Sleep" (10–11) takes on a vaguely menacing quality intensified by the description of the Princess in her "maiden bloom" (20): "Spell-bound she watches in one white room, / And is patient for thy sake" (23–4). Though the colour white suggests a bridal chamber, the room is quickly suffused by a profusion of flowers – roses, lilies, and red and white poppies – that explicitly symbolize death. They grow around the Princess's suspended body and cover her completely, as if she were a body in a waiting mortuary or a cemetery vault. These flowers are, as Psomiades writes, "so weighted by poetic tradition that it is difficult to tell whether they are literally present or purely metaphorical representations of living and dead sex and virginity," marking a contrast with the Prince, who is "surrounded by literal and mundane objects" in an "oddly domestic world" without particular aestheticist significance.[31] From this point on, the Princess enters a trance of emotional and physical withdrawal, a form of suspended animation that more closely resembles the apparently dead bodies of the Victorian medical gothic than the generally "lively bunch" of Rossetti's dead women who possess both "consciousness and language."[32]

In a broad sense, the spell-bound Princess and her too-soothing handmaidens represent the specifically lyric temporality that similarly characterizes their function in "The Fairy Prince Who Arrived Too Late," while the Prince, linked to *Progress* in the poem's title, bears the burden of narrative time. More than that, however, the intertwining of the stories of the suspended Princess and the slow-moving Prince in the opening section of the long poem instantiates an "anticipatory amalgam" in Heather Dubrow's sense of the term.[33] The predictions made by the handmaidens about the Prince's journey – "there's a mountain to climb, / A river to ford" (9–10) – are more specific than any of the information offered to the traveller himself, introducing the "fuzzy temporality"[34] of the lyric present into a narrative future that may or may not come to be. Any expectation of straightforward, actualized progress is undercut by this layering and hybridizing of temporalities. Where the Princess is encircled by whispering voices, the Prince is prodded forward by a chorus of others:

> "Time is short, life is short," they took up the tale:
>   "Life is sweet, love is sweet, use today while you may;
> Love is sweet, and tomorrow may fail;
>   Love is sweet, use today." (39–42)

These kinds of lines are often cited by those who read the poem as a cautionary tale. Yet, they are almost entirely devoid of content. At best, they advocate action in general, but they do not reveal even the vague information about the journey that the Princess received as she drifted off to sleep. Without the knowledge of mountains and rivers ahead, the Prince begins his journey singularly unprepared for what he will encounter:

> Forth he set in the breezy morn,
> Across green fields of nodding corn,
> As goodly a Prince as ever was born,
>   Carolling with the carolling lark; –
> Sure his bride will be won and worn,
>   Ere fall of the dark. (49–54)

Breaking through the inertia that surrounds both palaces, these lines propel the poem (and the Prince) into the narrative. He treats the success of his quest as a foregone conclusion, achievable within a defined period of time with a minimum of effort – essentially, a day trip. Yet even at this lighthearted, early moment, the poem registers its own ultimate failure. The repetition of "carolling," innocent as the image is, makes the line skip and repeat itself, foreshadowing the larger interruptions to come but also implicitly destabilizing the goal itself, the alleged object of the quest. The Prince's problem is not only that he envisions his task as the work of a day, but that he is fixated on the goal of winning the bride. While no one would argue that the biggest problem with Rossetti's Prince is that he is too goal-oriented, he nevertheless maintains ideas about his quest that do not include the possibility that he could fail, the sense that the object of the quest may not be worthy of his efforts, or the chance that his bride might not want to remain available to him.

Social Elements and Barren Boredom

When Dante Gabriel suggested that a tournament might liven up a poem that was, ostensibly, a medieval quest narrative, Christina responded with a defence of her own plan:

> [M]y actual *Prince* seems to me invested with a certain artistic congruity of construction not lightly to be despised: 1st, a prelude and outset; 2nd, an alluring milkmaid; 3rd, a trial of barren boredom; 4th, the social element again; 5th, barren boredom in a more uncompromising form; 6th, a wind-up and conclusion. See how the subtle elements balance each other, and fuse into a noble conglom![35]

While interpretations of *The Prince's Progress* by and large privilege the protagonist's interactions with other human characters, Rossetti elevates the "barren boredom" of the Prince's long hours of solitary walking to equal importance. Drawing attention to the intervals of vacancy between the interactions that drive the plot, Rossetti's description of *The Prince's Progress* shows how it both thematizes and enacts suspension. Her insistence on the two periods of "barren boredom," one more "uncompromising" than the other, for instance, draws attention away from the social dalliances that are typically blamed for the Prince's lack of appropriate progress, suggesting that narrative alone does not drive the poem. Her playful description of the "noble conglom" recasts the poem's failure to meet the expectations of genre, theme, or narrative structure as part of her broader project and suggests another kind of "amalgamation" that parallels the admixture of lyric and narrative temporality. Formally, too, the Prince's journey towards his own failure is marked by versions of what Tennyson, in *In Memoriam,* called "vast eddies in the flood / Of onward time" (128.5–6) – that is, by long pauses of seemingly lyric intensity that appear to dilate in an eternal present, even as narrative time slips away. In this section I offer an alternative account of the "social element" in *The Prince's Progress* and its relationship to a quest that foregrounds the intervals between encounters. At some level, of course, the Prince's miscalculations are obvious. But this circumstance implies that identifying the Prince's errors is not the endpoint of interpretation and may even obscure the more subtle workings of Rossetti's language and form.

The first of these interruptions, the dalliance with the "wave-haired milkmaid, rosy and white" (58), is the more seemingly straightforward of the social temptations that befall him – particularly for readers familiar with "Christabel."[36] After less than a mile of walking, the Prince encounters this charming young woman. "Was she a maid, or an evil dream?" (68) the poem asks, somewhat unnecessarily, given that her eyes "glitter and gleam" (69) and her hair turns into "shining serpent-coils" (94). A flicker of awareness on the Prince's part is registered as a hesitation that echoes Rossetti's "Remember": "He half-turned away, then he quite turned back" (86), agreeing to spend the night with her in return for the milk she has given him to drink. Although the milkmaid does not seem to be concealing any physical deformity, she perhaps exceeds Coleridge's Geraldine in her dangerous female wiles. She tempts the Prince join her in idleness – spending time that is not his to give. And much more so than Geraldine, this "insipid succubus of a milkmaid"[37] thwarts rehabilitation because she is an ultimately uninteresting character. All in all, it is not an auspicious beginning for a quest narrative or a spiritual pilgrimage – or even a pleasurable walking tour. That the Prince, having failed to resist even this most blatant of temptations, goes on to misinterpret more subtle encounters should surprise no one.

The poem, however, does not speak entirely in one voice; form and content are at odds. As the Prince struggles to rouse himself from sleep and leave the milkmaid, the poem almost aggressively pulls him back:

"Up, up, up," sad glad voices swelled:
"So the tree falls and lies as it's felled.
Be thy bands loosed, O sleeper, long held
 In sweet sleep whose end is not sweet.
Be the slackness girt and the softness quelled
  And the slowness fleet." (115–20)

The voices urge the Prince towards the actions that will ensure the successful completion of the quest. Yet a careful reader cannot help but notice how the structure of the stanza works against its putative message. Rather than performing the reveille it describes, much of the passage sounds like a lullaby. Some of the contradictions are obvious: the "up, up, up" of the first line "falls" in the second; the reference to "sweet sleep whose end is not sweet" appears in a line whose ending is, of course, the word "sweet." Paradoxical constructions such as "sad glad voices" and "slowness fleet" and the enjambment "long held / In sweet sleep" strengthen the bonds that the Prince is exhorted to escape. Repetition – "sleeper"/"sweet sleep" ... "not sweet" – and slippery alliteration trap this sleeper and the reader in an agitated, restless suspension: Do this! Don't do that! Don't wait! Hold on! Because the tone and content work against each other, it is also a somewhat difficult passage to read aloud. The line in which the "sleeper" is supposed to have his "bands loosed" is particularly challenging. Ultimately, it is impossible to attend both to the demands of the meaning and to the demands of the structure. The possible readings are irreducibly contradictory and, despite the assurances of Rossetti's more conservative interpreters, there is no clear guide for deciding which one takes precedence.

The Prince puts an abrupt end to the dilation of the "sad glad voices." With a decisiveness that somewhat belies the critical emphasis on indecision, the narrator declares simply, "Off he set" (121), cutting the Gordian knot woven by the preceding stanza. In a way, however, the Prince merely passes from one scene of suspension to another. His journey takes him to "A land of chasm and rent, a land / Of rugged blackness on either hand" (127–8). Here, in this first trial by "barren boredom," he encounters the "stagnant air" of a "land of neither life nor death" (144, 139):

> Untrodden before, untrodden since:
> Tedious land for a social Prince;
> Halting, he scanned the outs and ins,
>   Endless, labyrinthine, grim,
> Of the solitude that made him wince,
>   Laying wait for him. (151–6)

The gentle irony in the narrator's depiction of the "social Prince" unable to deal with his own solitude somewhat undercuts the image's gothic menace, although the rhyme of "Prince" and "wince" is especially suggestive of the relationship between physical and psychological stress. There is perhaps, as Rees proposes, a faint resonance with Coleridge's Ancient Mariner in the Prince's solitary path, even though, as she concedes, "Christina Rossetti's tone is different and she denies her prince the dignity of the ancient mariner in his suffering."[38] The landscape, however, bears more than a passing resemblance to that of Percy Shelley's

"Mont Blanc." The menace of solitude "Laying wait" recalls the creeping glaciers which had, in Shelley's poem, loomed "Like snakes that watch their prey" (101). As when Shelley scanned the riven landscape of the Mer de Glace for traces of a lesson to be learned and found only contingency, the landscape of the Prince's journey yields little consolation or guidance:

> Some old volcanic upset must
> Have rent the crust and blackened the crust;
> Wrenched and ribbed it beneath its dust
>   Above earth's molten centre at seethe,
> Heaved and heaped it by huge upthrust
>   Of fire beneath. (145–50)

The traces of "volcanic upset" mark the catastrophic temporality of absolute otherness – the geological events that have shaped a world independently of human consciousness. It pointedly does not gesture towards God's presence; the volcano does not appear to carry any specific scriptural resonance. Yet, no other symbolic protocol arises to fill this epistemological void. Thus this first trial of "barren boredom" evokes not only some of the darker images of "Mont Blanc," but also, more broadly, a Romantic discourse of sublimity that privileged the contemplation of rude, irregular landscapes and natural violence. In Rossetti's hands, these images no longer trigger an ecstatic trance; the Prince remains in what Shelley had characterized as a "separate phantasy" (36), estranged from the vacancy that surrounds him and longing for a human companion.

From the inhuman non-place of this "loveless land" (133), the Prince comes upon his second encounter with the "social element": a cave inhabited by a hundred-year-old alchemist who believes himself to be on the verge of creating a potion for eternal life. The alchemist is not particularly interested in convivial conversation, but he allows the Prince to enter his cave on the condition that he work the bellows to keep the fire going beneath the cauldron that holds the "Elixir of Life" (203). As in the scene with the milkmaid, it is rather difficult for a reader with even passing knowledge of literary conventions not to notice the ironies of the alchemist's position that somehow escape the Prince. Indications of death are all around: the fire inside the cave appears "Like a red-hot eye from a grave" (170), and the alchemist describes himself as having been "Buried alive from light and air" (199) and "mildewed for the grave" (213). In a somewhat predictable counter-movement, the alchemist must give his own life in the pursuit of eternal Life:

> The dead hand slipped, the dead finger dipped
> In the broth as the dead man slipped, –
> . . .
> The last ingredient was supplied
> (Unless the dead man mistook or lied). (242–3, 247–8)

The emphasis on the dead man's status as dead – a status also independently verified by the Prince himself, who "Made sure that his host had died" before he "filled a phial" (251, 252) – and the linking of that death to the production of the so-called elixir of life is nothing if not excessive. Whatever immediate miscalculations the Prince makes in this episode about his eventual ability to gain the Princess's forgiveness through a gift of distilled life are clear enough without the constant reminders that the alchemist is the "dead man in his cave" (260), let alone the persistence of the rhyming of "cave" with "grave." Yet, the narrator's parenthetical aside leaves the question of the efficacy of the elixir at least partially undecided. Whether the alchemist is "fool or knave, / Or honest seeker who had not found" (260–1) remains an unanswerable question. The poem's insistence on the connection between the alchemist's search for life and his actual, physical death points to a broader preoccupation with wasted or misdirected effort. The alchemist is nothing if not dedicated and sincere in his single-minded pursuit and, as such, is rather the opposite of the Prince himself. Yet, as Rees comments, this episode implies that sacrifice alone is not enough: "To lose one's life, it appears, may not necessarily be to save it, the light within may be darkness, a sacrifice may be polluted and be rejected."[39] Alchemy, as any reader of *Frankenstein* knows, has a tendency to seduce its practitioners into ultimately deleterious pursuits, even as it promises to address the most deeply felt human desires, particularly as regards life itself. For Rossetti, however, uncertainty must necessarily attend all exertions of effort, all sacrifices, even those that are not as explicitly proscribed as the alchemist's particular endeavour. In other words, we can never be certain that the cause to which we have dedicated ourselves is the correct one.[40] However, without this uncertainty – without, that is, a recognition of suspension and discontinuity as existential and absolute – no effort would be worth undertaking, nor would any act of faith be worthy of the name.

What further complicates the Prince's sojourn in the alchemist's cave is the way that the episode obscures its relationship to the passage of time. The dalliance with the milkmaid, however inadvisable, was clearly limited to a single night. The same *might* be the case for this next encounter with the "social element," but it is impossible to tell. The alchemist's self-imposed immurement has estranged him from even the most basic external temporal cycles, for "his eyes had scarcely brooked / The light of day" (185–6) while he worked with "sleepless care" (201). He measures time by the potion itself, watching it "wane or wax" (202). Even his claim that "This year is the hundredth year" (200) seems strikingly inexact, capable of referring either to the length of his toil or of his life. Once the Prince agrees to participate in this experiment, "Night turned to day and day to night" (230). Again, this line might refer either to the literal span of two nights and one day, or to a more abstract notion of time passing outside the cave. The latter possibility seems more likely, as the activities inside the cave continue to operate on a different scale – the potion is complete only "when the hundredth year was full" (235). The death of the alchemist thus not only fulfils the conditions necessary to create the elixir of life, it also appears to return the poem to its previous sense of time. Indeed, the Prince finds himself making a familiar set of plans, now with an additional expectation:

"One night's rest," thought the Prince: "This done,
Forth I speed with the rising sun:
With the morrow I rise and run,
  Come what will of wind or of weather.
This draught of Life when my Bride is won
    We'll drink together." (253–8)

Again, the irony of the Prince's position is underlined for Rossetti's readers. The effectiveness of the alchemist's potion is dubious at best, even if the fairy-tale frame of the poem authorizes a certain suspension of disbelief. The corpse of the alchemist signifies that the potion brewed in the cave is not meant to raise someone from the dead; it can only be consumed by those who are alive. And, having exited the cave, the Prince has voluntarily rejoined the temporal scheme that already dictates that he will arrive "too late" to implement his plans. Without that last bit of knowledge, he clings tightly to the phial for the rest of the poem, even when that clinging places his own life in peril. The irony of clinging to an occult potion while one's beloved is dying the death that will place her beyond that potion's reach is abundantly clear and, in its form at least, quintessentially Rossettian. At the same time, the phial does provide a thread of symbolic continuity in the second half of the poem. With each successive reappearance of the object, it seems more and more reasonable to conclude that part of the Prince's problem, part of his failure, is this inappropriate fixation. However, to insist too firmly on the status of *The Prince's Progress* as a parable of non-attachment is itself a kind of attachment. And, indeed, the same scene which purportedly secures the ironic status of the elixir of life – a flash flood in which the Prince nearly perishes – also formalizes suspension as the ontological ground of the poem's world view.

"Which way – which way?"

According to Rossetti's schema, the Prince should emerge from his temporary immurement with the alchemist into another trial of "barren boredom in a more uncompromising form." Yet, the poem and the Prince take a strange turn at this point away from the plan for "artistic congruity" that had been previously laid out. For the Prince almost immediately realizes that "the black land was travelled o'er" (283) and he now journeys through a "flowering country" (285). Granted, he is again palpably restless, as his attention leaps from the details of the natural world – the nest of a kingfisher, the path of a field-mouse – to the comparative monotony of his situation. The sigh of "Leaves, still leaves, and nothing new" (297) suggests the weariness of a traveller and of a reader paging through a book that has failed to hold his interest. Still, if this is understood as the second trial of boredom to which Rossetti's outline refers, it does not possess the same barren intensity as the earlier episode, and it passes much more quickly. At one moment, the Prince languidly expresses his yearnings for female human company:

> It's oh for a second maiden, at least,
> To bear the flagon, and taste it too,
> And flavour the feast. (298–300)

The "fl" sounds from "flagon" and "flavour" ooze into the "l" sounds of the next stanza – until the poem takes an abrupt turn:

> Lagging he moved, and apt to swerve;
> Lazy of limb, but quick of nerve.

At length the water-bed took a curve,
The deep river swept the bankside bare;
Waters streamed from the hill-reserve –
Waters here, waters there. (301–6)

The flash flood appears from nowhere, the sharp "-rve" line endings quickly overwhelming the Prince's lagging, lazy limbs. For a fleeting moment, the curving "water-bed" offers a reminder of the Princess who remains in deep sleep; the next line erupts into catastrophe. The devastation is swift and complete. Overflowing its existing boundaries and violently carving new ones, the river carries with it the force of contingency itself – a contingency that, as we have seen in "Mont Blanc," is capable of erasing all alternative stories from the surface of the earth. Breaking through a "reserve" that can be understood as both a physical space and, in the context of Rossetti's Tractarian commitments, a theological doctrine, the passage provokes an experience of sublime awe for which the Prince and the poem's readers are eminently unprepared.

Powerfully disorienting and physically terrifying, the flood quickly overwhelms the poem's protagonist. At no other point in the story is the Prince so much at the mercy of forces outside of his control. He is swept off his feet by the "dizzying whirl," "thunderous downshoot," and "lashing spray" (314, 315, 316), the watery equivalent of the volcanic blast that had haunted the bleak passage between the milkmaid and the alchemist:

High above, and deep below,
Bursting, bubbling, swelling the flow,
Like hill-torrents after the snow, –
Bubbling, gurgling, in the whirling strife,
Swaying, sweeping, to and fro, –
He must swim for his life. (307–12)

The repeated "-ing" sounds and the hard consonants strain the boundaries of Rossetti's form. The internal echoes erupt from the lines that cannot fully contain them and in some sense drown out the end-rhymes of "below," "flow," "snow," and "fro." Thus the violently churning flood, described in language that explicitly evokes the Romantic nature-sublime, raises the spectre of nature that does not follow a divine plan – at least, not a divine plan that is in any way legible. The Prince's cognitive powers are also overwhelmed. It takes nearly eight lines for him to realize that he must "swim for his life":

Which way? – which way? – his eyes grew dim
With the dizzying whirl – which way to swim?
The thunderous downshoot deafened him;
  Half he choked in the lashing spray:
Life is sweet, and the grave is grim –
    Which way? – which way? (313–18)

The dashes suggest the flailing of limbs in rough waters; one can almost feel the Prince's body being pulled under by the current. This is the only time in the poem where the "way" has been put into question – the Prince may not like the path he must follow and he may take longer than recommended to complete it, but he has not, at least up until this point, had to spend much time wondering whether he has been moving in the right direction. The "life is sweet" cliché – an echo of the platitudes offered by the voices earlier in the poem – surfaces here with a heavy uselessness; it cannot answer the more urgent question of "which way?" Rescue arrives in the following stanza, in the form of a voice from the beach that helps the Prince reorient himself and, more concretely, in the form of a rope thrown to his aid. Yet, this timely intervention nearly fails because the Prince continues to grasp the phial, now a comically inappropriate "life preserver." The "slipping" that had marked the moment of the alchemist's death reappears here: while the bottle remains "clutched in one drowning hand" (321), the Prince fumbles for the rope with his free hand, and "His feet slip on the slipping sand" (323).

Somewhat in spite of himself, the Prince does survive this experience: he is "Just saved, without pulse or breath, – / Scarcely saved from the gulp of death" (325–6) by shadowy female figures who restore him to full animation through their kind ministrations. At the moment of his rescue, the Prince is not the interpreter but the object of interpretation, a body in suspended animation. The image of the drowned Prince thus marks the point where knowledge, expectation, and attachment all encounter a dead end. As I discussed in the previous chapter, this is a vulnerable position, for an extreme state of suspended animation could cause a living body to be mistaken for dead, and, throughout much of the nineteenth century, there was no reliable method for determining, in the moment, whether a drowning victim was alive or dead. Therefore, while the Prince's suspended animation renders him an object of interpretation, it does so in such a way that rules of interpretation are also themselves suspended. The questions that the poem poses about the Prince's body in the preceding line – "Is there life? – Is there hope?" (324) – reflect not only two of the central emotional preoccupations of Rossetti's poetry but also the popular uncertainty about the signs of death described in the previous chapter. Granted, a similar set of questions is posed about the Princess later on: "Is there life? – the lamp burns low; / Is there hope? – the coming is slow" (379–80). In that context, however, the epistemological dimension is more explicit: these are questions that will receive answers. In the flood scene, however, the caesura visually reinforces the lingering, absolute uncertainty of this moment. In a literal sense, there is no way to "know" the status of the Prince's body, no index of reading practices that will enable a determination in that moment. The dash itself reproduces this sense of ruptured temporality, for there is no easy transition from the concern with the present ("Is there life?") to confidence in the future ("Is there hope?"). Without a way to verify the presence of either life or hope, the Prince's rescuers act spontaneously and on faith to save his life. In so doing they perform the only unambiguously successful act of interpretation in *The Prince's Progress* – if it can be called interpretation at all. The drowned body represents nothing less than the limits of methodology, the evasion of reading practices, and the spectre of an ineradicable uncertainty.[41] What it does not allow is fixation or attachment to a single rule, a reading that depends upon a single "symbolic protocol" that will make the poem's multiple levels of signification "manageable."[42] As we discovered in the previous chapter, no single protocol can account for every possible combination of consciousness and insensibility that places a suspended body in danger of being mistaken for a dead one; the unmanageability cannot be effaced.

For all of its excitement and suspense, the flood scene has received relatively little attention. Most critics assume that the floodwaters possess some general Christian significance, though they disagree on what that significance actually is. Arseneau, for instance, emphasizes the flood's "many biblical counterparts" and proposes that it "could restore the Prince and offer him a second chance"[43] or at least the possibility of reform. Rees categorically denies that any such possibility exists, claiming that "The prince experiences no ... purgation and salvation, though saved he is in what in effect is a parody of Christian salvation."[44] The symbolic excess of nature out of control, a nature only partly reconciled with the designs of an active, Christian God, draws attention to vulnerability and contingency that attend even the lives of the faithful. The show of sublime natural force in a poem that seems otherwise preoccupied with the working through of Christian images situates *The Prince's Progress* as an extension of what David Collings has described as a Romantic tradition of "disastrous transcendence," texts that "juxtapose the representation of ... contingency with allusions to aspects of the Christian tradition" in ways that are not fully resolvable.[45] If God is at work in a scene like this, then one must conclude that such a deity is bound by no rule and that his actions cannot be predicted with any certainty. Drawing upon the language of Shelley more than that of Bunyan (despite the fact that Christian and Hopeful do pass through the waters of death), this flood seems to recall the "flood of ruin" caused by the glaciers of "Mont Blanc." As in Shelley's poem, the violence is general and seemingly unmotivated. The unmistakable echo of the Ancient Mariner's lament in Rossetti's "Waters here, waters there" further complicates any attempts to establish cause and effect. Her citational practices obscure as much as they reveal.

A subtle but significant change in tone marks the end of the Prince's dalliance with his rescuers. The languidly expressed suggestions about taking action that characterize many of the interludes earlier in the poem disappear in favour of a more urgent and straightforward emphasis on impermanence:

Slip past, slip fast,
Uncounted hours from first to last,
Many hours till the last is past,
  Many hours dwindling to one –
One hour whose die is cast,
  One last hour gone. (361–6)

The stanza's uncharacteristically short first line, composed of just four beats, brings the poem up short, as if shifting it into another gear. Reversing the ambiguous time of the poem's opening lines, this stanza shakes the poem out of its soporific suspension, setting it and the Prince in motion at last. Repetition loses its suspensive powers and serves rather to intensify the forward pressures of time:

Come, gone – gone forever –
Gone as an unreturning river –

Gone as to death the merriest liver –
  Gone as the year at the dying fall –
Tomorrow, today, yesterday, never –
    Gone once for all. (366–72)

The word "gone" cascades through the stanza, replicating the flow of the "unreturning river" and the receding floodwaters. If the end rhymes provide the melody, "gone," which appears at or near the beginning of five of the stanza's six lines, is the harmony that marks loss and operates beyond the dominant structure of the passage. Although the sentiment "Gone once for all" suggests closure and finality, the stanza as a whole resists containment. It slips away as it is read, performing the evanescence it describes.

After this, there are approximately one hundred lines of verse left to describe the rest of the Prince's journey to his late arrival in the Princess's kingdom. In this interval, the Prince accomplishes more than he has in the rest of the poem – including those tasks that had been predicted with such portentousness in the opening lines. Chastened, one can only assume, by his recent near-death experience in the floodwaters, he "crossed the stream where a ford was plain" (393) and carefully climbs the steep bank on the other side. He summits a snow-capped mountain at heights "where the goat scarce clings, / Up where the eagle folds her wings, / Past the green line of living things" (409–11). Having finally solidified his intention and exerted his strength, the Prince seems, at last, to have overcome his laggardly habits. Curiously, however, the depiction of these seemingly crucial events is, at best, perfunctory. The dalliance with the milkmaid unfolded over eleven stanzas; the entirety of the Prince's feats of bravery and strength are dispensed with in five. Most scholars do not even mention them, skipping over these lines in order to note that the Prince's first glimpse of the Princess's kingdom offers the interpretive consolations of rich biblical and sexual imagery – another set of unfulfilled promises whose whispers disappear into the cries of "too late" that end the poem.

Reading against Roothold

Dawn Henwood cites inappropriate readerly expectations in her assessment of why *The Prince's Progress* has failed to achieve the popularity enjoyed by some of Rossetti's other poems. "If the sequel to *Goblin Market* disappoints," she writes, "it is not, as many have claimed, because it is one-dimensional or monotonous. The poem only disappoints those readers who delight more in answers than in questions."[46] To delight in questions more than in answers is undoubtedly a prerequisite for being a "good" reader in a literary-critical sense. But Henwood's defence of *The Prince's Progress* would be more appropriate for a lyric like "Winter: My Secret," which achieves partial legibility through its performance of concealment. In that case, a "good" reader will be able to apprehend the limits of knowledge and action. She will take care not to identify with the epistemological desires of the imagined addressee, knowing that the implied disappointment is part of the pleasure. But where "Winter: My Secret" flaunts its own secrecy in a way that allows a cannily positioned reader to take pleasure in its suspension, *The Prince's Progress* is more simply frustrating, its questions more tedious than enjoyable. These frustrations are not meant to be fully recoverable, even as traces of a knowledge endlessly deferred. Much less may they be mitigated by the application of a more refined reading process. As figured by the drowned, radically illegible body of the Prince, the poem performs a general, structural critique of expectation *as such*, prior to its being attached to any specific desire, hope, or goal. In other words, *The Prince's Progress* resists attempts to reify its lack of closure into a quasi-resolution, asking its readers to accept suspension and belatedness not as limitations but as potentially – if paradoxically – generative conditions that are the foundation for the experience of faith. Its coherence as a text comes largely from its refusal of coherence, from a reluctance to have done with instability. Moreover, this refusal of stability does not arise in spite of Rossetti's religious faith, but because of it. Where a scholar such as Mary Arseneau claims that the poem's portrayal of the "difficulties and dangers inherent in symbolic interpretations" does not amount to "suggesting that the world is intrinsically undecipherable," my own reading of *The Prince's Progress* reveals rather that the intrinsic undecipherability of the world is not a threat to Rossetti's "uncompromising orthodoxy."[47] Instead, it is one of the most fundamental tenets of that orthodoxy. As a result, Rossetti's practices of poetic suspension remain attentive to what she calls, in her devotional work *The Face of the Deep* (1892), the "incalculable if not infinite variety" that constitutes the world. "Divergences," she observes, "are the order of our day; insomuch that it even has been alleged that no two leaves can be found alike; and I for one am ready to believe it."[48] Rossetti makes it clear that divergence as such is not what separates man from God. Rather, it is separation from God that makes differences appear as problems – divergences from some arbitrary standard. In other words, divergences only appear to be so when they disappoint expectations that are always already inadequate and misplaced. Only a poetics of radical suspension can respond in faith to a world that has been created to be constitutively contingent.

Thus she continues,

> Foothold we must needs have, at least until we be made equal unto the angels; but let us pray against roothold. A foot may spurn the ground it cannot choose but tread; a root grasps and holds fast to the soil whence it sucks subsistence, and whence it oftentimes cannot be wrenched except to die.[49]

The image of a root that "sucks subsistence" from ground that can never satisfy it calls to mind the language of *Goblin Market*, where Laura's desire becomes fixated on an object: the "kernel-stone" (138) that she kept as a souvenir of her goblin-fruit feast:

> One day remembering the kernel-stone
> She set it by a wall that faced the south;
> Dewed it with tears, hoped for a root,
> Watched for a waxing shoot,
> But there came none ... (281–5)

Ripped from the fruit it came in, the kernel-stone is just another dead object, a fact that underscores the tragic nature of Laura's fixation. Though "kernel" suggests fecundity and possibility, the potential for growth and expansion, "stone," suggests hardening and opacity, a certain limitation: it can multiply only by being broken or shattered.

However, what is perhaps most striking about *The Face of the Deep*'s counsel to "pray against roothold" is the fact that Rossetti does not distinguish between "good" and "bad" objects of attachment. Neither does she advocate a wholesale project of renunciatory transcendence, of holding oneself "above it all." Foothold cannot be dispensed with; to cling to one's future transcendence is still clinging. Even the most admirable attitudes and interpretations, the most orthodox beliefs and practices, can become objects of attachment or sites of fixation. To be "made equal unto the angels" is not to be redeemed from the condition of change and illegibility, but is rather a liberation from the condition of attachment itself, a state of suspension without object. Because she sees each act of expression as a foothold – temporary and ultimately incomplete – Rossetti is able to maintain a posture of radical acceptance, not the imposed self-denial and depletion that have so often been attributed to her. The suspension of disbelief is not, for Rossetti, the *exclusion* of anything, not repression or forgetting, but a way of bracketing, keeping something present, including it, even though it no longer serves the same inhibiting function – making genuine disbelief constitutive of poetic faith.

A series of entries in Rossetti's devotional "reading diary," *Time Flies* (1882), offers an example of what it might mean not only to pray, but also to read, against roothold. In the entries for 17 and 18 July, Rossetti unfolds the implications of an experience she had as a child of waiting patiently for a wild strawberry to ripen. On 17 July she recalls the realization that she had "watched in vain: for a snail, or some such marauder, must have forestalled us at a happy moment. One fatal day we found it half-eaten, and good for nothing." The anecdote plots the meeting of reasonable expectation with seemingly arbitrary disappointment to which the speaker must accommodate herself. However, Rossetti frames the story of the strawberry in a way that emphasizes her interpretive agency as well as her capacity for ethical action. She is actively engaged in rereading and rethinking her story, deferring its conclusion: "Thus then had we watched in vain: or was it altogether in vain?" she wonders, acknowledging that she and her childhood companion had learned lessons other than the ones they were expecting. Rossetti's work of self-revision continues in the entry for 18 July, where she returns to the phrasing of the day before: "'Half-eaten and good for nothing,' said I of the strawberry. I need not have expressed myself with such sweeping contempt."[50] Widening her gaze to include "other living creatures, including creepers on the earth" who also have "a share in strawberries" allows Rossetti to consider the problem of anthropocentric greed and the ethical demands of living in "a world in which plenitude and dearth and the consequent *intensity* of desire and lack are not individually created, not solely caused by the self, but arise from the given conditions of experience."[51] This realization parallels the one that the Prince perhaps failed to learn in his journey through the inhuman "land of neither life nor death" – a lesson in contingency that profoundly decentres the human subject.

Time Flies participates in a complex action of suspension and self-revision, one temporary "foothold" in the project of cultivating faith. The unhappy ending that Coleridge could not bear to write in

"Christabel" – the ending, that is, that left his protagonist's prayers unanswered – is transformed, by Rossetti, into the absolute substance of faith. The underlying anxiety in poems like "Mont Blanc" and even, to some extent, *Maud* had to do with the presence of a contingency that could not be subsumed by some higher power. For Rossetti, that higher power becomes identified with contingency itself, without becoming any less worthy of obedience and worship. The divergences that arise in the practice of daily life, the order and the ordering of the day, are, in the final analysis, the most real, ineradicable elements of the reality that Rossetti relentlessly incorporated into her poetics. Taking nothing for granted, Rossetti's faith resists the urge to remake the world in the image of its own desire, even a desire for a coherent, undivided reality.

Conclusion

Over, Again

> Sometimes I said: This thing shall be no more;
> My expectation wearies and shall cease;
> I will resign it now and be at peace:
> Yet never gave it o'er.[1]

How does a book about suspension end? The question is more easily deferred than answered. One is always too early or too late. One says too much or too little. One form of suspension is traded for another, usually more bombastic, version of itself. Coleridge leaves "Christabel" in a seemingly permanent suspension, its "true" ending one of those many projected works that remain speculative and unrealized. Shelley ends "Mont Blanc" with a rhetorical question as unreadable as the mountain itself. The speaker of Tennyson's *Maud* celebrates his loss of self, which is also the resolution of the uncertainties that plague him, in a patriotic apotheosis that has all the signs of a redoubled illusion; if he is no longer considered to be mad, it is only because his condition now speaks a language interpretable by others. Rossetti's Prince will always arrive too late because it is never clear that he arrives at all. Spells are made to be broken. Sublime ecstasy fades. These endings are both inevitable and necessary; the knocking always comes to reveal that the suspension had been operating in the first place. The return of calculation, the closing of the awful parenthesis is what enables the perception of discontinuity and the memory of how the comparing powers had just been suspended.

At the same time, suspension marks an irreducible paradox, the "to be continued" implied by the ellipsis, or "suspension points." David Collings describes modernity as "the management of its aimlessness, the routinization of its (un)founding, a practice of perpetual suspension." It has its roots in the Romantic era's recognition of human vulnerability in a cosmos that is not yet fully secular, but in which the covenant binding the human and the divine is no longer in force. God is not dead, but "alien, disfigured, and utterly unreadable, a mode of disastrous transcendence."[2] The Brocken Spectre and the secret lodger, the "secret springs" of human inhumanity, illegible bodies threatened by living graves, flash floods and false progress: all of these figure that vulnerability, revealed at moments of sublimity but also persisting past their time as reminders of constitutive discontinuity in otherwise stable contexts. Suspension must come to an end, but, at the same time, those endings are both premature and too long deferred. Of the authors discussed in this book, perhaps only Rossetti manages fully to realize a "practice of perpetual suspension" by placing absolute faith in an absolutely unpredictable God who operates through radical contingency. The poetry and devotional prose of Rossetti thus represent a certain limit of suspension, a way of closing the awful parenthesis in this chapter of literary history.

At the same time, suspension gestures towards what remains unconditioned and contingent, to "an essential *unfinishedness* that cannot be reduced to an incompleteness or an inadequacy."[3] To adopt these practices requires an assent to a certain experience of never-having-done, continuing to take contingency and instability seriously, not allowing these concepts to become domesticated through frequent use. It is necessary to remain in "the state of suspension in which it's over – *and* over again, and you'll never have done with that suspension itself ."[4] I take these phrases from Jacques Derrida's essay "Living On," which is something of a classic deconstructionist meditation on suspension, in the context of an essay that is, ostensibly, a reading of Percy Shelley's "The Triumph of Life."[5] Suspension undoes finality, turning cessation ("it's over") into repetition ("*and* over again"). Suspension is not, for Derrida, the *exclusion* of anything, not repression or forgetting, but a way of bracketing, keeping contingency present, including it, even though it no longer serves the same inhibiting function as it did in the Kantian-influenced accounts of the sublime that operated in the nineteenth-century texts at the centre of this study.

By the end of the Victorian era, the encounter with the essential discontinuity of the world no longer needs to be presented as the jolt of the sublime. As narrative forms become increasingly experimental towards the end of the nineteenth and the beginning of the twentieth century, the intimacy of poetry, suspension, and the sublime becomes, in a certain sense, less urgent and perhaps even less strange. In the last decades of the nineteenth century, suspension does, to some extent, become routine and perpetual – something manageable, something given. Over time, even estrangement becomes familiar. The process is already in progress by the time Walter Pater, in his conclusion to *The Renaissance* (1873), codifies his sense of a life lived through "impressions unstable, flickering, inconsistent," a life that is also a life lived through suspension:

> those impressions of the individual mind to which, for each one of us, experience dwindles down, are in perpetual flight … all that is actual in it being a single moment, gone while we try to apprehend it, of which it may ever be more truly said that it has ceased to be than that it is … It is with the movement, the passage and dissolution of impressions, images, sensations, that analysis leaves off, – that continual vanishing away, that strange perpetual weaving and unweaving of ourselves.[6]

It is possible to discern in this foundational text of late Victorian aestheticism the hints of the experience that Thomas De Quincey had been exploring much earlier in the century: the moment apprehended only in its passing away, a present moment always in motion yet mysteriously still. In the influential essay "Formalism and Time," Catherine Gallagher argues that Pater's aestheticism radicalizes that of Shelley. While both writers, to her mind, are committed to the "hope that attention to literary form might at least cheat time," she sees in Pater a potentially disastrous conflation of art and life, the pursuit of an impossible version of "success in life." Paterian formalism – or, in Gallagher's coinage, "formula-ism" – becomes, in essence, a practice of running to stand still. More than that, however, Pater's language of a "perpetual weaving and unweaving" implies an increasing level of comfort with certain kinds of instability. Gallagher associates the "sudden accessions of aesthetic illumination" in the works of writers like Virginia Woolf and James Joyce with "tropes such as epiphany, syncope, fragmentation, discontinuity, and rupture"[7] – terms that are strikingly similar to those that have dominated this book. As certain kinds of cognitive estrangement become the rule rather than the exception, suspension becomes normalized, its sublimity more elusive.

How does one live in a state of perpetual suspension, holding back and giving over, prior to and separate from decision and calculation? *Awful Parenthesis* has sought to recover some of the textual traces of a world in which reality was increasingly unstable. This world remains very much our own in the twenty-first century; then, as now, the question of how to construct liveable, reasonably coherent lives across a discontinuous present imposes itself with a quiet urgency. "We cannot ever," as Caroline Levine observes, "apprehend the totality of the networks that organize us."[8] To suspend the notion that reality is by default fixed and unchangeable is to open oneself at once to the sublime terror of a contingent world that could become otherwise at any moment and to the sublime relief – even joy – of the possibilities of the new, of a world that will not simply replicate itself in the lockstep of the same. Such practices do not constitute an escape from the world as it is, a rejection of the historical or the political, but a potentially more profound, if non-totalizing, sense of the way the world may be engaged to bring about change that remains both proximate to and unimaginable in the present moment. A recent essay by Claire Colebrook reminds us that "our decisions – our modes of knowing – are never finally our own but are marked by traces that will make our future never reducible to the limits of our now."[9] Naught may endure but Mutability – our poetic faith has always been a faith in the incalculable, a faith in the very unknowability not only of the future but of the present. Still, it is difficult, even impossible, to remain always on the edge of the abyss, to embrace the discomfort of the aporia. On the one hand, the demand for decision, beyond calculation, beyond the horizon of the possible; on the other, the impossibility of deciding, inflexible and equally demanding. Only a posture of suspension – holding back, giving over – can meet this contradictory situation of "infinite speculation"[10] in an uncertain future.

Notes

Introduction

1 Thomas De Quincey, *The Works of Thomas De Quincey*, gen. ed. Grevel Lindop, 21 vols. (London: Pickering & Chatto, 2000–3), 3.151. Further citations from this essay will be given in the text.

2 All of Wordsworth's poems are cited from William Wordsworth, *The Major Works*, ed. Stephen Gill (Oxford: Oxford University Press, 1984); line numbers will be given in the text.

3 David Bromwich, *Disowned by Memory: Wordsworth's Poetry of the 1790s* (Chicago: University of Chicago Press, 1998), 72.

4 Thomas Weiskel, *The Romantic Sublime: Studies in the Structure and Psychology of Transcendence* (Baltimore: Johns Hopkins University Press, 1976), 29.

5 Timothy Corrigan, "Interpreting the Uncitable Text: The Literary Criticism of Thomas De Quincey," *Ineffability: Naming the Unnamable from Dante to Beckett*, ed. Peter S. Hawkins and Anne Howland Schotter (New York: AMS Press, 1984), 143.

6 Markus Iseli, for instance, cites the thought process represented in "Knocking" as "an instance of unconscious problem-solving that is being studied by cognitive psychologists today." "Thomas De Quincey and the Cognitive Prospects of the Unconscious," *European Romantic Review* 24, no. 3 (2013): 327. See also Joel Faflak, *Romantic Psychoanalysis: The Burden of the Mystery* (Albany: State University of New York Press, 2008), 151–98.

7 Steven Knapp, *Personification and the Sublime: Milton to Coleridge* (Cambridge, MA: Harvard University Press, 1985), 5. This phrase refers specifically to Coleridge's definition of the sublime, but is broadly applicable to the general concept of suspension I outline here.

8 Matthew Arnold, *The Poetical Works of Matthew Arnold* (New York: Thomas Y. Crowell & Co., 1897), 428.

9 On this last point, see Clyde de L. Ryals, *A World of Possibilities: Romantic Irony in Victorian Literature* (Columbus: Ohio State University Press, 1990).

10 Letter to George and Thomas Keats, 21 or 27 December 1817. *The Letters of John Keats, 1814–1821*, ed. Hyder Edward Rollins, 2 vols. (Cambridge, MA: Harvard University Press, 1958), 1.193.

11 Ou Li, *Keats and Negative Capability* (London: Continuum, 2009). See also Michael Theune, "~~Negative Capability~~ T wang dillo dee," *Jacket* 2 40 (late 2010), accessed 7 June 2017, http://jacketmagazine.com/40/theune-keats.shtml.

12 Henry Sidgwick, *Miscellaneous Essays and Addresses* (London: Macmillan, 1904), 60.

13 Caroline Levine, *The Serious Pleasures of Suspense: Victorian Realism and Narrative Doubt* (Charlottesville: University of Virginia Press, 2003), 3.

14 *Oxford English Dictionary Online*, s.v. "suspension," accessed 27 September 2017, http://www.oed.com/view/Entry/195164?.

15 Brian Massumi, *Parables for the Virtual: Movement, Affect, Sensation* (Durham, NC: Duke University Press, 2002), 220.

16 Stefanie Markovits, *The Crisis of Action in Nineteenth-Century English Literature* (Columbus: Ohio State University Press, 2006), 4.

17 Elisha Cohn, *Still Life: Suspended Development in the Victorian Novel* (Oxford: Oxford University Press, 2016), 5.

18 Jonathan Crary, *Suspensions of Perception: Attention, Spectacle, and Modern Culture* (Cambridge, MA: MIT Press, 1999), 10.

19 Victor Shklovsky, "Art as Technique," *Russian Formalist Criticism: Four Essays*, trans. Lee T. Lemon and Marion J. Rees (Lincoln: University of Nebraska Press, 1965), 22.

20 Robert Mitchell, *Experimental Life: Vitalism in Romantic Science and Literature* (Baltimore: Johns Hopkins University Press, 2013), 53.

21 Gavin Budge, *Romanticism, Medicine and the Natural Supernatural: Transcendent Vision and Bodily Spectres, 1789–1852* (Houndmills: Palgrave Macmillan, 2013); and Simone Natale, *Supernatural Entertainments: Victorian Spiritualism and the Rise of Modern Media Culture* (University Park: Penn State University Press, 2016).

22 Cohn, *Still Life*, 3, 5.

23 Jonathan Culler, *The Pursuit of Signs: Semiotics, Literature, Deconstruction*, augmented ed. (Ithaca: Cornell University Press, 2002), 149, 148.

24 Monique R. Morgan, *Narrative Means, Lyric Ends: Temporality in the Nineteenth-Century British Long Poem* (Columbus: Ohio State University Press, 2009), 9.

25 J. Hillis Miller, *The Linguistic Moment: From Wordsworth to Stevens* (Princeton: Princeton University Press, 1985), 15. Cf. Brian McHale, "Beginning to Think about Narrative in Poetry," *Narrative* 17, no. 1 (January 2009): 11–30, particularly his discussion of the "segmentivity" of poetry and the use of the gap as a tool of meaning making.

26 Meredith Martin and Yisrael Levin, "Victorian Prosody: Measuring the Field," *Victorian Poetry* 49, no. 2 (Summer 2011): 157.

27 Ibid., 158.

28 Anne-Lise François, *Open Secrets: The Literature of Uncounted Experience* (Stanford: Stanford University Press, 2008), 27.

29 Immanuel Kant, *Critique of Judgment*, trans. Werner S. Pluhar (Indianapolis: Hackett, 1987), 128.

30 The German *Aufhebung*, though usually translated as "sublime" or "sublimation," also contains resonances related to suspension. Cf. Christopher Lauer, *The Suspension of Reason in Hegel and Schelling* (London: Continuum, 2010), 3–5; see also François, *Open Secrets*, 46–65.

31 Kant, *Critique of Judgment*, 98.

32 Christopher Hitt, "Toward an Ecological Sublime," *New Literary History* 30, no. 3 (Summer 1999): 617.

33 Jean-François Lyotard, *The Differend: Phrases in Dispute*, trans. Georges Van Den Abbeele (Minneapolis: University of Minnesota Press, 1988), 66.

34 See Jean-François Lyotard, "The Sublime and the Avant-Garde," *The Inhuman: Reflections on Time*, trans. Geoffrey Bennington and Rachel Bowlby (Stanford: Stanford University Press, 1991), 89–107.

35 Philippe Lacoue-Labarthe, *Poetry as Experience*, trans. Andrea Tarnowski (Stanford: Stanford University Press, 1999), 19.

36 Angela Esterhammer, *The Romantic Performative: Language and Action in British and German Romanticism* (Stanford: Stanford University Press, 2000), 18.

37 Jerome Christensen, *Lord Byron's Strength: Romantic Writing and Commercial Society* (Baltimore: Johns Hopkins University Press, 1993), xxi.

38 Anne K. Mellor, *English Romantic Irony* (Cambridge, MA: Harvard University Press, 1980); James Chandler, *England in 1819: The Politics of Literary Culture and the Case of Romantic Historicism* (Chicago: University of Chicago Press, 1998).

39 See Ann C. Colley, *Victorians in the Mountains: Sinking the Sublime* (Farnham: Taylor and Francis, 2010). For a general consideration of the

cultural overdetermination of the Alps at the turn of the nineteenth century, see Cian Duffy, *The Landscapes of the Sublime, 1700–1830: Classic Ground* (Houndmills: Palgrave Macmillan, 2013), 28–67.

40 Charlotte Brontë, *Villette*, ed. Mark Lilly (London: Penguin Classics, 1985), 237.

41 George Eliot, *Scenes of Clerical Life*, ed. David Lodge (Harmondsworth: Penguin Classics, 1973), 215.

42 Ibid., 216.

43 Jill Matus, *Shock, Memory and the Unconscious in Victorian Fiction* (Cambridge: Cambridge University Press, 2009), 20.

44 See, for instance, David Riede's discussion of Tennyson's early poem "On Sublimity," which argues that "To avoid total incoherence, the poet must move beyond the speaker's foundering in the abyss of the inexpressible and introduce comprehensible content into the sublime, which he accomplishes by mediating his inwardness with publicly available discourses … to give content to his vision." *Allegories of One's Own Mind: Melancholy in Victorian Poetry* (Columbus: Ohio State University Press, 2005), 66.

45 Joel Faflak and Julia M. Wright, "Introduction," *Nervous Reactions: Victorian Recollections of Romanticism* (Albany: State University of New York Press, 2004), 10.

46 Morgan, *Narrative Means, Lyric Ends*, 3.

47 Dino Franco Felluga, *The Perversity of Poetry: Romantic Ideology and the Popular Male Poet of Genius* (Albany: State University of New York Press, 2005), 107.

48 Elaine Freedgood and Maureen McLane, "'Romantic Realism/Victorian Romance': An Introduction to Four Provocations," *Romanticism and Victorianism on the Net* 64 (October 2013), par. 2, accessed 12 May 2017, doi: 10.7202/1025674ar.

49 Caroline Levine, *Forms: Whole, Rhythm, Hierarchy, Network* (Princeton: Princeton University Press, 2015), 6.

50 Paul Youngquist, *Monstrosities: Bodies and British Romanticism* (Minneapolis: University of Minnesota Press, 2003); Colin Jager, *Unquiet Things: Secularism in the Romantic Age* (Philadelphia: University of Pennsylvania Press, 2015).

1. Coleridge, Suspension, and the Sublime

1 William Hazlitt, unsigned review of *Christabel, Kubla Khan, and The Pains of Sleep* in the *Examiner* (*CCH* 205).

2 Kenneth Johnston, *Unusual Suspects: Pitt's Reign of Alarm and the Lost Generation of the 1790s* (Oxford: Oxford University Press, 2013), 231.

3 Susan Wolfson, "'Comparing Power': Coleridge and Simile," *Coleridge's Theory of Imagination Today*, ed. Christine Gallant (New York: AMS Press, 1989), 167, 168.

4 See Jennifer Ford, *Coleridge on Dreaming: Romanticism, Dreams and the Medical Imagination* (Cambridge: Cambridge University Press, 1998); on Coleridge and mesmerism, see Tim Fulford, "Conducting the Vital Fluid: The Politics and Poetics of Mesmerism in the 1790s," *Studies in Romanticism* 43, no. 1 (Spring 2004): 57–78.

5 David Vallins, editor's introduction to *Coleridge's Writings, Volume 5: On the Sublime* (Houndmills: Palgrave Macmillan, 2003), 1.

6 John Beer, *Coleridge's Poetic Intelligence* (Houndmills: Macmillan, 1977), 136.

7 Christopher Stokes, *Coleridge, Language and the Sublime: From Transcendence to Finitude* (Houndmills: Palgrave Macmillan, 2011), 55.

8 Felicity James, *Charles Lamb, Coleridge and Wordsworth: Reading Friendship in the 1790s* (Houndmills: Palgrave Macmillan, 2008), 121–2.

9 Tim Fulford, *Coleridge's Figurative Language* (Houndmills: Macmillan, 1991), 47.

10 Unless otherwise noted, quotations from Coleridge's poetry are taken from *CPW* and are cited by line number throughout.

11 Judith Thompson, "An Autumnal Blast, a Killing Frost: Coleridge's Poetic Conversation with John Thelwall," *Studies in Romanticism* 36, no. 3 (Fall 1997): 438.

12 The alteration first appears in the the errata of 1817's *Sibylline Leaves* (see *CPP* 121n5).

13 In notes on a printer's copy of *Sibylline Leaves*, Coleridge glosses "trances" as "the brief moments of profound silence" (cf. *CPP* 122n8).

14 Thompson, "An Autumnal Blast, a Killing Frost," 450.

15 See *CPW* 1.1.453 and 1.1.456n74.

16 David Simpson, *Romanticism and the Question of the Stranger* (Chicago: University of Chicago Press, 2013), 56.

17 Paul de Man, *The Rhetoric of Romanticism* (New York: Columbia University Press, 1984), 89.

18 Heather Dubrow, "The Interplay of Narrative and Lyric: Competition, Cooperation, and the Case of the Anticipatory Amalgam," *Narrative* 14, no. 3 (October 2006): 265.

19 Cf. the *OED*'s entry for "suspend," particularly I.5.a: "To keep in a state of mental fixity, attention, or contemplation; to rivet the attention of" (*Oxford English Dictionary Online*, s.v. "suspend," accessed 7 June 2017, http://www.oed.com/view/Entry/195150?).

20 Edmund Burke, *A Philosophical Enquiry into the Origin of Our Ideas of the Sublime and Beautiful*, ed. David Womersley (London: Penguin Classics, 2004), 79.
21 In section 54 of *In Memoriam* (1850), Tennyson will describe himself as "An infant crying in the night: / An infant crying for the light: / And with no language but a cry" (54.17–20).
22 Thomas Weiskel, *The Romantic Sublime: Studies in the Structure and Psychology of Transcendence* (Baltimore: Johns Hopkins University Press, 1976), 23–4.
23 Stokes, *Coleridge, Language and the Sublime*, 4.
24 Nicola Trott, "The Picturesque, the Beautiful and the Sublime," *A Companion to Romanticism*, ed. Duncan Wu (Oxford: Blackwell Publishers, 1998), 88n45.
25 Stokes, *Coleridge, Language and the Sublime*, 136.
26 See *CPW* 1.1.14–15.
27 Immanuel Kant, *Critique of Judgment*, trans. Werner S. Pluhar (Indianapolis: Hackett, 1987), 105. Italics in original.
28 For fuller treatments of Coleridge's philosophical development, see Elinor S. Shaffer, "The Metaphysics of Culture: Kant and Coleridge's *Aids to Reflection*," *Journal of the History of Ideas* 31, no. 2 (April–June 1970): 199–218; Paul Hamilton, *Coleridge and German Philosophy: The Poet in the Land of Logic* (London: Continuum, 2007); and Alexander M. Schlutz, *Mind's World: Imagination and Subjectivity from Descartes to Romanticism* (Seattle: University of Washington Press, 2009), especially chapter 6.
29 Monika Class, *Coleridge and Kantian Ideas in England, 1796–1817: Coleridge's Responses to German Philosophy* (London: Bloomsbury, 2012), 154.
30 Schlutz, *Mind's World*, 216.
31 Kant, *Critique of Judgment*, 120–1.
32 Ibid., 119.
33 Seamus Perry, *Coleridge and the Uses of Division* (Oxford: Oxford University Press, 1999), 159.
34 Alan Vardy, "Coleridge on Broad Stand," *Romanticism and Victorianism on the Net* 61 (April 2012), par. 9, accessed 6 August 2014, doi: 10.7202/1018600ar.
35 Cf. *Oxford English Dictionary Online*, s.v. "palsy," A.1.a. and A.1.b., accessed 7 June 2017, http://www.oed.com/view/Entry/136554?.
36 Robert Mitchell, *Experimental Life: Vitalism in Romantic Science and Literature* (Baltimore: Johns Hopkins University Press, 2013), 45.
37 Ford, *Coleridge on Dreaming*, 52.
38 As with many of Coleridge's other borrowings, this instance was identified by Thomas De Quincey after Coleridge's death. See Alan Vardy's revisionary account of the scandal surrounding De Quincey's *Edinburgh*

Review articles in *Constructing Coleridge: The Posthumous Life of the Author* (Houndmills: Palgrave Macmillan, 2010), 26–44.

39 Luke 19:40, KJV.

40 Stuart Curran, *Poetic Form and British Romanticism* (New York: Oxford University Press, 1986), 60.

41 Stokes, *Coleridge, Language and the Sublime*, 126.

42 Noel B. Jackson, "Coleridge's Criticism of Life," *Coleridge Bulletin* n.s. 37 (Summer 2011): 22.

43 Ibid., 26–32.

44 Ibid., 28.

45 See also Celeste Langan's comparison of this passage to Coleridge's poetical experiments in "Christabel." "Pathologies of Communication from Coleridge to Schreber," *South Atlantic Quarterly* 102, no. 1 (Winter 2003): 136.

46 Karen Swann, "'Christabel': The Wandering Mother and the Enigma of Form," *Studies in Romanticism* 23, no. 4 (Winter 1984): 540.

47 Michael Tomko, *Beyond the Willing Suspension of Disbelief: Poetic Faith from Coleridge to Tolkien* (London: Bloomsbury 2016), 3.

48 See, for instance, Anthony J. Ferri, *Willing Suspension of Disbelief: Poetic Faith in Film* (Lanham, MD: Lexington Books, 2007). For a humorous treatment of the concept that suggests its cultural ubiquity, see "Suspension of Disbelief Goes Unrewarded," *The Onion*, 18 February 2011, http://www.theonion.com/article/suspension-of-disbelief-goes-unrewarded-19194.

49 Michael Tomko, "Politics, Performance, and Coleridge's 'Suspension of Disbelief,'" *Victorian Studies* 49, no. 2 (Winter 2007): 245. His expanded argument in chapters 1 and 2 of *Beyond the Willing Suspension of Disbelief* revisits these claims at greater length.

50 Tomko, "Politics, Performance," 244.

51 For accounts of the "gothic" reading practices that Coleridge deplores here, see Jon P. Klancher, *The Making of English Reading Audiences, 1790–1832* (Madison: University of Wisconsin Press, 1987); and E.J. Clery, *The Rise of Supernatural Fiction, 1762–1800* (Cambridge: Cambridge University Press, 1995).

52 Cf. Coleridge's gloss on this passage: "i.e. – By deep feeling we make our *Ideas dim* – & this is what we mean by our Life – ourselves. I think of the Wall – it is before me, a distinct Image – here. I necessarily think of the *Idea* & the Thinking I as two distinct and opposite Things. Now <let me> think of *myself* – of the thinking Being – the Idea becomes dim whatever it be – so dim that I know not what it is – but the Feeling is deep & steady – and this I call *I* – ~~the~~ identifying the Percipient & Perceived" (*CN* 1.921).

2. Semblances of Truth in "Christabel" and *Aids to Reflection*

1 Paul Hamilton, *Coleridge's Poetics* (Oxford: Basil Blackwell, 1983), 7.

2 Many of these qualities have been explored in the criticism. See especially Karen Swann, "'Christabel': The Wandering Mother and the Enigma of Form," *Studies in Romanticism* 23, no. 4 (Winter 1984): 533–53; Marjorie Levinson, *The Romantic Fragment Poem* (Chapel Hill: University of North Carolina Press, 1986); Swann, "Teaching *Christabel*: Gender and Genre," *Approaches to Teaching Coleridge's Poetry and Prose*, ed. Richard Matlak (New York: Modern Language Association, 1991), 121–7; Celeste Langan, "Pathologies of Communication from Coleridge to Schreber," *South Atlantic Quarterly* 102, no. 1 (Winter 2003): 117–52; and Jerrold E. Hogle, "'Christabel' as Gothic: The Abjection of Instability," *Gothic Studies* 7, no. 1 (May 2005): 18–27.

3 Elinor S. Shaffer, "Illusion and Imagination: Derrida's Parergon and Coleridge's Aid to Reflection. Revisionary Readings of Kantian Formalist Aesthetics," *Aesthetic Illusion: Theoretical and Historical Approaches*, ed. Frederick Burwick and Walter Pape (Berlin: Walter de Gruyter, 1990), 146.

4 Coleridge altered this preface in later editions. The version in *Poetical Works* (1834) replaces the comment about suspended animation with a more general reference to his "indolence" and removes any plans for finishing the poem (see *CPW* 1.1.481).

5 Tim Fulford, *The Late Poetry of the Lake Poets: Romanticism Revised* (Cambridge: Cambridge University Press, 2013), 115.

6 See, for instance, Walter Jackson Bate, *Coleridge* (New York: Macmillan, 1968); and John Beer, "Coleridge, Hazlitt, and 'Christabel,'" *Review of English Studies* 37, no. 145 (February 1986): 40–54. Susan Eilenberg casts the story within a larger structure of "dispossession": just as Christabel falls victim to Geraldine's influence, "Christabel" falls to Wordsworth's poetic presence in *Lyrical Ballads*. See *Strange Power of Speech: Wordsworth, Coleridge, and Literary Possession* (New York: Oxford University Press, 1992), 97–101.

7 Douglas Hedley, *Coleridge, Philosophy and Religion:* Aids to Reflection *and the Mirror of the Spirit* (Cambridge: Cambridge University Press, 2000), 90.

8 Anya Taylor, "Coleridge's 'Christabel' and the Phantom Soul," *SEL* 42, no. 4 (Autumn 2002): 707.

9 Hedley, *Coleridge, Philosophy and Religion*, 95.

10 Robert Mitchell, *Experimental Life: Vitalism in Romantic Science and Literature* (Baltimore: Johns Hopkins University Press, 2013), 93.

11 John Beer, "Coleridge and Wordsworth on Reflection," *Wordsworth Circle* 20, no. 1 (Winter 1989): 21, 23.

12 David Vallins, "The Feeling of Knowledge: Insight and Delusion in Coleridge," *ELH* 64, no. 1 (Spring 1997): 159. See also Alexander Schlutz's discussion of method and intuition in *The Friend* in *Mind's World: Imagination and Subjectivity from Descartes to Romanticism* (Seattle: University of Washington Press, 2009), 219–22.

13 Stephen Prickett, *Coleridge and Wordsworth: The Poetry of Growth* (Cambridge: Cambridge University Press, 1970), 26.

14 Sebastian Mitchell, "Dark Interpreter: Literary Uses of the Brocken Spectre from Coleridge to Pynchon," *Dalhousie Review* 87, no. 2 (2007): 168.

15 Prickett, *Coleridge and Wordsworth*, 23.

16 Mitchell, "Dark Interpreter," 171.

17 Morton Paley, *Coleridge's Later Poetry* (Oxford: Clarendon Press, 1996), 104.

18 Jennifer Ford, *Coleridge on Dreaming: Romanticism, Dreams and the Medical Imagination* (Cambridge: Cambridge University Press, 1998), 94.

19 Gavin Budge, *Romanticism, Medicine and the Natural Supernatural: Transcendent Vision and Bodily Spectres, 1789–1852* (Houndmills: Palgrave Macmillan, 2013), 105. Rei Terada finds similar lines of thought in the *Notebooks*. "Phenomenality and Dissatisfaction in Coleridge's *Notebooks*," *Studies in Romanticism* 43, no. 2 (Summer 2004): 257–81.

20 David Ward, *Coleridge and the Nature of Imagination: Evolution, Engagement with the World, and Poetry* (Houndmills: Palgrave Macmillan, 2013), 162.

21 Coleridge removed this line and the following one – "As on her bed she lay in sleep" – after 1816 (*CPP* 163n5).

22 Judith Halberstam defines the gothic as "the crisis occasioned by the inability to 'tell,' meaning both the inability to narrate and the inability to categorize." *Skin Shows: Gothic Horror and the Technology of Monsters* (Durham, NC: Duke University Press, 1995), 23. This remark is quoted by Leslie Ann Minot and Walter Minot, "*Frankenstein* and *Christabel*: Intertextuality, Biography, and Gothic Ambiguity," *European Romantic Review* 15, no. 1 (March 2004): 44.

23 Langan, "Pathologies of Communication," 126.

24 For examples of these interpretations, see Claire B. May, "'Christabel' and Abjection: Coleridge's Narrative in Process/on Trial," *SEL* 37, no. 4 (Autumn 1997): 699–721; Mark M. Hennelly, Jr, "'As Well Fill Up the Space Between': A Liminal Reading of *Christabel*," *Studies in Romanticism* 38, no. 2 (Summer 1999): 203–22; and Taylor, "Coleridge's 'Christabel' and the Phantom Soul."

25 Swann, "'Christabel': The Wandering Mother," 534.

26 Bate, *Coleridge*, 68.

27 Swann, "'Christabel': The Wandering Mother," 534.

28 Ibid., 543.
29 See Karen Swann, "Literary Gentlemen and Lovely Ladies: The Debate on the Character of *Christabel*," *ELH* 52, no. 2 (Summer 1985): 397–418.
30 Mary Favret, "The Questions of *Christabel*," *Approaches to Teaching Coleridge's Poetry and Prose*, ed. Richard Matlak (New York: Modern Language Association, 1991), 110.
31 Deborah Channick, "'A Logic of Its Own': Repetition in Coleridge's 'Christabel,'" *Romanticism and Victorianism on the Net* 50 (May 2008): par. 6, doi: 10.7202/018144ar.
32 Ford, *Coleridge on Dreaming*, 45. See also her longer discussion of "Christabel" as a poem of disturbed (and disturbing) sleep, 46–7.
33 Ward, *Coleridge and the Nature of Imagination*, 171.
34 *Oxford English Dictionary Online*, s.v. "askance," accessed 10 January 2017, http://www.oed.com/view/Entry/11511. See especially definitions A.1.b. and A.2.
35 Edmund Burke, *A Philosophical Enquiry into the Origin of Our Ideas of the Sublime and Beautiful*, ed. David Womersley (London: Penguin Classics, 2004), 101.
36 Eilenberg, *Strange Power*, 89. Ford makes a similar point about the unspeakable quality of dreams: "Both the language of the dream and the language in which to express the experience of a dream are unutterable" (*Coleridge on Dreaming*, 98–9).
37 Michael F. Andrews, "How (Not) to Find God in All Things: Derrida, Levinas, and St. Ignatius of Loyola on Learning How to Pray for the Impossible," *The Phenomenology of Prayer*, ed. Bruce Ellis Benson and Norman Wirzba (New York: Fordham University Press, 2005), 196.
38 Rom. 8:26 (KJV).
39 J. Robert Barth, "'In the Midnight Wood': The Power and Limits of Prayer in *Christabel*," *Wordsworth Circle* 32, no. 2 (Spring 2001): 81.
40 Andrew M. Cooper, "Who's Afraid of the Mastiff Bitch? Gothic Parody and Original Sin in *Christabel*," *Critical Essays on Samuel Taylor Coleridge*, ed. Leonard Orr (New York: G.K. Hall & Co., 1994), 93.
41 Matt. 6:5 (KJV).
42 Christopher Stokes, "Coleridge's Philosophy of Prayer: Responsibility, Parergon, and Catachresis," *Journal of Religion* 89, no. 4 (October 2009): 543.
43 Mitchell, "Dark Interpreter," 174. See also William S. Davis's reading of "The Pains of Sleep," which casts it as a poetic exploration of subjectivity. "'The Pains of Sleep': Philosophy, Poetry, Melancholy," *Prism(s): Essays In Romanticism* 9, no. 1 (2001): 51–64.

44 Ford, *Coleridge on Dreaming*, 47. See also Tim Fulford, "Coleridge's Visions of 1816: The Political Unconscious and the Poetic Fragment," *Romanticism and Victorianism on the Net* 61 (April 2012), doi: 10.7202/1018601ar.
45 Ford, *Coleridge on Dreaming*, 143–4.
46 Schlutz, *Mind's World*, 235.
47 For an overview of this period, see Richard Holmes, *Coleridge: Darker Reflections, 1804–1834* (New York: Pantheon Books, 1998), 343–72. See also Alan Vardy's account of the composition of *Aids to Reflection* as a process that began in these fraught years. *Constructing Coleridge: The Posthumous Life of the Author* (Houndmills: Palgrave Macmillan, 2010), 86–92.
48 I am indebted here to Vardy's reading of the Cottle letter as a prototype for the composition of *Aids to Reflection* (*Constructing Coleridge*, 88).
49 Beer, "Editor's Introduction," *AR* xlix.
50 Vardy, *Constructing Coleridge*, 88, 94.
51 Hedley, *Coleridge, Philosophy and Religion*, 117. Italics in original.
52 Murray J. Evans, "Sublime Discourse and Romantic Religion in Coleridge's *Aids to Reflection*," *Wordsworth Circle* 47, no. 1 (Winter 2016): 27.
53 John Beer points out this connection in his gloss on the passage (*AR* 86n31).
54 Michael S. Macovski, *Dialogue and Literature: Apostrophe, Auditors, and the Collapse of Romantic Discourse* (New York: Oxford University Press, 1994), 84; Anya Taylor, "Coleridge's Self-Representations," *The Oxford Handbook of Samuel Taylor Coleridge*, ed. Frederick Burwick (New York: Oxford University Press, 2012), 115.
55 Christopher Stokes, *Coleridge, Language and the Sublime: From Transcendence to Finitude* (Houndmills: Palgrave Macmillan, 2011), 102.
56 Douglas Hedley, "Was Coleridge a Romantic?" *Wordsworth Circle* 22, no. 1 (Winter 1991): 71.
57 Evans, "Sublime Discourse," 31.
58 Thomas De Quincey, *Susperia De Profundis*, in *The Works of Thomas De Quincey*, gen. ed. Grevel Lindop, 21 vols. (London: Pickering & Chatto, 2000–3), 15.142. See also the section of *Susperia De Profundis* on "The Apparition of the Brocken" (15.182–5), where De Quincey introduces the figure of the "dark interpreter."
59 Prickett, *Coleridge and Wordsworth*, 25.
60 On this point, see Prickett's discussion of Coleridge's influence on Maurice in *Romanticism and Religion: The Tradition of Coleridge and Wordsworth in the Victorian Church* (Cambridge: Cambridge University Press, 1976), 120–51; as well as Beer's "Editor's Introduction," *AR* cxxxiii–cxlix.

61 Frederick Denison Maurice, "To the Rev. Derwent Coleridge, Stanley Grove, Chelsea" (Dedication), *The Kingdom of Christ; or Hints Respecting the Principles, Constitution, and Ordinances of the Catholic Church*, 2nd ed. (New York: D. Appleton & Co., 1843), 11.

3. Ecstatic Suspension in Shelley's "Universe of Things"

1 See Sally West, *Coleridge and Shelley: Textual Engagement* (Aldershot: Ashgate, 2007), 22–3; and Michael O'Neill, "The Gleam of those Words: Coleridge and Shelley," *Keats-Shelley Review* 19 (2005): 76–96.

2 [Thomas Allsop], *Letters, Conversations, and Recollections of S.T. Coleridge* (New York: Harper & Brothers, 1836), 151.

3 See Edward Trelawny, *Records of Shelley, Byron, and the Author* (1878), 2 vols. (New York: Benjamin Blom, 1968), 1.163–4; and Ann Wroe, "Resolutions, Destinations: Shelley's Last Year," *The Oxford Handbook of Percy Bysshe Shelley*, ed. Michael O'Neill and Anthony Howe (New York: Oxford University Press, 2012), 48–64.

4 Percy Bysshe Shelley, *The Complete Poetry of Percy Bysshe Shelley*, ed. Donald Reiman, Neil Fraistat, and Nora Crook, 3 vols. (Baltimore: Johns Hopkins University Press, 2000–), 2.294.

5 Unless otherwise noted, Shelley's poetry is quoted from *Shelley's Poetry and Prose*, ed. Donald H. Reiman and Neil Fraistat, 2nd ed. (New York: W.W. Norton, 2002).

6 Christoph Bode, "A Kantian Sublime in Shelley: 'Respect for our Own Vocation' in an Indifferent Universe," *1650–1850: Ideas, Aesthetics, and Inquiries in the Early Modern Era* 3 (1997): 342. For discussions of Shelley's relationship to travel writing, see Benjamin Colbert, *Shelley's Eye: Travel Writing and Aesthetic Vision* (Aldershot: Ashgate, 2005); Christopher Hitt, "Shelley's Unwriting of Mont Blanc," *Texas Studies in Literature and Language* 47, no. 2 (Summer 2005): 139–66; and Michael Erkelenz, "The Poetry of Wandering: 'Mont Blanc' in *History of a Six Weeks' Tour*," *Keats-Shelley Journal* 63 (2014): 78–101.

7 Earl Wasserman, *Shelley: A Critical Reading* (Baltimore: Johns Hopkins University Press, 1971), 237.

8 Frances Ferguson, "Shelley's *Mont Blanc*: What the Mountain Said," *Romanticism and Language*, ed. Arden Reed (Ithaca: Cornell University Press, 1984), 213.

9 David S. Miall, "Foregrounding and the Sublime: Shelley in Chamonix," *Language and Literature* 16, no. 2 (2007): 157, 158.

10 Bode, "Kantian Sublime," 337.

11 Ibid., 358.

12 This remains one of the most widespread readings of "Mont Blanc." See especially Geoffrey Hartman, "Gods, Ghosts, and Shelley's 'Atheos,'" *Literature and Theology* 24, no. 1 (March 2010): 4–18. For an extended discussion of the relationship between Coleridge and Shelley that seeks to go beyond the parameters of the traditional influence study, see West, *Coleridge and Shelley*.

13 Immanuel Kant, *Critique of Judgment*, trans. Werner S. Pluhar (Indianapolis: Hackett, 1987), 120, 119.

14 Nigel Leask, "Mont Blanc's Mysterious Voice: Shelley and Huttonian Earth Science," *The Third Culture: Literature and Science*, ed. Elinor S. Shaffer (Berlin: de Gruyter, 1998), 187.

15 See Steven Shaviro, *The Universe of Things: On Speculative Realism* (Minneapolis: University of Minnesota Press, 2014), 57–9. Shaviro is one of several recent scholars to have read "Mont Blanc" as an early articulation of speculative realist philosophy or as a challenge to idealism. See also Louise Economides, "'Mont Blanc' and the Sublimity of Materiality," *Cultural Critique* 61 (Fall 2005): 87–114; Greg Ellermann, "Speculative Romanticism," *SubStance* 44, no. 1 (2015): 154–74; and Evan Gottlieb, *Romantic Realities: Speculative Realism and British Romanticism* (Edinburgh: Edinburgh University Press, 2016), 161–71. I develop my own speculative reading of "Mont Blanc" in "The Aesthetics of Contingency in the Shelleyan Universe of Things, or, 'Mont Blanc' without Mont Blanc," *Studies in Romanticism* 54, no. 3 (Fall 2015): 355–75.

16 Donald H. Reiman, ed., *Shelley and His Circle, 1773–1822*, 8 vols. (Cambridge, MA: Harvard University Press, 1986), 7.41.

17 Jeanne Moskal, "Travel Writing," *The Cambridge Companion to Mary Shelley*, ed. Esther Schor (Cambridge: Cambridge University Press, 2003), 243.

18 Zoe Bolton, "Collaborative Authorship and Shared Travel in *History of a Six Weeks' Tour*," *Mary Shelley: Her Circle and Her Contemporaries*, ed. L. Adam Meckler and Lucy Morrison (Newcastle-upon-Tyne: Cambridge Scholars, 2010), 8.

19 Jonathan Culler, *The Pursuit of Signs: Semiotics, Literature, Deconstruction*, augmented ed. (Ithaca: Cornell University Press, 2002), 152.

20 Ferguson, "Shelley's *Mont Blanc*," 205.

21 Jerrod E. Hogle, *Shelley's Process: Radical Transference and the Development of His Major Works* (New York: Oxford University Press, 1988), 76–7.

22 Ferguson, "Shelley's *Mont Blanc*," 212–13.

23 Cf. Noah Heringman, *Romantic Rocks, Aesthetic Geology* (Ithaca: Cornell University Press, 2004), 49–53.
24 Wasserman, *Shelley: A Critical Reading*, 228.
25 Leask, "Mont Blanc's Mysterious Voice," 189.
26 John Keats, *The Complete Poems*, 3rd ed., ed. John Barnard (New York: Penguin, 1988), 348.
27 For a reading of "Mont Blanc" as a critique of natural and political violence, see Matthew Borushko, "The Politics of Subreption: Resisting the Sublime in Shelley's 'Mont Blanc,'" *Studies in Romanticism* 52, no. 2 (Summer 2013): 225–52.
28 See Leask, "Mysterious Voice," 189–94.
29 Ferguson, "Shelley's *Mont Blanc*," 210.
30 See Michael Erkelenz, "Shelley's Draft of 'Mont Blanc' and the Conflict of 'Faith,'" *Review of English Studies*, 40, no. 157 (February 1989): 100–3.
31 Borushko, "Politics of Subreption," 225.
32 Laura Wells Betz's discussion of *Prometheus Unbound* explores the extent to which Shelley was both fascinated and troubled by the spellbinding capacities of poetic language. "'At once mild and animating': *Prometheus Unbound* and Shelley's Spell of Style," *European Romantic Review* 21, no. 2 (April 2010): 161–81.
33 William Keach, *Shelley's Style* (New York: Methuen, 1984), 199.
34 For a planetary perspective on the effects of the eruption, see Gillen D'Arcy Wood, *Tambora: The Eruption That Changed the World* (Princeton: Princeton University Press, 2014).
35 Kant, *Critique of Judgment*, 113, 114.
36 Zachary Sng, *The Rhetoric of Error from Locke to Kleist* (Stanford: Stanford University Press, 2010), 80.
37 Kant, *Critique of Judgment*, 105, 120.
38 Wasserman, *Shelley: A Critical Reading*, 182.
39 Percy Bysshe Shelley, *The Posthumous Poems of Percy Bysshe Shelley*, ed. Mary Wollstonecraft Shelley (London: John and Henry L. Hunt, 1824).
40 On Mary Shelley's editing of *Posthumous Poems*, see the essays by Mary Favret and Susan Wolfson in *The Other Mary Shelley: Beyond Frankenstein*, ed. Audrey Fisch, Anne Mellor, and Esther Schor (Oxford: Oxford University Press, 1993), 17–38 and 39–72, respectively.
41 Shelley, *Posthumous Poems*, 198.
42 Judith Chernaik comments, "Carpe diem poems usually have two parts; a statement of the brevity of life's pleasures, and an admonition to enjoy them while they last; and Shelley's lyric follows the pattern." *The Lyrics of Shelley* (Cleveland: Press of Case Western Reserve University, 1972), 155.

43 Mary Shelley, *Frankenstein, or The Modern Prometheus* (1818), 3rd ed., ed. D.L. Macdonald and Kathleen Scherf (Peterborough: Broadview Press, 2012), 116.
44 Ibid., 116–17.
45 For examples of this reading, see Mark Hansen, "'Not thus, after all, would life be given': *Technesis*, Technology and the Parody of Romantic Poetics in *Frankenstein*," *Studies in Romanticism* 36, no. 4 (Winter 1997): 595–600; and Sara Guyer, *Romanticism after Auschwitz* (Stanford: Stanford University Press, 1997), 79–88.
46 I follow the dating scheme proposed by Charles Robinson, who makes the case that Mary Shelley had in mind the period of time that runs from her conception to thirteen days after her birth in the years 1796–7. See *The Frankenstein Notebooks, Part 1*, ed. Charles E. Robinson (New York: Garland Publishing: 1996), lxv–lxvi.
47 Mary Shelley, *Frankenstein*, 142.

4. Tennyson and the Rhetoric of Suspended Animation

1 William Wordsworth, "Ode" ["There was a time"], *The Major Works*, ed. Stephen Gill (Oxford: Oxford University Press, 1984), 300.
2 All quotations from Tennyson's poetry are taken from *The Poems of Tennyson*, 2nd ed., ed. Christopher Ricks, 3 vols. (Essex: Longman, 1987). Subsequent line numbers and, where appropriate, section numbers will be given parenthetically.
3 Hallam Tennyson, *Alfred Lord Tennyson: A Memoir, by his son*, 2 vols. (London: Macmillan, 1897), 1.396.
4 Ruth Richardson, *Death, Dissection and the Destitute*, 2nd ed. (Chicago: University of Chicago Press, 2000), 7.
5 For a detailed account of the debates concerning the Anatomy Act, see ibid., 75–215.
6 George K. Behlmer, "Grave Doubts: Victorian Medicine, Moral Panic, and the Signs of Death," *Journal of British Studies* 42, no. 2 (April 2003): 214.
7 Ibid., 208.
8 E. Warwick Slinn, *The Discourse of Self in Victorian Poetry* (Houndmills: Macmillan, 1991), 82.
9 Qtd. in Hallam Tennyson, *Alfred Lord Tennyson: A Memoir*, 1.398.
10 George Levine, who has written extensively on the connections between Victorian narrative fiction and scientific experimentation, remarks that "Epistemology, one might say, is something like a Victorian novel." *Dying to Know: Scientific Epistemology and Narrative in Victorian England* (Chicago: University of Chicago Press, 2002), 20.

11 See, for instance, Jonathan Wordsworth, "'What is it, that has been done?' The Central Problem of *Maud*," *Essays in Criticism* 24, no. 4 (1974): 356–62.
12 Seamus Perry, *Alfred Tennyson* (Tavistock: Northcote Press, 2005), 118.
13 Slinn, *Discourse of Self*, 76.
14 Paul de Man, *Allegories of Reading: Figural Language in Rousseau, Nietzsche, Rilke, and Proust* (New Haven: Yale University Press, 1979), 9.
15 Ibid., 12.
16 Richardson, *Death*, 227. Carolyn J. Lawes notes a similar connection between accounts of live burial panics and cholera outbreaks in antebellum American periodicals. "Buried Alive? Fear of Failure in Antebellum America," *Journal of American Culture* 37, no. 3 (September 2014): 301.
17 See Jan Bondeson, *Buried Alive! The Terrifying History of Our Most Primal Fear* (New York: W.W. Norton, 2001), 137–54.
18 James Curry, *Observations on Apparent Death from Drowning, Hanging, Suffocation &c. with an Account of the Means to be Employed for Recovery* (Northampton: Dicey and Co., 1792), 3, 4.
19 Edgar Allan Poe, "The Premature Burial," *Poetry and Tales* (New York: Library of America, 1984), 667.
20 Ibid., 667, 668.
21 A.T. Thomson, "Lectures on Medical Jurisprudence, Now in the Course of Delivery at the University of London. Lecture XXX: Sudden Death," *Lancet* 2, no. 713 (29 April 1837): 178. Thomson was a respected physician trained in Edinburgh and London and one of the first professors of medicine at University College, London. See "Notice on the Life and Writings of Dr Antony Todd Thomson," *Edinburgh Medical and Surgical Journal* 78 (1 October 1852): 446–61.
22 Elizabeth Gaskell, "Clopton House," *The Works of Mrs. Gaskell*, ed. Adolphus William Ward, 8 vols. (London: Smith, Elder & Co., 1906), 1.506.
23 Poe, "The Premature Burial," 667.
24 Ibid., 673.
25 Horace Smith, "Posthumous Memoir of Myself," *New Monthly Magazine and Humorist* 87, no. 345 (September 1849): 9. Further instalments appeared in the issues of October and November 1849. That Smith, according to the editor's note, died just before the first instalment went to press almost too perfectly intensifies the posthumous nature of the "Posthumous Memoir." Smith was for many years the financial adviser and friend of Percy Bysshe Shelley, who wrote in the "Letter to Maria Gisborne" (1820) that "Wit and sense, / Virtue and human knowledge, all that might / Make this dull world a business of delight, / Are all combined in Horace Smith" (247–50).

26 [George Henry Lewes], "Death-in-Life," *Fraser's Magazine for Town and Country* 36, no. 211 (July 1847): 110.

27 Ibid., 109.

28 Unlikely, but not entirely implausible, as suggested by research on anaesthesia awareness. Patients who suffer from this condition, which can only be diagnosed after the fact, recall having experienced consciousness and sensations of pain when they have supposedly been put under general anaesthesia for major surgery. See Michael S. Avidan et al., "Anesthesia Awareness and the Bispectral Index," *New England Journal of Medicine* 358, no. 11 (13 March 2008): 1097–1107. I am grateful to Mira Batra for alerting me to this connection.

29 Lawes, "Buried Alive?" 310.

30 Behlmer, "Grave Doubts," 208–9.

31 See Erin E. Forbes, "From Prison Cell to Slave Ship: Social Death in 'The Premature Burial,'" *Poe Studies* 46 (2013): 32–58.

32 Lawes, "Buried Alive?" 299.

33 Clyde de L. Ryals, "The 'Weird Seizures' in *The Princess*," *Texas Studies in Literature and Language* 4, no. 2 (Summer 1962): 268.

34 Barbara Herb Wright, "Tennyson, the Weird Seizures in *The Princess*, and Epilepsy," *Literature and Medicine* 6 (1987): 62.

35 Eve Kosofsky Sedgwick, *Between Men: English Literature and Male Homosocial Desire* (New York: Columbia University Press, 1985), 130.

36 D.B. Ruderman, *The Idea of Infancy in Nineteenth-Century British Poetry: Romanticism, Subjectivity, Form* (New York and London: Routledge, 2016), 205.

37 Poe, "Premature Burial," 675–6.

38 Andrew Mangham, "Buried Alive: The Gothic Awakening of Taphophobia," *Journal of Literature and Science* 3, no. 1 (2010): 13.

39 Robert Browning, *Robert Browning's Poetry*, 2nd ed., ed. James F. Loucks and Andrew M. Stauffer (New York: W.W. Norton, 2007), 182.

40 Scott Dransfield, "The Morbid Meters of *Maud*," *Victorian Poetry* 46, no. 3 (Fall 2008): 286.

41 Francis O'Gorman, "What Is Haunting Tennyson's *Maud* (1855)?" *Victorian Poetry* 48, no. 3 (Fall 2010): 293.

42 Dransfield, "Morbid Meters," 283.

43 Qtd. in Tennyson, *Poems of Tennyson*, 2.551–2n.

44 O'Gorman, "What Is Haunting," 304.

45 Of course, if Maud is truly not the child of her father, the most obvious reason would be that her mother had been unfaithful to her husband. Considering that the only other father figure in the poem is the speaker's, there may even be the implication of incest in this attempt to revise Maud's parentage.

46 See Susan Shatto, ed., *Tennyson's Maud: A Definitive Edition* (London: Athlone Press, 1986), 208–9.
47 Aidan Day, *Tennyson's Scepticism* (Houndmills: Palgrave Macmillan, 2005), 156.
48 Gerhard Joseph, *Tennyson and the Text: The Weaver's Shuttle* (Cambridge: Cambridge University Press, 1992), 36.
49 See Anna Barton, *Tennyson's Name: Identity and Responsibility in the Poetry of Alfred Lord Tennyson* (Aldershot: Ashgate, 2008), 73.
50 Richardson, *Death*, 273.
51 Eve Kosofsky Sedgwick, *The Coherence of Gothic Conventions* (New York: Methuen, 1986), 20.
52 Herbert F. Tucker, *Tennyson and the Doom of Romanticism* (Cambridge, MA: Harvard University Press, 1988), 426.
53 Slinn, *Discourse of Self*, 84.
54 Kirstie Blair, *Victorian Poetry and the Culture of the Heart* (Oxford: Oxford University Press, 2006), 171.
55 Tucker, *Tennyson and the Doom of Romanticism*, 380–1.
56 Matthew Rowlinson, "The Thing in the Poem: *Maud*'s Hymen," *differences: A Journal of Feminist Cultural Studies* 12, no. 3 (Fall 2001): 148.
57 Tucker, *Tennyson and the Doom of Romanticism*, 351.
58 George Eliot, *Selected Critical Writings*, ed. Rosemary Ashton (Oxford: Oxford World's Classics, 2000), 173.
59 Ibid., 178.
60 Samuel Schulman, "Mourning and Voice in *Maud*," *SEL* 23 (1983), 645.
61 See Peter McCandless, "Liberty and Lunacy: The Victorians and Wrongful Confinement," *Journal of Social History* 11, no. 3 (Spring 1978): 366–86; and "Dangerous to Themselves and Others: The Victorian Debate over the Prevention of Wrongful Confinement," *Journal of British Studies* 23, no. 1 (Autumn 1983): 84–104.
62 Ryals, "'Weird Seizures,'" 271.
63 Hallam Tennyson, *Alfred Lord Tennyson: A Memoir*, 1.320.
64 Perry, *Alfred Tennyson*, 95, 82.
65 Hallam Tennyson, *Alfred Lord Tennyson: A Memoir*, 1.395–6.
66 Tucker, *Tennyson and the Doom of Romanticism*, 406.

5. Christina Rossetti's Poetic Faith

1 All quotations from Rossetti's poetry are taken from *The Complete Poems of Christina Rossetti*, ed. Rebecca Crump, 3 vols. (Baton Rouge: Louisiana State University Press, 1979–2000). Line numbers will be given parenthetically.

2 Isobel Armstrong, *Victorian Poetry: Poetry, Poetics and Politics* (London: Routledge, 1993), 357.
3 Antony H. Harrison, *Christina Rossetti in Context* (Chapel Hill: University of North Carolina Press, 1988), 84–5.
4 Dinah Roe, *Christina Rossetti's Faithful Imagination: The Devotional Poetry and Prose* (Houndmills: Palgrave Macmillan, 2007); Emma Mason, "Christina Rossetti and the Doctrine of Reserve," *Journal of Victorian Culture* 7, no. 2 (Autumn 2002): 196–219; Andrew D. Armond, "Limited Knowledge and the Tractarian Doctrine of Reserve in Christina Rossetti's *The Face of the Deep*," *Victorian Poetry* 48, no. 2 (Summer 2010): 219–41; and Elizabeth Ludlow, *Christina Rossetti and the Bible: Waiting with the Saints* (London: Bloomsbury, 2014).
5 G.B. Tennyson, *Victorian Devotional Poetry: The Tractarian Mode* (Cambridge, MA: Harvard University Press, 1991), 45.
6 Roe, *Christina Rossetti's Faithful Imagination*, 13.
7 Mason, "Christina Rossetti and the Doctrine of Reserve," 208.
8 Roe, *Christina Rossetti's Faithful Imagination*, 9.
9 See Isobel Armstrong's discussion of Rossetti's "pausal poetics" in *A Pageant and other poems* (1881). "Christina Rossetti in the Era of the New Woman and *fin de siècle* Culture," *Journal of Pre-Raphaelite Studies* 13 (2004): 32.
10 Constance Hassett, *Christina Rossetti: The Patience of Style* (Charlottesville: University of Virginia Press, 2005), 87.
11 William Michael Rossetti, comp., *Rossetti Papers: 1862 to 1870* (New York: Charles Scribner's Sons, 1903), 83.
12 William M. Rossetti, "Preface," *Poems of Christina Rossetti*, ed. William Michael Rossetti (London: Macmillan and Co., 1904), ix.
13 Mary Arseneau, *Recovering Christina Rossetti* (Houndmills: Palgrave Macmillan, 2004), 144–5.
14 See, for instance, Linda Peterson, "Restoring the Book: The Typological Hermeneutics of Christina Rossetti and the PRB," *Victorian Poetry* 32, no. 3/4 (Autumn–Winter 1994): 209–32.
15 Dawn Henwood, "Christian Allegory and Subversive Poetics: Christina Rossetti's *Prince's Progress* Reconsidered," *Victorian Poetry* 35, no. 1 (Spring 1997): 84, 86.
16 Arseneau, *Recovering*, 156. See also Joan Rees, "Christina Rossetti: Poet," *Critical Quarterly* 26, no. 3 (September 1984): 59–72.
17 Mary Arseneau, "Pilgrimage and Postponement: Christina Rossetti's *The Prince's Progress*," *Victorian Poetry* 32, no. 3/4 (Autumn–Winter 1994): 295.
18 Henwood, "Christian Allegory," 87.

19 Simon Humphries, "Who Is the Alchemist in Christina Rossetti's 'The Prince's Progress'?" *Review of English Studies* 58, no. 237 (November 2007): 685.

20 See Kerry McSweeney's discussion of *Goblin Market* in *What's the Import? Nineteenth-Century Poems and Contemporary Critical Practice* (Montreal and Kingston: McGill-Queen's University Press, 2007), 57–62.

21 Kathy Alexis Psomiades, "Whose Body? Christina Rossetti and Aestheticist Femininity," *Women and British Aestheticism*, ed. Talia Schaffer and Kathy Alexis Psomiades (Charlottesville: University Press of Virginia, 1999), 113.

22 Susan Shatto, ed., *Tennyson's Maud: A Definitive Edition* (London: Athlone Press, 1986), 20.

23 Dolores Rosenblum, *Christina Rossetti: The Poetry of Endurance* (Carbondale: Southern Illinois University Press, 1986), 46–7. For alternative interpretations of Dante Gabriel's influence on *The Prince's Progress*, see Hassett, *Christina Rossetti*, 86–9; Katherine J. Mayberry, *Christina Rossetti and the Poetry of Discovery* (Baton Rouge: Louisiana State University Press, 1989), 10, 41–2; and Arseneau, *Recovering*, 158–62. For a broader critical reading of the siblings' creative relationship, see Allison Chapman, *The Afterlife of Christina Rossetti* (Houndmills: Palgrave Macmillan, 2000), especially chapters 4 and 5.

24 Crump dates the composition of lines 481–540 ("The Fairy Prince Who Arrived Too Late") to October 1861 and the rest of the poem to January 1865 (*Complete Poems of Christina Rossetti*, 1.266).

25 The line numbers given refer to *The Prince's Progress* as a whole.

26 Rees, "Christina Rossetti: Poet," 69.

27 Diane D'Amico groups *The Prince's Progress*, along with *Goblin Market* and the less well known "Maiden-Song," under the general rubric of "Christian Fairy-Tale poems" in *Christina Rossetti: Faith, Gender, and Time* (Baton Rouge: Louisiana State University Press, 1999), 68.

28 Harrison, *Christina Rossetti in Context*, 117.

29 Chapman, *Afterlife*, 75.

30 Kathryn Burlinson, *Christina Rossetti* (Plymouth: Northcote House, 1988), 23.

31 Psomiades, "Whose Body?" 110.

32 Anne Jamison, *Poetics en Passant: Redefining the Relationship between Victorian and Modern Poetry* (Houndmills: Palgrave Macmillan, 2009), 132.

33 Heather Dubrow, "The Interplay of Narrative and Lyric: Competition, Cooperation, and the Case of the Anticipatory Amalgam," *Narrative* 14, no. 3 (October 2006): 254–71.

34 Ibid., 265.

35 William Michael Rossetti, ed., *Rossetti Papers*, 77–8.

36 Rees hints at this connection in passing, observing that "The glittering and gleaming of her eyes are reminiscent of Coleridge's Geraldine" ("Christina Rossetti: Poet," 62).

37 Noelle Bowles, "A Chink in the Armour: Christina Rossetti's 'The Prince's Progress,' 'A Royal Princess,' and Victorian Medievalism," *Women's Writing* 12, no. 1 (2005): 120.

38 Rees, "Christina Rossetti: Poet," 62.

39 Ibid., 70.

40 See also Humphries' discussion of the alchemist as the allegorical figure of the Jew and thus the avatar of the "old dispensation of labour under the law [that] must pass away in order that man may emerge from that bondage" ("Who Is the Alchemist?" 692).

41 Cf. Robert Mitchell, *Experimental Life: Vitalism in Romantic Science and Literature* (Baltimore: Johns Hopkins University Press, 2013), 45–7.

42 Humphries, "Who Is the Alchemist?" 697.

43 Arseneau, "Pilgrimage and Postponement," 288.

44 Rees, "Christina Rossetti: Poet," 64.

45 David Collings, "After the Covenant: Romanticism, Secularization, and Disastrous Transcendence," *European Romantic Review* 21, no. 3 (June 2010): 347.

46 Henwood, "Christian Allegory," 92.

47 Arseneau, *Recovering*, 156.

48 Christina Rossetti, *The Face of The Deep: A Devotional Commentary on the Apocalypse* (London: Society for Promoting Christian Knowledge, 1892), 118.

49 Ibid., 119.

50 Christina Rossetti, *Time Flies: A Reading Diary* (London: Society for Promoting Christian Knowledge, 1902), 137.

51 Armstrong, "Christina Rossetti in the Era of the New Woman," 31.

Conclusion

1 Christina Rossetti, "A Pause of Thought," *The Complete Poems of Christina Rossetti*, ed. Rebecca Crump, 3 vols. (Baton Rouge: Louisiana State University Press, 1979–2000), lines 9–12.

2 David Collings, "After the Covenant: Romanticism, Secularization, and Disastrous Transcendence," *European Romantic Review* 21, no. 3 (June 2010): 351, 352.

3 Jacques Derrida, "Living On/Border Lines," trans. J. Hulbert, *Deconstruction and Criticism* (London: Continuum, 2004), 85.

4 Ibid., 63.

5 I have argued elsewhere for the status of suspension as a constitutive, though largely unexplored, term in Derrida's thought. See Anne C. McCarthy, "Suspension," *Jacques Derrida: Key Concepts*, ed. Claire Colebrook (London and New York: Routledge, 2015), 23–30.

6 Walter H. Pater, *Studies in the History of the Renaissance* (London: Macmillan and Co., 1873), 209–10.

7 Catherine Gallagher, "Formalism and Time," *MLQ* 61, no. 1 (March 2000): 240, 242, 247.

8 Caroline Levine, *Forms: Whole, Rhythm, Hierarchy, Network* (Princeton: Princeton University Press, 2015), 129.

9 Claire Colebrook, "Not Kant, Not Now: Another Sublime," *Speculations: A Journal of Speculative Realism* 5 (2014): 137.

10 Jacques Derrida, "Psyche: Invention of the Other," trans. Catherine Porter, *Psyche: Inventions of the Other, Vol. 1*, ed. Peggy Kamuf and Elizabeth Rottenberg (Stanford: Stanford University Press, 2007), 15.

Bibliography

[Allsop, Thomas.] *Letters, Conversations, and Recollections of S.T. Coleridge*. New York: Harper & Brothers, 1836.

Andrews, Michael F. "How (Not) to Find God in All Things: Derrida, Levinas, and St. Ignatius of Loyola on Learning How to Pray for the Impossible." *The Phenomenology of Prayer*, edited by Bruce Ellis Benson and Norman Wirzba, 195–208. New York: Fordham University Press, 2005.

Armstrong, Isobel. "Christina Rossetti in the Era of the New Woman and *fin de siècle* Culture." *Journal of Pre-Raphaelite Studies* 13 (2004): 21–48.

– *Victorian Poetry: Poetry, Poetics and Politics*. London: Routledge, 1993.

Armond, Andrew D. "Limited Knowledge and the Tractarian Doctrine of Reserve in Christina Rossetti's *The Face of the Deep*." *Victorian Poetry* 48, no. 2 (Summer 2010): 219–41.

Arnold, Matthew. *The Poetical Works of Matthew Arnold*. New York: Thomas Y. Crowell & Co., 1897.

Arseneau, Mary. "Pilgrimage and Postponement: Christina Rossetti's *The Prince's Progress*." *Victorian Poetry* 32, no. 3/4 (Autumn–Winter 1994): 279–98.

– *Recovering Christina Rossetti*. Houndmills: Palgrave Macmillan, 2004.

Avidan, Michael S., et al. "Anesthesia Awareness and the Bispectral Index." *New England Journal of Medicine* 358, no. 11 (13 March 2008): 1097–1108.

Barth, J. Robert. "'In the Midnight Wood': The Power and Limits of Prayer in *Christabel*." *Wordsworth Circle* 32, no. 2 (Spring 2001): 78–83.

Barton, Anna. *Tennyson's Name: Identity and Responsibility in the Poetry of Alfred Lord Tennyson*. Aldershot: Ashgate, 2008.

Bate, Walter Jackson. *Coleridge*. New York: Macmillan, 1968.

Beer, John. "Coleridge and Wordsworth on Reflection." *Wordsworth Circle* 20, no. 1 (Winter 1989): 20–9.

– "Coleridge, Hazlitt, and 'Christabel.'" *Review of English Studies* 37, no. 145 (February 1986): 40–54.

– *Coleridge's Poetic Intelligence*. Houndmills: Macmillan, 1977.

Behlmer, George K. "Grave Doubts: Victorian Medicine, Moral Panic, and the Signs of Death." *Journal of British Studies* 42, no. 2 (April 2003): 206–35.

Betz, Laura Wells. "'At once mild and animating': *Prometheus Unbound* and Shelley's Spell of Style." *European Romantic Review* 21, no. 2 (April 2010): 161–81.

Blair, Kirstie. *Victorian Poetry and the Culture of the Heart*. Oxford: Oxford University Press, 2006.

Bode, Christoph. "A Kantian Sublime in Shelley: 'Respect for our Own Vocation' in an Indifferent Universe." *1650–1850: Ideas, Aesthetics, and Inquiries in the Early Modern Era* 3 (1997): 329–58.

Bolton, Zoe. "Collaborative Authorship and Shared Travel in *History of a Six Weeks' Tour*." *Mary Shelley: Her Circle and Her Contemporaries*, edited by L. Adam Meckler and Lucy Morrison, 7–25. Newcastle-upon-Tyne: Cambridge Scholars, 2010.

Bondeson, Jan. *Buried Alive! The Terrifying History of Our Most Primal Fear*. New York: W.W. Norton, 2001.

Borushko, Matthew. "The Politics of Subreption: Resisting the Sublime in Shelley's 'Mont Blanc.'" *Studies in Romanticism* 52, no. 2 (Summer 2013): 225–52.

Bowles, Noelle. "A Chink in the Armour: Christina Rossetti's 'The Prince's Progress,' 'A Royal Princess,' and Victorian Medievalism." *Women's Writing* 12, no. 1 (2005): 115–26.

Bromwich, David. *Disowned by Memory: Wordsworth's Poetry of the 1790s*. Chicago: University of Chicago Press, 1998.

Brontë, Charlotte. *Villette*. Edited by Mark Lilly. London: Penguin Classics, 1985.

Browning, Robert. *Robert Browning's Poetry*. 2nd ed., edited by James F. Loucks and Andrew M. Stauffer. New York: W.W. Norton, 2007.

Budge, Gavin. *Romanticism, Medicine and the Natural Supernatural: Transcendent Vision and Bodily Spectres, 1789–1852*. Houndmills: Palgrave Macmillan, 2013.

Burke, Edmund. *A Philosophical Enquiry into the Origin of Our Ideas of the Sublime and Beautiful*. Edited by David Womersley. London: Penguin Classics, 2004.

Burlinson, Kathryn. *Christina Rossetti*. Plymouth: Northcote House, 1998.

Chandler, James. *England in 1819: The Politics of Literary Culture and the Case of Romantic Historicism*. Chicago: University of Chicago Press, 1998.

Channick, Deborah. "'A Logic of Its Own': Repetition in Coleridge's 'Christabel.'" *Romanticism and Victorianism on the Net* 50 (May 2008). doi: 10.7202/018144ar.

Chapman, Allison. *The Afterlife of Christina Rossetti*. Houndmills: Palgrave Macmillan, 2000.

Chernaik, Judith. *The Lyrics of Shelley*. Cleveland: Press of Case Western Reserve University, 1972.

Christensen, Jerome. *Lord Byron's Strength: Romantic Writing and Commercial Society*. Baltimore: Johns Hopkins University Press, 1993.

Class, Monika. *Coleridge and Kantian Ideas in England, 1796–1817: Coleridge's Responses to German Philosophy*. London: Bloomsbury, 2012.

Clery, E.J. *The Rise of Supernatural Fiction, 1762–1800*. Cambridge: Cambridge University Press, 1995.

Cohn, Elisha. *Still Life: Suspended Development in the Victorian Novel*. Oxford: Oxford University Press, 2016.

Colbert, Benjamin. *Shelley's Eye: Travel Writing and Aesthetic Vision*. Aldershot: Ashgate, 2005.

Colebrook, Claire. "Not Kant, Not Now: Another Sublime." *Speculations: A Journal of Speculative Realism* 5 (2014): 127–57.

Coleridge, Samuel Taylor. *Aids to Reflection*. Edited by John Beer. Princeton: Princeton University Press, 1993. (*AR*)

– *Biographia Literaria*. 2 vols., edited by James Engell and W. Jackson Bate. Princeton: Princeton University Press, 1983. (*BL*)

– *Coleridge's Poetry and Prose*. Edited by Nicholas Halmi, Paul Magnuson, and Raimonda Modiano. New York: W.W. Norton, 2004. (*CPP*)

– *Collected Letters of Samuel Taylor Coleridge*. 6 vols., edited by Earl Leslie Griggs. Oxford: Clarendon Press, 1956–71. (*CL*)

– *The Friend*. 2 vols., edited by Barbara E. Rooke. Princeton: Princeton University Press, 1967. (*Friend*)

– *Notebooks*. 5 vols., edited by Kathleen Coburn, Merton Christensen, and Anthony John Harding. Princeton: Princeton University Press, 1957–2002. (*CN*)

– *Poetical Works*. 2 vols., edited by J.C.C. Mays. Princeton: Princeton University Press, 2001. (*CPW*)

– *Shorter Works and Fragments*. 2 vols., edited by H.J. Jackson and J.R. de J. Jackson. Princeton: Princeton University Press, 1995. (*SWF*)

Colley, Ann C. *Victorians in the Mountains: Sinking the Sublime*. Farnham: Taylor and Francis, 2010.

Collings, David. "After the Covenant: Romanticism, Secularization, and Disastrous Transcendence." *European Romantic Review* 21, no. 3 (June 2010): 345–61.

Cooper, Andrew M. "Who's Afraid of the Mastiff Bitch? Gothic Parody and Original Sin in *Christabel*." *Critical Essays on Samuel Taylor Coleridge*, edited by Leonard Orr, 81–107. New York: G.K. Hall & Co., 1994.

Corrigan, Timothy. "Interpreting the Uncitable Text: The Literary Criticism of Thomas De Quincey." *Ineffability: Naming the Unnamable from Dante to Beckett*, edited by Peter S. Hawkins and Anne Howland Schotter, 131–46. New York: AMS Press, 1984.

Crary, Jonathan. *Suspensions of Perception: Attention, Spectacle, and Modern Culture*. Cambridge, MA: MIT Press, 1999.

Culler, Jonathan. *The Pursuit of Signs: Semiotics, Literature, Deconstruction*. Augmented edition. Ithaca: Cornell University Press, 2002.

Curran, Stuart. *Poetic Form and British Romanticism*. New York: Oxford University Press, 1986.

Curry, James. *Observations on Apparent Death from Drowning, Hanging, Suffocation &c. with an Account of the Means to be Employed for Recovery*. Northampton: Dicey and Co., 1792.

D'Amico, Diane. *Christina Rossetti: Faith, Gender, and Time*. Baton Rouge: Louisiana State University Press, 1999.

Davis, William S. "'The Pains of Sleep': Philosophy, Poetry, Melancholy." *Prism(s): Essays in Romanticism* 9, no. 1 (2001): 51–64.

Day, Aidan. *Tennyson's Scepticism*. Houndmills: Palgrave Macmillan, 2005.

de Man, Paul. *Allegories of Reading: Figural Language in Rousseau, Nietzsche, Rilke, and Proust*. New Haven: Yale University Press, 1979.

– *The Rhetoric of Romanticism*. New York: Columbia University Press, 1984.

De Quincey, Thomas. *The Works of Thomas De Quincey*. 21 vols., general editor Grevel Lindop. London: Pickering & Chatto, 2000–3.

Derrida, Jacques. "Living On/Border Lines." Translated by J. Hulbert in *Deconstruction and Criticism*, 62–142. London: Continuum, 2004.

– "Psyche: Invention of the Other." Translated by Catherine Porter in *Psyche: Inventions of the Other, Vol. 1*, edited by Peggy Kamuf and Elizabeth Rottenberg, 2–47. Stanford: Stanford University Press, 2007.

Dransfield, Scott. "The Morbid Meters of *Maud*." *Victorian Poetry* 46, no. 3 (Fall 2008): 279–97.

Dubrow, Heather. "The Interplay of Narrative and Lyric: Competition, Cooperation, and the Case of the Anticipatory Amalgam." *Narrative* 14, no. 3 (October 2006): 254–71.

Duffy, Cian. *The Landscapes of the Sublime, 1700–1830: Classic Ground*. Houndmills: Palgrave Macmillan, 2013.

Economides, Louise. "'Mont Blanc' and the Sublimity of Materiality." *Cultural Critique* 61 (Fall 2005): 87–114.

Eilenberg, Susan. *Strange Power of Speech: Wordsworth, Coleridge, and Literary Possession*. New York: Oxford University Press, 1992.

Eliot, George. *Scenes of Clerical Life*. Edited by David Lodge. Harmondsworth: Penguin Classics, 1973.

– *Selected Critical Writings*. Edited by Rosemary Ashton. New York: Oxford World's Classics, 2000.

Ellermann, Greg. "Speculative Romanticism." *SubStance* 44, no. 1 (2015): 154–74.

Erkelenz, Michael. "The Poetry of Wandering: 'Mont Blanc' in *History of a Six Weeks' Tour*." *Keats-Shelley Journal* 63 (2014): 78–101.

– "Shelley's Draft of 'Mont Blanc' and the Conflict of 'Faith.'" *Review of English Studies* 40, no. 157 (February 1989): 100–3

Esterhammer, Angela. *The Romantic Performative: Language and Action in British and German Romanticism*. Stanford: Stanford University Press, 2000.

Evans, Murray J. "Sublime Discourse and Romantic Religion in Coleridge's *Aids to Reflection*." *Wordsworth Circle* 47, no. 1 (Winter 2016): 27–31.

Faflak, Joel. *Romantic Psychoanalysis: The Burden of the Mystery*. Albany: State University of New York Press, 2008.

Faflak, Joel, and Julia M. Wright, eds. *Nervous Reactions: Victorian Recollections of Romanticism*. Albany: State University of New York Press, 2004.

Favret, Mary. "The Questions of *Christabel*." *Approaches to Teaching Coleridge's Poetry and Prose*, edited by Richard Matlak, 110–20. New York: Modern Language Association, 1991.

Felluga, Dino Franco. *The Perversity of Poetry: Romantic Ideology and the Popular Male Poet of Genius*. Albany: State University of New York Press, 2005.

Ferguson, Frances. "Shelley's *Mont Blanc*: What the Mountain Said." *Romanticism and Language*, edited by Arden Reed, 202–14. Ithaca: Cornell University Press, 1984.

Ferri, Anthony J. *Willing Suspension of Disbelief: Poetic Faith in Film*. Lanham, MD: Lexington Books, 2007.

Fisch, Audrey, Anne Mellor, and Esther Schor, eds. *The Other Mary Shelley: Beyond Frankenstein*. Oxford: Oxford University Press, 1993.

Forbes, Erin E. "From Prison Cell to Slave Ship: Social Death in 'The Premature Burial.'" *Poe Studies* 46 (2013): 32–58.

Ford, Jennifer. *Coleridge on Dreaming: Romanticism, Dreams and the Medical Imagination*. Cambridge: Cambridge University Press, 1998.

François, Anne-Lise. *Open Secrets: The Literature of Uncounted Experience*. Stanford: Stanford University Press, 2008.

Freedgood, Elaine, and Maureen McLane. "'Romantic Realism/Victorian Romance': An Introduction to Four Provocations." *Romanticism and Victorianism on the Net* 64 (October 2013), doi: 10.7202/1025674ar.

Fulford, Tim. *Coleridge's Figurative Language*. Houndmills: Macmillan, 1991.
– "Coleridge's Visions of 1816: The Political Unconscious and the Poetic Fragment." *Romanticism and Victorianism on the Net* 61 (April 2012). doi: 10.7202/1018601ar.
– "Conducting the Vital Fluid: The Politics and Poetics of Mesmerism in the 1790s." *Studies in Romanticism* 43, no. 1 (Spring 2004): 57–78.
– *The Late Poetry of the Lake Poets: Romanticism Revised*. Cambridge: Cambridge University Press, 2013.
Gallagher, Catherine. "Formalism and Time." *MLQ* 61, no. 1 (March 2000): 229–51.
Gaskell, Elizabeth. *The Works of Mrs. Gaskell*. 8 vols., edited by Adolphus William Ward. London: Smith, Elder & Co., 1906.
Gottlieb, Evan. *Romantic Realities: Speculative Realism and British Romanticism*. Edinburgh: Edinburgh University Press, 2016.
Guyer, Sara. *Romanticism after Auschwitz*. Stanford: Stanford University Press, 1997.
Halberstam, Judith. *Skin Shows: Gothic Horror and the Technology of Monsters*. Durham, NC: Duke University Press, 1995.
Hamilton, Paul. *Coleridge and German Philosophy: The Poet in the Land of Logic*. London: Continuum, 2007.
– *Coleridge's Poetics*. Oxford: Basil Blackwell, 1983.
Hansen, Mark. "'Not thus, after all, would life be given': *Technesis*, Technology and the Parody of Romantic Poetics in *Frankenstein*." *Studies in Romanticism* 36, no. 4 (Winter 1997): 575–609.
Harrison, Antony H. *Christina Rossetti in Context*. Chapel Hill: University of North Carolina Press, 1988.
Hartman, Geoffrey. "Gods, Ghosts, and Shelley's 'Atheos.'" *Literature and Theology* 24, no. 1 (March 2010): 4–18.
Hassett, Constance. *Christina Rossetti: The Patience of Style*. Charlottesville: University of Virginia Press, 2005.
Hedley, Douglas. *Coleridge, Philosophy and Religion:* Aids to Reflection *and the Mirror of the Spirit*. Cambridge: Cambridge University Press, 2000.
– "Was Coleridge a Romantic?" *Wordsworth Circle* 22, no. 1 (Winter 1991): 71–5.
Hennelly, Mark M., Jr. "'As Well Fill Up the Space Between': A Liminal Reading of *Christabel*." *Studies in Romanticism* 38, no. 2 (Summer 1999): 203–22.
Henwood, Dawn. "Christian Allegory and Subversive Poetics: Christina Rossetti's *Prince's Progress* Reconsidered." *Victorian Poetry* 35, no. 1 (Spring 1997): 83–94.

Heringman, Noah. *Romantic Rocks, Aesthetic Geology*. Ithaca: Cornell University Press, 2004.

Hitt, Christopher. "Shelley's Unwriting of Mont Blanc." *Texas Studies in Literature and Language* 47, no. 2 (Summer 2005): 139–66.

– "Toward an Ecological Sublime." *New Literary History* 30, no. 3 (Summer 1999): 603–23.

Hogle, Jerrold E. "'Christabel' as Gothic: The Abjection of Instability." *Gothic Studies* 7, no. 1 (May 2005): 18–27.

– *Shelley's Process: Radical Transference and the Development of His Major Works*. New York: Oxford University Press, 1988.

Holmes, Richard. *Coleridge: Darker Reflections, 1804–1834*. New York: Pantheon Books, 1998.

Humphries, Simon. "Who Is the Alchemist in Christina Rossetti's 'The Prince's Progress'?" *Review of English Studies* 58, no. 237 (November 2007): 684–97.

Iseli, Markus. "Thomas De Quincey and the Cognitive Prospects of the Unconscious." *European Romantic Review* 24, no. 3 (2013): 325–33.

Jackson, J.R. de J., ed. *Coleridge: The Critical Heritage*. New York: Barnes & Noble, 1970. (*CCH*)

Jackson, Noel B. "Coleridge's Criticism of Life." *Coleridge Bulletin* n.s., 37 (Summer 2011): 21–34.

Jager, Colin. *Unquiet Things: Secularism in the Romantic Age*. Philadelphia: University of Pennsylvania Press, 2015.

James, Felicity. *Charles Lamb, Coleridge and Wordsworth: Reading Friendship in the 1790s*. Houndmills: Palgrave Macmillan, 2008.

Jamison, Anne. *Poetics en Passant: Redefining the Relationship between Victorian and Modern Poetry*. Houndmills: Palgrave Macmillan, 2009.

Johnston, Kenneth. *Unusual Suspects: Pitt's Reign of Alarm and the Lost Generation of the 1790s*. Oxford: Oxford University Press, 2013.

Joseph, Gerhard. *Tennyson and the Text: The Weaver's Shuttle*. Cambridge: Cambridge University Press, 1992.

Kant, Immanuel. *Critique of Judgment*. Translated by Werner S. Pluhar. Indianapolis: Hackett, 1987.

Keach, William. *Shelley's Style*. New York: Methuen, 1984.

Keats, John. *The Complete Poems*. 3rd ed., edited by John Barnard. New York: Penguin, 1988.

– *The Letters of John Keats, 1814–1821*. 2 vols., edited by Hyder Edward Rollins. Cambridge, MA: Harvard University Press, 1958.

Klancher, Jon P. *The Making of English Reading Audiences, 1790–1832*. Madison: University of Wisconsin Press, 1987.

Knapp, Steven. *Personification and the Sublime: Milton to Coleridge*. Cambridge, MA: Harvard University Press, 1985.

Lacoue-Labarthe, Philippe. *Poetry as Experience*. Translated by Andrea Tarnowski. Stanford: Stanford University Press, 1999.

Langan, Celeste. "Pathologies of Communication from Coleridge to Schreber." *South Atlantic Quarterly* 102, no. 1 (Winter 2003): 117–52.

Lauer, Christopher. *The Suspension of Reason in Hegel and Schelling*. London: Continuum, 2010.

Lawes, Carolyn J. "Buried Alive? Fear of Failure in Antebellum America." *Journal of American Culture* 37, no. 3 (September 2014): 299–313.

Leask, Nigel. "Mont Blanc's Mysterious Voice: Shelley and Huttonian Earth Science." *The Third Culture: Literature and Science*, edited by Elinor S. Shaffer, 182–203. Berlin: De Gruyter, 1998.

Levine, Caroline. *Forms: Whole, Rhythm, Hierarchy, Network*. Princeton: Princeton University Press, 2015.

– *The Serious Pleasures of Suspense: Victorian Realism and Narrative Doubt*. Charlottesville: University of Virginia Press, 2003.

Levine, George. *Dying to Know: Scientific Epistemology and Narrative in Victorian England*. Chicago: University of Chicago Press, 2002.

Levinson, Marjorie. *The Romantic Fragment Poem*. Chapel Hill: University of North Carolina Press, 1986.

[Lewes, George Henry.] "Death-in-Life." *Fraser's Magazine for Town and Country* 36, no. 211 (July 1847): 108–12.

Li, Ou. *Keats and Negative Capability*. London: Continuum, 2009.

Ludlow, Elizabeth. *Christina Rossetti and the Bible: Waiting with the Saints*. London: Bloomsbury, 2014.

Lyotard, Jean-François. *The Differend: Phrases in Dispute*. Translated by Georges Van Den Abbeele. Minneapolis: University of Minnesota Press, 1988.

– "The Sublime and the Avant-Garde." *The Inhuman: Reflections on Time*, translated by Geoffrey Bennington and Rachel Bowlby, 89–107. Stanford: Stanford University Press, 1991.

Macovski, Michael S. *Dialogue and Literature: Apostrophe, Auditors, and the Collapse of Romantic Discourse*. New York: Oxford University Press, 1994.

Mangham, Andrew. "Buried Alive: The Gothic Awakening of Taphophobia." *Journal of Literature and Science* 3, no. 1 (2010): 10–22.

Markovits, Stefanie. *The Crisis of Action in Nineteenth-Century English Literature*. Columbus: Ohio State University Press, 2006.

Martin, Meredith, and Yisrael Levin. "Victorian Prosody: Measuring the Field." *Victorian Poetry* 49, no. 2 (Summer 2011): 149–60.

Mason, Emma. "Christina Rossetti and the Doctrine of Reserve." *Journal of Victorian Culture* 7, no. 2 (Autumn 2002): 196–219.

Massumi, Brian. *Parables for the Virtual: Movement, Affect, Sensation*. Durham, NC: Duke University Press, 2002.

Matus, Jill. *Shock, Memory and the Unconscious in Victorian Fiction*. Cambridge: Cambridge University Press, 2009.

Maurice, Frederick Denison. *The Kingdom of Christ; or, Hints Respecting the Principles, Constitution, and Ordinances of the Catholic Church*. 2nd ed. New York: D. Appleton & Co., 1843.

May, Claire B. "'Christabel' and Abjection: Coleridge's Narrative in Process/on Trial." *SEL* 37, no. 4 (Autumn 1997): 699–721.

Mayberry, Katherine J. *Christina Rossetti and the Poetry of Discovery*. Baton Rouge: Louisiana State University Press, 1989.

McCandless, Peter. "Dangerous to Themselves and Others: The Victorian Debate over the Prevention of Wrongful Confinement." *Journal of British Studies* 23, no. 1 (Autumn 1983): 84–104.

– "Liberty and Lunacy: The Victorians and Wrongful Confinement." *Journal of Social History* 11, no. 3 (Spring 1978): 366–86.

McCarthy, Anne C. "The Aesthetics of Contingency in the Shelleyan Universe of Things, or, 'Mont Blanc' without Mont Blanc." *Studies in Romanticism* 54, no. 3 (Fall 2015): 355–75.

– "Suspension." *Jacques Derrida: Key Concepts*, edited by Claire Colebrook, 23–30. London and New York: Routledge, 2015.

McHale, Brian. "Beginning to Think about Narrative in Poetry." *Narrative* 17, no. 1 (January 2009): 11–30.

McSweeney, Kerry. *What's the Import? Nineteenth-Century Poems and Contemporary Critical Practice*. Montreal and Kingston: McGill-Queen's University Press, 2007.

Mellor, Anne K. *English Romantic Irony*. Cambridge, MA: Harvard University Press, 1980.

Miall, David S. "Foregrounding and the Sublime: Shelley in Chamonix." *Language and Literature* 16, no. 2 (2007): 155–68.

Miller, J. Hillis. *The Linguistic Moment: From Wordsworth to Stevens*. Princeton: Princeton University Press, 1985.

Minot, Leslie Ann, and Walter Minot. "*Frankenstein* and *Christabel*: Intertextuality, Biography, and Gothic Ambiguity." *European Romantic Review* 15, no. 1 (March 2004): 23–49.

Mitchell, Robert. *Experimental Life: Vitalism in Romantic Science and Literature*. Baltimore: Johns Hopkins University Press, 2013.

Mitchell, Sebastian. "Dark Interpreter: Literary Uses of the Brocken Spectre from Coleridge to Pynchon." *Dalhousie Review* 87, no. 2 (2007): 167–87.

Morgan, Monique R. *Narrative Means, Lyric Ends: Temporality in the Nineteenth-Century British Long Poem*. Columbus: Ohio State University Press, 2009.

Moskal, Jeanne. "Travel Writing." *The Cambridge Companion to Mary Shelley*, edited by Esther Schor, 242–58. Cambridge: Cambridge University Press, 2003.

Natale, Simone. *Supernatural Entertainments: Victorian Spiritualism and the Rise of Modern Media Culture*. University Park: Penn State University Press, 2016.

"Notice on the Life and Writings of Dr Antony Todd Thomson." *Edinburgh Medical and Surgical Journal* (1 October 1852): 446–61.

O'Gorman, Francis. "What Is Haunting Tennyson's *Maud* (1855)?" *Victorian Poetry* 48, no. 3 (Fall 2010): 293–312.

O'Neill, Michael. "The Gleam of those Words: Coleridge and Shelley." *Keats-Shelley Review* 19 (2005): 76–96.

Paley, Morton. *Coleridge's Later Poetry*. Oxford: Clarendon Press, 1996.

Pater, Walter H. *Studies in the History of the Renaissance*. London: Macmillan and Co., 1873.

Perry, Seamus. *Alfred Tennyson*. Tavistock: Northcote Press, 2005.

– *Coleridge and the Uses of Division*. Oxford: Oxford University Press, 1999.

Peterson, Linda. "Restoring the Book: The Typological Hermeneutics of Christina Rossetti and the PRB." *Victorian Poetry* 32, no. 3/4 (Autumn–Winter 1994): 209–32.

Poe, Edgar Allan. *Poetry and Tales*. New York: Library of America, 1984.

Prickett, Stephen. *Coleridge and Wordsworth: The Poetry of Growth*. Cambridge: Cambridge University Press, 1970.

– *Romanticism and Religion: The Tradition of Coleridge and Wordsworth in the Victorian Church*. Cambridge: Cambridge University Press, 1976.

Psomiades, Kathy Alexis. "Whose Body? Christina Rossetti and Aestheticist Femininity." *Women and British Aestheticism*, edited by Talia Schaffer and Kathy Alexis Psomiades, 101–18. Charlottesville: University Press of Virginia, 1999.

Rees, Joan. "Christina Rossetti: Poet." *Critical Quarterly* 26, no. 3 (September 1984): 59–72.

Reiman, Donald H., ed. *Shelley and His Circle, 1773–1822*. 8 vols. Cambridge, MA: Harvard University Press, 1986.

Richardson, Ruth. *Death, Dissection and the Destitute*. 2nd ed. Chicago: University of Chicago Press, 2000.

Riede, David. *Allegories of One's Own Mind: Melancholy in Victorian Poetry*. Columbus: Ohio State University Press, 2005.

Robinson, Charles E., ed. *The Frankenstein Notebooks, Part 1*. New York: Garland Publishing, 1996.

Roe, Dinah. *Christina Rossetti's Faithful Imagination: The Devotional Poetry and Prose*. Houndmills: Palgrave Macmillan, 2007.

Rosenblum, Dolores. *Christina Rossetti: The Poetry of Endurance*. Carbondale: Southern Illinois University Press, 1986.

Rossetti, Christina. *The Complete Poems of Christina Rossetti*. 3 vols., edited by Rebecca Crump. Baton Rouge: Louisiana State University Press, 1979–2000.

– *The Face of the Deep: A Devotional Commentary on the Apocalypse*. London: Society for Promoting Christian Knowledge, 1892.

– *Time Flies: A Reading Diary*. London: Society for Promoting Christian Knowledge, 1902.

Rossetti, William Michael, ed. *Poems of Christina Rossetti*. London: Macmillan and Co., 1904.

– *Rossetti Papers: 1862 to 1870*. New York: Charles Scribner's Sons, 1903.

Rowlinson, Matthew. "The Thing in the Poem: *Maud*'s Hymen." *differences: A Journal of Feminist Cultural Studies* 12, no. 3 (Fall 2001): 128–65.

Ruderman, D.B. *The Idea of Infancy in Nineteenth-Century British Poetry: Romanticism, Subjectivity, Form*. New York and London: Routledge, 2016.

Ryals, Clyde de L. "The 'Weird Seizures' in *The Princess*." *Texas Studies in Literature and Language* 4, no. 2 (Summer 1962): 268–75.

– *A World of Possibilities: Romantic Irony in Victorian Literature*. Columbus: Ohio State University Press, 1990.

Schlutz, Alexander M. *Mind's World: Imagination and Subjectivity from Descartes to Romanticism*. Seattle: University of Washington Press, 2009.

Schulman, Samuel. "Mourning and Voice in *Maud*." *SEL* 23 (1983): 633–46.

Sedgwick, Eve Kosofsky. *Between Men: English Literature and Male Homosocial Desire*. New York: Columbia University Press, 1985.

– *The Coherence of Gothic Conventions*. New York: Methuen, 1986.

Shaffer, Elinor S. "Illusion and Imagination: Derrida's Parergon and Coleridge's Aid to Reflection. Revisionary Readings of Kantian Formalist Aesthetics." *Aesthetic Illusion: Theoretical and Historical Approaches*, edited by Frederick Burwick and Walter Pape, 138–57. Berlin: Walter de Gruyter, 1990.

– "The Metaphysics of Culture: Kant and Coleridge's *Aids to Reflection*." *Journal of the History of Ideas* 31, no. 2 (April–June 1970): 199–218.

Shatto, Susan, ed. *Tennyson's Maud: A Definitive Edition*. London: Athlone Press, 1986.

Shaviro, Steven. *The Universe of Things: On Speculative Realism*. Minneapolis: University of Minnesota Press, 2014.

Shelley, Mary. *Frankenstein, or The Modern Prometheus*. 1818. Edited by D.L. MacDonald and Kathleen Scherf. 3rd ed. Peterborough, ON: Broadview Press, 2012.

– *History of a Six Weeks' Tour through a Part of France, Switzerland, Germany, and Holland; with Letters Descriptive of a Sail Round the Lake of Geneva, and of the Glaciers of Chamouni*. London: T. Hookham, Jun., and C. and J. Ollier, 1817. (*HSWT*)

Shelley, Percy Bysshe. *The Complete Poetry of Percy Bysshe Shelley*. Edited by Donald H. Reiman, Neil Fraistat, and Nora Crook. 3 vols. Baltimore: Johns Hopkins University Press, 2000–.

– *The Posthumous Poems of Percy Bysshe Shelley*. Edited by Mary Wollstonecraft Shelley. London: John and Henry L. Hunt, 1824.

– *Shelley's Poetry and Prose*. 2nd ed., edited by Donald H. Reiman and Neil Fraistat. New York: W.W. Norton, 2002.

Shklovsky, Victor. "Art as Technique." *Russian Formalist Criticism: Four Essays*, translated by Lee T. Lemon and Marion J. Rees, 3–24. Lincoln: University of Nebraska Press, 1965.

Sidgwick, Henry. *Miscellaneous Essays and Addresses*. London: Macmillan, 1904.

Simpson, David. *Romanticism and the Question of the Stranger*. Chicago: University of Chicago Press, 2013.

Slinn, E. Warwick. *The Discourse of Self in Victorian Poetry*. Houndmills: Macmillan, 1991.

Smith, Horace. "Posthumous Memoir of Myself." *New Monthly Magazine and Humorist* 87, no. 345 (September 1849): 1–9.

Sng, Zachary. *The Rhetoric of Error from Locke to Kleist*. Stanford: Stanford University Press, 2010.

Stokes, Christopher. *Coleridge, Language and the Sublime: From Transcendence to Finitude*. Houndmills: Palgrave Macmillan, 2011.

– "Coleridge's Philosophy of Prayer: Responsibility, Parergon, and Catachresis." *Journal of Religion* 89, no. 4 (October 2009): 541–63.

"Suspension of Disbelief Goes Unrewarded." *The Onion*, 18 February 2011, http://www.theonion.com/article/suspension-of-disbelief-goes-unrewarded-19194.

Swann, Karen. "'Christabel': The Wandering Mother and the Enigma of Form." *Studies in Romanticism* 23, no. 4 (Winter 1984): 533–53.

– "Literary Gentlemen and Lovely Ladies: The Debate on the Character of *Christabel*." *ELH* 52, no. 2 (Summer 1985): 397–418.

– "Teaching *Christabel*: Gender and Genre." *Approaches to Teaching Coleridge's Poetry and Prose*, edited by Richard Matlak, 121–7. New York: Modern Language Association, 1991.

Taylor, Anya. "Coleridge's 'Christabel' and the Phantom Soul." *SEL* 42, no. 4 (Autumn 2002): 707–30.

– "Coleridge's Self-Representations." *The Oxford Handbook of Samuel Taylor Coleridge*, edited by Frederick Burwick, 107–24. New York: Oxford University Press, 2012.

Tennyson, Alfred. *The Poems of Tennyson*. 2nd ed., 3 vols., edited by Christopher Ricks. Essex: Longman, 1987.

Tennyson, G.B. *Victorian Devotional Poetry: The Tractarian Mode*. Cambridge, MA: Harvard University Press, 1991.

Tennyson, Hallam. *Alfred Lord Tennyson: A Memoir, by his son*. 2 vols. London: Macmillan, 1897.

Terada, Rei. "Phenomenality and Dissatisfaction in Coleridge's *Notebooks*." *Studies in Romanticism* 43, no. 2 (Summer 2004): 257–81.

Theune, Michael. "~~Negative Capability~~ T wang dillo dee." *Jacket* 2 40 (late 2010), http://jacketmagazine.com/40/theune-keats.shtml.

Thompson, Judith. "An Autumnal Blast, a Killing Frost: Coleridge's Poetic Conversation with John Thelwall." *Studies in Romanticism* 36, no. 3 (Fall 1997): 427–56.

Thomson, A.T. "Lectures on Medical Jurisprudence, Now in the Course of Delivery at the University of London. Lecture XXX: Sudden Death." *Lancet* 2, no. 713 (29 April 1837): 177–83.

Tomko, Michael. *Beyond the Willing Suspension of Disbelief: Poetic Faith from Coleridge to Tolkien*. London: Bloomsbury, 2016.

– "Politics, Performance, and Coleridge's 'Suspension of Disbelief.'" *Victorian Studies* 49, no. 2 (Winter 2007): 241–49.

Trelawny, Edward. *Records of Shelley, Byron, and the Author*. 2 vols. 1878. New York: Benjamin Blom, 1968.

Trott, Nicola. "The Picturesque, the Beautiful and the Sublime." *A Companion to Romanticism*, edited by Duncan Wu, 72–90. Oxford: Blackwell Publishers, 1998.

Tucker, Herbert F. *Tennyson and the Doom of Romanticism*. Cambridge, MA: Harvard University Press, 1988.

Vallins, David. "The Feeling of Knowledge: Insight and Delusion in Coleridge." *ELH* 64, no. 1 (Spring 1997): 157–87.

Vallins, David, ed. *Coleridge's Writings, Volume 5: On the Sublime*. Houndmills: Palgrave Macmillan, 2003.

Vardy, Alan. "Coleridge on Broad Stand." *Romanticism and Victorianism on the Net* 61 (April 2012), doi: 10.7202/1018600ar.

– *Constructing Coleridge: The Posthumous Life of the Author*. Houndmills: Palgrave Macmillan, 2010.

Ward, David. *Coleridge and the Nature of Imagination: Evolution, Engagement with the World, and Poetry*. Houndmills: Palgrave Macmillan, 2013.

Wasserman, Earl. *Shelley: A Critical Reading*. Baltimore: Johns Hopkins University Press, 1971.

Weiskel, Thomas. *The Romantic Sublime: Studies in the Structure and Psychology of Transcendence*. Baltimore: Johns Hopkins University Press, 1976.

West, Sally. *Coleridge and Shelley: Textual Engagement*. Aldershot: Ashgate, 2007.

Wolfson, Susan. "'Comparing Power': Coleridge and Simile." *Coleridge's Theory of Imagination Today*, edited by Christine Gallant, 167–95. New York: AMS Press, 1989.

Wood, Gillen D'Arcy. *Tambora: The Eruption That Changed the World*. Princeton: Princeton University Press, 2014.

Wordsworth, Jonathan. "'What is it, that has been done?' The Central Problem of *Maud*." *Essays in Criticism* 24, no. 4 (1974): 356–62.

Wordsworth, William. *The Major Works*. Edited by Stephen Gill. Oxford: Oxford University Press, 1984.

Wright, Barbara Herb. "Tennyson, the Weird Seizures in *The Princess*, and Epilepsy." *Literature and Medicine* 6 (1987): 61–76.

Wroe, Ann. "Resolutions, Destinations: Shelley's Last Year." *The Oxford Handbook of Percy Bysshe Shelley*, edited by Michael O'Neill and Anthony Howe, 48–64. New York: Oxford University Press, 2012.

Youngquist, Paul. *Monstrosities: Bodies and British Romanticism*. Minneapolis: University of Minnesota Press, 2003.

Index